Savoir-Flair!

...It never occurred to me that he (Hitler) might destroy France, because it would have been as hard for me to prefigure a world without France as survival with one lobe of my brain gone. France represented for me the historical continuity of intelligence and reasonable living. When this continuity is broken, nothing anywhere can have meaning until it is reestablished.

A.J.Liebling, *The Road Back to Paris*, 1944

Savoir-Flair!

211 Tips for Enjoying France and the French

Polly Platt

Illustrations by Ande Grchich

Published by Culture Crossings, Ltd., London

Distributed in the UK by Plymbridge
      Estover, Plymouth, Devon PL6 7P2, England
      tel: 44 1752 202 301
      fax: 44 1752 202 330

Distributed in the US by Distribooks
      8120 ▒▒▒geway Avenue
      ▒koki▒ ▒0076
      tel 1▒ ▒ 5 1596
      ax: ▒ ▒ 76 1195
      e-mail: Info@Distribooks.com

First American edition published in June 2000
Second Printing May 2001

Feedback to the author: tel (33)1 45 56 04 62
                             e-mail: polly@pollyplatt.com
                             web site: www.pollyplatt.com

Cover and layout design by Ian Heard

ISBN 0-9646684-1-6

Printed in the United States by Edwards Brothers,
      Lillington, North Carolina

To Sashie
sunlight to me, and to so many
my daughter and best friend

To Grace
who adopted me as sister and has been more than one

To Taitsie and Walter
who made things possible

Acknowledgments

I may be breaking a taboo, but instead of ending with last-but-not-least-helpful-supportive-spouse, Ande is at top of my list for grateful thanks: first in my heart, first in my life, he encouraged me to start another book, read the chapters, put up with my misgivings and hasty meals, made me laugh even when NATO bombs were falling on his country -- and drew the illustrations.

Far away across the ocean in Saint Louis, Tom McTigue, Boeing executive and cross-cultural colleague, harassed me to get myself wired years ago, when I had barely heard of the Internet, and used it for a flow of e-mailed corrections, suggestions and Dilbert-quality anecdotes. Thanks to Tom, readers of *French or Foe?* and others of my message at Amazon.com, begging for their anecdotes about France, could e-mail me, and they did. A great big thank you to all of them.

The editorial advisor I'm immeasurably indebted to and grateful for, both for her enthusiasm and her professional attention, is my friend Julie Winn, a former copy editor. From her delightful scribbled comments and anecdotes in the margins, it is clear that she must write her own book about France. On the subject of thanks, huge ones go to Gail Chaddock, Frances Jones, Anne-Elisabeth Moutet and Susan Rosenberg for lending me their wits, professional and otherwise, and to Gail and Anne-Elisabeth for letting me include parts of their own writing about France. Eve François, whose responses in reading the manuscript have been as cheering as her sharp eyes have been exacting, Sylvie Hester, Sylvia Couturié and Brani and Emmanuella, my son and daughter-in-law, have been much-appreciated French mentors. Other readers of the manuscript to whom I am indebted for their time and for the typos and errors they found are Sarah Davis, Andrea Rose, Shari Segall, Ted Simpson and Elizabeth Turqué. Special thanks for enthusiasm and support go to Tricia Hawkes and to everyone who wrote, said or phoned cheering comments about *French or Foe?* Such comments help a doubtful author to get going again, more than they can know.

Finally, the book might never have been written but for the vision, encouragement and expertise of a French ex-pat bibliophile, Jean Gabriel, of the European Book Company, San Francisco. Thank you, Jean. And thank you, Yves Mengin, also a literary French ex-pat, of Distribooks, Chicago, who has not only distributed *French or Foe?* and *Savoir-Flair!* in stores all over the US, but has also been of immense help in the various complications of printing and marketing.

Table of Contents

Introduction   9

Chapter 1: Enjoying Your Arrival   13
  • emergency assistance at Orly Sud Airport
  • at Charles de Gaulle Airport: ATM's, phone cards
  • which transportation to Paris? Bus, train, shuttle, taxi?
Chapter 2: Enjoying Your Hotel   25
  • where is it? how is it?
  • what is its name?
  • my adventure in Toulouse
Chaper 3: Enjoying French Bathrooms   40
  • in hotels
  • in cafés
  • in other public places
Chapter 4: Enjoying Paris on Foot   50
  • helpfulness of Parisians
  • crossing streets!
  • a stroll through 1,000 years
Chapter 5: Enjoying Speaking French   64
  • the French appreciate your (even bad) French
  • short cuts (bluffs)
  • street expressions to avoid
  • deceptive French words (faux amis)
Chapter 6: Enjoying Paris on Wheels and Water   77
  • in taxis
  • on the Métro and the RER, in buses , on the Seine Batobus shuttle
  • driving, cycling, rollerblading
Chapter 7: Enjoying French Dogs   101
  • dogs are different in France
  • City Hall's dog-poop wars
Chapter 8: Enjoying Getting Information   108
  • knowing how
  • mistaken assumptions
Chapter 9: Enjoying French Customer Service   115
  • French and American expectations
  • travelers who got it and travelers who didn't
Chapter 10: Enjoying the Local Scene   126
  • the post office, open markets, the barber/ hairdresser, the movies
  • the pharmacy, department stores , the flea market, church
Chapter 11: Enjoying Finding Something You've Lost   139

Chapter 12: Enjoying Being Young in Paris: Teens and Early Twenties   144
- in French families: hot water, long meals, etc.
- flirting, *la bise*, where to meet a young man/young woman
- in the Métro, on the street
- early teens

Chapter 13: Enjoying Being a Woman in France   160
- enjoying being a man meeting French women
- enjoying being a woman flirting with French men

Chapter 14: Enjoying Cafés   173
- the corner café, café geos, literary cafés, café philos
- café customs

Chapter 15: Enjoying French Food   181
- the great French delicacies
- the great chefs: what they say and write

Chapter 16: Enjoying French Restaurants   193
- French restaurants are special
- French waiters are special: their language and prestige
- travelers' tales
- the celestial 3-stars

Chapter 17: Enjoying Business (and Pleasure) Meals   213
- suggestions of where to go, with whom and when
- restaurant manners
- hosting a business lunch: seating, eating, drinking

Chapter 18: Enjoying the SNCF (the French Railroad)   224
- why the TGV (the bullet train) is wonderful
- the Savoir-Flair of taking the right train
- six foreign-passenger SNCF adventures

Chapter 19: Enjoying Motoring in France   239
- French expressway habits
- road regulations
- handling a rented car
- handling road maps
- an American accident that turned out well

Chapter 20: Enjoying Bicycle Tours   254
- your own tour or a group tour
- following the Tour de France

Chapter 21: Enjoying Rural Living   263
- renting: why, where and who from
- the Dordogne, an English "colony": what are the amenities
- dealing with local tradespeople

Conclusion   280

Introduction

"It was the best of times, it was the worst of times."
Dickens's opening line of *A Tale of Two Cities* echoes across time to the millennium. He was writing about the French Revolution, but he might have been quoting travelers today. France is different. Some love it and come home with stars in their eyes. Others return frustrated and vengeful, complaining. Too many monuments. Too many stairs. Too many rude people who don't speak English.

The purpose of this book is to put those stars in *your* eyes. To give you confidence that the French are wonderful. That they'll be wonderful to you. That they've made a wonderful country.

If you're attracted to the grand, the brilliant, the beautiful, the far out, the delicious, the elegant, the quaint, the spiritual, the turbulent, the serene, the tender, the brave, the controversial, the stupendous and the small but perfect... then France -- all of it, not just Paris -- is the place for you. You'll love it. You'll love the French. You'll be dazzled at the unexpected and laugh at the misunderstandings.

Savoir-Flair is about *being* in the French sense: knowing how and knowing where, about the things you might do in France and how to do them smoothly. France is a new, different game, with different rules that you need to know, just the same as if you wanted to learn how to play tennis or golf. *Savoir-Flair* is about the basics and also about the unexpected that might happen... and how it happened to me and to lots of foreigners and what we did about it -- or , in some cases, failed to do, might have done had we known better.

Along the way, it's about aspects of Frenchness, about Paris and Parisians, and about rural France, *la France profonde*. Travelers tell their tales of generous French help, and the automatic French response: "It's nothing. *C'est normal!"*

France is a very old country, always changing, yet, like a river, always recognizably the same. Knowing the rules is a basic part of feeling comfortable. The French call their rules *savoir-faire*, or knowing how. Celebrated for their *savoir-vivre* (knowing how to live), they're convinced that there is no *savoir-vivre* without that discipline -- without *savoir-faire*. Which also leads to *savoir-être*... knowing how to be ... and the title of this book, *Savoir-Flair*.

Once you know the how-to's, you can handle the cultural differences.

It's helpful, but not absolutely essential, to know what they are.

Paul Salacain, a director at the Heidelberg Web Press in Beauvais, spotted them very soon. He arrived in 1997 and took a 2-week total immersion Berlitz course on arrival.

"I came assuming that the French were like us, only they spoke a different language," he said. "This was 350 percent wrong. The correct sentence is, 'The French are not like us and in addition, they speak a different language.' The French think differently, they approach everything, including work, differently, and if you think you're going to change them, you might as well pack up right now and go home."

Michel Goget, the French director of the Dolce International Hotel near Aix-en-Provence, married an American and lived in the U.S. long enough to become an enthusiastic detective of Franco-American cultural differences. He put together this chart:

FRANCE		U.S.A
One	CULTURE	Multi
Labor laws	SOCIAL	Union contract
Fixed	LABOR	Flexible
A risk	VENTURE	A chance
Elitist	MANAGEMENT	Participation
A profession	CAREER	Job
King/serf	HISTORY	New world
Formal	BOSS/SUBORDINATE	Informal
One pure wool suit	CLOTHING	5 Washable suits
Suspicious/	BEHAVIOR	Open/
traditionalist		adventurous
Cash	SPENDING	Credit
Family togetherness	SOCIAL	Club/
		individuality
To keep	ACQUISITIONS	Use and
		dispose of
Soccer	SPORT	Football
(tactic)		(strategic)
Academic	HIGH SCHOOL	Sport/social
2CV(Escort)	SALESMAN	Cadillac
Live to	EAT	To live
To be earned/lasting	TRUST (SOCIAL)	Friendly/short

You don't have to be an anthropologist to see that the people in these cultures are going to be as different as Paul Salacain found them. Which is why foreigners who don't know much about the French, and have a cultural need to simplify, fall back on stereotypes and pass them on to their children in the nursery. Such as:

• *The French are quarrelsome eggheads who are obsessed with sex and don't tell the truth.*

Quarrelsome? Instead of avoiding their differences, French people confront them, discussing, arguing, honing their critical skills. Eggheads? Intellectuals are admired; being a philosopher is a profession. Sex-obsessed? They call it love, and male-female encounters are the ambrosia of their daily life. As for truth, what is truth? Your truth may not be mine, and if it were, we would not have the civil wars we have in Kosovo, Afghanistan, Indonesia. "Like justice," said prominent writer, and member of the Académie Française, Jean d'Ormesson on television (Sept 1999), "truth can never be attained, but that doesn't mean we shouldn't continue to strive for it."

• *Wimps at war in 1940.* They weren't. Far from it. This is the English version of World War II. Read a thin book which is the best existing WWII account from the French front, *The Strange Defeat* by the eminent French medievalist and executed (Jewish) Resistance leader, Marc Bloch. Read about the bravery of the French military in Bosnia and Vietnam, not to mention Napoleon's armies.

Do travelers to France really have to worry about all this? Not really. The thing to do is wipe out your assumptions and received ideas about stereotypes and be like Mary Ann Rateau, a nurse, a grandmother of generous girth who lives in Anchorage, Alaska. She looks happy. She laughs a lot. So much so that it makes you -- and probably her patients -- feel happy to look at her. Apparently French people react this way to her too.

"I think it's a matter of attitude," she said during a 5-day visit to Paris in 1999. "If you expect people to be nice to you, and if you're nice to them, they will be. People have gotten up to give me their seat on the Métro and in buses, especially young girls. My French isn't very good, but the waiters are patient. They even bring me coffee with my main dish. I love the people here. It's a mistake to demand that things happen the way they do at home."

Other Americans are less serene than Mary Ann. Judy Grozsman, who moved without a word of French from Maplewood, N.J., to France in

1995 with her husband and three children, gives strategy talks to newly arrived parents at the American School of Paris.

"I tell Americans that this place is great and the people are wonderful -- but it's a different game they'll be playing here, with different rules. Of course we'll make mistakes. But that doesn't make us inferior. We have to learn to laugh at ourselves, the way they do, among themselves. I tell people to write **'I am intelligent'** on a piece of paper, tape it to their bedside table, and look at it every night and every morning ."

Then there are the joyful travelers who love France and thrive on confusion and cultural differences. Each time they spot something unexpected and different from anything at home, they pounce on it and examine it in awe and delight. Tom McTigue, a Boeing executive in St. Louis, who is also a professor of cross-cultural management at Webster University Graduate School, is one of these. Some of his gems appear in later chapters.

As Robert Lovenheim, a television producer from Los Angeles, said after living in France for four years, "Maybe *everything* doesn't work here -- the taxes are too high, unemployment is too high and so forth -- but *life* works."

So -- let's go!

Chapter One

Enjoying Your Arrival

Chris Pinet's Emergency at Orly Airport
Airport Arrival Essentials, Transportation to Paris

French people love to solve problems. It's the national sport. The worse the odds are, the more they're intrigued. It helps if you speak French, but it's not essential. The important word -- problem -- is the same: problème. The critical element is asking politely, and psychologically filling them in on the details of your urgent need of their expertise. The more personal and intimate the better.

Savoir-Flair Tip No. 1:
Help is at hand, all you have to do is ask for it!

Welcome to Paris. Please, relax. French airport personnel are now falling over themselves to make you feel welcome. Remember, the welcome is a French welcome. They may not smile, although then again, they might. But they will rush to answer your questions and steer you around. In addition, they have the quick minds and reflexes plus the comforting *sympa* feeling you need in an emergency, should there be an emergency.

Most travelers land in Paris at Charles de Gaulle Airport. I'm going to run you through there in a minute, with all the critical arrival steps in that sensational New Age building. But first, in case you're dubious about the welcome, and in case you're one of those inclined to panic at the unexpected, particularly at an airport, Chris Pinet's rescue at Orly, the other and much smaller Paris airport, should give you a shot of joyful reassurance.

Orly Airport has two divisions, Orly Sud (South) for international flights and, about a kilometer away, Orly Ouest (West) for domestic flights.

Normally, Orly Sud is as free from surprises and as easy to handle as any airport in the U.S.

But Chris Pinet had a problem.

Anyone but Chris, ebullient American professor of French at Montana State University, would have been in an advanced heart-pounding panic, landing that day in June 1998 at Orly Sud. Even Chris was close to it.

Chris and his wife, Carol, were on their way to Ajaccio, in Corsica, from Bozeman, Montana to celebrate their 25th wedding anniversary. Since boarding their flight from Bozeman the day before at 4:30 am, they'd changed planes in Salt Lake City and then in New York, where they waited on the ground for four hours before takeoff. The plane made up two hours over the Atlantic, but they were still two hours late at Orly Sud at 12:50 pm. Their connection to Ajaccio was 10 minutes later at 1:00 from Orly Ouest, a kilometer away.

Hopeless? You'd think so. Except for two if's:

• For one, if Chris knew the catastrophe approach to the French

• For another, if he found an airline hostess who believed in Napoleon's slogan, *"L'impossible n'est pas français"* (Impossible is not French)

"We were wrecks," Chris said. "By that time we'd been traveling for 29 hours. The next flight to Ajaccio wasn't until 10 that evening. There was no way I was going to be stuck at that airport for 12 more hours without giving it everything I had. I told Carol to forget about the luggage, we'd worry about that later. We dashed off the plane. I ran up to the first hostess I saw -- luckily she was young -- and breathlessly croaked the Magic Words,* 'Excuse me, I need your help, we have a problem!'

"When I told her what it was, she first blinked and then she said, 'Did you check your luggage through?'

"Luggage! Time was wasting! I was frantic. I said as calmly as possible, no, I'd only checked it to Paris. She told me that was a big mistake -- *scolding* me -- as if we had all day!

"I went along with it -- I said, yes it was a big mistake -- I even told her I was sorry! By now there were only five minutes left! Then I said forget the luggage and could she help? -- telling her what wrecks we were, and that it was our 25th wedding anniversary, please..."

"This triggered something. She opened up her walkie talkie and began talking to Orly Ouest. They apparently didn't say no, but didn't say

---

For more on the Magic Words ("Excusez-moi de ... etc"*) see *French or Foe?* pp. 30-34

yes either, because she turned to me and said, 'Can you run?'

"Well, Carol and I had both chosen running shoes for this long trip -- but the hostess had on high heels! High spike heels! And she began running! She waved at the airport police and customs people and took us through a side door.

"Then out on the street, we sprinted towards the other airport, this hostess running in her high spike heels and phoning into her mobile as she ran, to tell Orly Ouest to hold the plane! They said it was too late -- but she was undaunted!"

Chris continued: "At Orly Ouest we didn't even go into the airport building, she knew where the plane for Ajaccio would leave from on the tarmac. And there it was, already *moving!* The stairs were gone, the door was closed! She waved to the pilot. He stopped the plane! They opened the door, threw down the steps -- and up we went! Whew!

"I thanked the hostess -- as you can imagine -- and asked for her name so that I could write a letter to the top brass at Air France. But she said, 'Oh no, don't bother. *C'est normal,*' she added. That's what she said! It's normal! And then said she'd send on the luggage."

And normal it seems to be. Tom and Carolyn Kavunedus, of Yorktown Heights, NY, arrived at Orly Ouest at 8 am to drop off their rented car at the agency before their 10 am flight to New York. They found the airport surrounded by soldiers with machine guns, waving them away. Apparently there was a bomb scare. They wrote to the *Herald Tribune* about it:

"In desperation, we drove to Orly Sud, parked our car in the garage there and dashed inside to find a car rental desk. No such luck! By now it was 9:30. We could only find the information desk. There, an airline hostess took care of our car and got us on that plane!"

Charles de Gaulle Airport

Terminal Two of Charles de Gaulle Airport is new, simplified and traditional, not that different from Orly. It's only for Air France airplanes.

Terminal One of Charles de Gaulle Airport, incomparably bigger with many times the traffic, is for the world's other aviation companies. If you took some melatonin, had a good night's sleep and know where you're going, landing at this futuristic phenomenon is thrilling: Gay Paree, here I come!

But lots of non-melatonin foreigners arrive there in a sleepy fog, unprepared for its galactic atmosphere. After stepping off the plane, you walk a short gangway and enter a circular, mostly all-glass "satellite," one of seven similar boarding and landing areas with underground arms to the gigantic glass sphere which is the main building of Terminal One. To get there you follow the other passengers onto a moving sidewalk. This one has a slight roller-coaster effect at first, conveying you down steeply to enter a long low-ceilinged white tunnel, its rough-plastered walls lit indirectly. It's silent. You pass a few seductive French poster-ads hanging from the ceiling. No crowds, just you cruising along in pleasant, effortless strangeness. You've been spared lugging your carry-on bag for a discouraging stretch of bustling airport corridors without a visible goal, to enjoy, instead, this long white ride, saving your energy, slowing down your arrival at the luggage carrousel and thereby reducing the wait for it.

You begin to wake up. Terminal One looms ahead. You're really in France, the country which has hurtled into the 21st century as a high-tech leader not without pain, not leaving behind its historical treasures, its gift for style, for design, for pushing the art envelope.

Savoir-Flair Tip No. 2:
Greeting before any exchange sparks a warm welcome

From the moving sidewalk in the white tunnel, you step inside the outer rim of the sphere, the main airport building. Here you have your first encounter with a French inhabitant, the passport police inspector. Sweeten it with the local coded politeness, *"Bonjour, monsieur,"* and he'll most likely look up in pleased surprise and respond with a *"Bonjour, monsieur"* (or madame) of his own. This will cheer your morning. He might even smile a little, but don't take it personally if he doesn't.

Then you step onto a steeply pitched ramp moving you up -- hang onto the railing! -- inside a transparent tube, a kind of covered, upwardly sloping diagonal gangway in the sphere, which now seems to be a global space station. Other gangways criss-cross the sphere all around you, with motionless people inside them being moved up or down. It's crazy, surrealist, wonderful.

The gangway lands you near a luggage carrousel, but not yours. It's empty. You look around for one of the small overhead electronic monitors listing your flight's carrousel number, and discover that it's a few degrees around the side of the sphere. You note lots more big framed poster-ads -- some in English! -- hanging from the ceiling, and whole trains of luggage carts (*caddies*). You detach one. First happy surprise: it's free.

Riot Police

You retrieve your luggage, nod in passing to the customs people (*la douane*) if you have nothing to declare, and head for the *Sortie* (Exit). Now you're in the vast main area of the sphere. Several members of the CRS (the riot police) carrying automatic machine guns are moving around looking fierce. Don't worry. It doesn't mean they expect trouble. They're there to prevent it.

ATM Machines

The first thing to do now is to find an ATM (*Point Argent* or *distributeur*) for some local currency. Bankers agree that ATMs in the foreign country you're in give you the best going rate -- without charging a commission.

French airport ATMs often give screen instructions in French and English. Others invite you to choose a language among several. They operate in several steps. First, insert your credit card. (Master and Visa cards are the most reliably accepted all over France.) The machine will then ask you to punch your 4-digit PIN number, called a *code secret* in French, and then the green button marked *valider* to confirm the order. Next you'll be given a choice of desired amounts of cash -- in francs, remember -- and queried if you want a receipt (*reçu*). Push *oui* (yes). Then study it. The rate may have changed since yesterday, but if you multiply by seven, you'll be close enough for the first try.

"I didn't understand at all how this worked in a foreign country," said Judy M., from London. "It was my first trip outside the U.K.... and when I punched 100, I expected one hundred pounds worth of francs would pop out. Was I ever surprised!"

Savoir-Flair Tip No. 3:
Crowding at the ATM machine isn't threatening

While you're working the ATM, someone may be looking over your shoulder behind you. In fact, well, breathing down your neck. Be vigilant, but don't worry. He's not going to snatch your wallet. Spatial codes are different here. If the machine's instructions aren't clear to you, he'll be happy to explain.

Telephone Cards

Next, look for a "Tabac" (tobacconist shop) to buy a French telephone card (*télécarte*). Public telephones in France now accept only cards, not change. Your American mobile phone will be non-compatible in France. (French ones work anywhere in the world except in the U.S.) The least expensive phone card is 41 francs for 50 *unités* (units). A Tabac is indicated by its emblem above the door: usually white letters spelling T A B A C vertically on a red diamond. Tabacs are licensed by the French government to sell tobacco, and in return are obliged to sell other products of government-owned companies. Besides cigarettes and telephone cards (also available in post offices), you can buy matches, Métro tickets, postage stamps, special government stamps demanded by bureaucrats, lotto numbers and automobile tax stickers. You can also buy paper supplies, chewing gum and postcards... and, guess what, place your racing bets. If you're planning to rent a car, this is the place to get a card for the Paris parking meters.

Savoir-Flair Tip No. 4:
Get also a booklet of Paris districts at the TABAC

If you haven't already got one, also get a pocket-sized *Plan de Paris par Arrondissements*. This clever guide is full of daily and emergency information, including above all, maps of Paris by arrondissements (districts), page by page. Keep one with you at all times, like your passport.

Paris is not organized in a grid, but in circles, the newer, outer arrondissements sweeping in a spiral around the older arrondissements at the center. You learn to perceive the city through the feeling of the arrondissements. Street listings in the guide identify their district, where to find them on the district maps, where they begin and end, and the nearest Métro. This guide also has Métro maps, bus itineraries and useful addresses: movies, museums, embassies, hospitals, churches, and *monuments* such as the Arc de Triomphe, the Opera, and the Pyramid of the Louvre.

A new boon to foreigners in Paris, and complement to the guide above, has just come out, called *Le petit parisien*. It has three pages per arrondissement, each mercifully clear, one showing the bus routes in different colors, one showing the Métro (subway) routes and stations, and one showing the streets in detail, including their direction.

Savoir-Flair Tip No. 5:
Your telephone card is user-friendly in several languages at the airports

To use your telephone card, just insert it and wait for directions on the screen. Its chip keeps track of your call units. Like the ATMs, some, in airports, railroad stations and post offices, give instructions in both French and English, or ask you to choose a language. It will tell you to *décrochez* (lift the receiver) or *raccrochez* (hang up). Probably then it will ask you to *patientez* (be patient), a good word to connect with in France. You will often be asked to *patienter*. The French are impatient because they're highstrung, not because they feel time leaking away, lost, like Americans and Britons. French impatience tends to be emotional and aggressive. So one of their rules of *politesse* is not to show it. To *patienter*.

Savoir-Flair Tip No. 6:
Don't travel into Paris by rail from Charles de Gaulle

Going by rail (RER, or surburban express) from Charles de Gaulle Airport to the city of Paris is complicated and exhausting, except for Paris veterans whose hotel is next to an RER station. It involves a change to the Métro, which, as the RER and Métro escalators never seem to be working, means dragging your luggage up and down a series of stairways, and then looking for a taxi to get to your hotel.

In addition, thieves love this RER line. The American Consul General in Paris warns: "Gangs of thieves operate on the rail link from Charles de Gaulle Airport to downtown Paris by preying on jet-lagged, luggage-burdened tourists. One thief distracts the tourist with a question about directions while an accomplice takes a momentarily unguarded backpack, briefcase, or purse. Thieves often time their thefts to coincide with train stops, for a quick exit."

Savoir-Flair Tip No. 7:
Share a taxi with another airplane passenger

Air France buses are great, but why not take a taxi? You'll need to take one to your hotel anyway from the bus terminal. If there are two of you, the two bus tickets (FF 65 each at this writing) plus the taxi from the terminal to your hotel would be not much different than a taxi all the way, about FF 250 in January 2000. Think of it as part of the price of your airplane ticket. Besides, there are often no taxis at the bus terminal, which is not a building, but simply a stop on a street. (See below about transportation from Orly Airport.)

The best airport-city tip I've heard for penny-wise singles comes from a Baltimore consultant, Mary Zaske, a Francophile and frequent Paris visitor. On the plane she asks the passenger next to her how he's planning to get to center city... and then suggests sharing a cab.

Sometimes it's hard to find a cab, even at the airport. Nevertheless, it's usually better to wait, no matter how long. You might be lucky, as I was last week when there was no taxi anywhere, and be approached by a shuttle chauffeur heading back empty to Paris. If he looks credible, take him. He won't have a meter, so bargain on the rate before you get in. But you might also be hustled by a rogue taxi without the roof lights and the white sign with blue letters saying Taxi Parisien, required by legal taxis. Ignore him. *Patientez.*

Andy Stewart, widow of Supreme Court Justice Potter Stewart, known to the Washington press as "First Friend" because of her close friendship with Barbara Bush, had visited Paris many times before she arrived at Orly airport with her son, Potter Jr., and his wife in the fall of 1999. It was raining. They couldn't find a taxi. They didn't *patienter.*

"Oh, don't get me started!" she laughed, when I asked about her trip to town. "I drop with exhaustion just thinking about it! When we gave up finding a taxi at Orly, we took the Air France bus to the Montparnasse stop. There wasn't any taxi there either. The closest Métro station was under the train station. This was three long blocks away. We lugged our baggage there, we lugged it down two long stairways to the Métro platform -- no escalator was working -- and at our station, Vaneau, we lugged it *up* two more long stairways, where there wasn't any escalator at all. Then we lugged it down the street to the hotel. Next question?"

Before getting in the taxi, check the details about your hotel: its name, address, and nearest Métro. Then write all this on a piece of paper for the taxi driver. They need help. Lots of Paris hotels have similar names (see Chapter 2 about hotels). If you suspect that your pronunciation is off, stop by the airport information counter, marked *Accueil* or *Renseignements*, check the right pronunciation and practice it. Garbled pronunciation is one of the Franco-American frustrations. A French manager once asked me about a college that sounded like Ah-VOD. I was ashamed to admit I'd never heard of it. He was talking about Harvard.

Charles Feldman arrived at Charles de Gaulle after a sleepless night for a visit with his daughter, Wendy, married to a Parisian. He groggily hailed what he thought was a taxi. He'd forgotten to ask Wendy if the *"bis"* part of her address meant anything, and simply told the driver to take him to 11 rue Pigalle, without mentioning the *bis.*

The door at no. 11 was locked. The driver asked if there was a door code, numbers you push on a little plaque inside the door jamb to open doors of Paris dwellings. Feldman said he didn't know anything about that. He now mentioned the vital little word *bis* to the taxi driver. *Bis* comes from the Latin word for twice. Two separate houses now stood where a bigger one had been torn down, so that to solve the problem of two no. 11's, the *bis* was added to the one closer to no. 13. Wendy's house was next door. (If three buildings had been squeezed into the plot at the former 11, the third would have been 11 *ter*.)

The door at no. 11 *bis* opened nicely. The driver brought Feldman's suitcase inside. Noting that there was no elevator, he offered to carry the suitcase up to the apartment. The light went out just as they reached the staircase.

"Blackout!" Feldman said later. "First I was locked out -- I thought -- and now it was total darkness! All I had to do was arrive in the City of Light to trigger a major power shutdown! Well, the driver was unfazed. He explained that the hall light was timed. Wendy had said her apartment was on the fourth floor -- but he insisted on taking it up to the fifth! It seems the French count differently -- they don't start with the ground floor! He was extremely helpful -- but when he said I owed him 600 francs, I went into shock. Then he said he wasn't a taxi at all -- but a limousine! Well, at the top of five flights of stairs I decided that it was 600 francs well spent."

The Friendly Air France Buses

If you're alone, and decide to take a bus, you have choices.

Air France buses are swift, pleasant and comfortable. Air France buses from Charles de Gaulle have two itineraries (with two prices): one that stops at the Gare de Lyon on the Right Bank and the Gare Montparnasse on the Left Bank; and one that stops twice on the Right Bank: at the Palais des Congrès (Porte Maillot Métro) and at the Avenue Carnot near the Arc de Triomphe (Etoile Métro). There is no terminal building at any of these stops. There will *probably* be taxis near all of them. (See Chapter 6, Paris on Wheels.)

Here you need to check your pocket map to see which terminal is closest to your hotel. The bus driver probably won't know. During the summer, I was in the same bus with a large American in his fifties wearing neon-blue shorts that looked like bathing trunks, and a purple upper garment cut like an undershirt (not the kind of getup to touch the hearts of French people). In the aggressive voice you're likely to hear from foreigners suffering from Extremely Frazzled Tourist Nerves, or EFTN, he asked the bus driver which stop he should get off at for his hotel, which he named. Or tried to. The bus driver didn't understand but was very pleasant. The man repeated the name of the hotel in an even more aggressive voice. The driver remained pleasant, but still didn't understand. Near enough to hear him, I also couldn't decipher the name of his hotel. I suggested he write it on a piece of paper. It turned out to be the Hotel Saint Honoré, one of the easy names, I'd have thought. But his pronunciation was under water. He almost missed his stop.

When he got out, I noticed that the bus driver seemed cheery and fresh as a daisy, unperturbed by the brusque treatment. I asked him how he kept his happy temper. Easy, he said, smiling. It was his first day on the job.

More Arrival Savoir-Flair Tips

Air France buses

- Air France buses also go to or from Charles de Gaulle Airport directly to Orly Sud and Orly Ouest.
- From Orly Sud and Ouest to the city, they stop at the Porte d'Orléans and near the Gare Montparnasse before ending at the Invalides terminal, which, unlike the Charles de Gaulle Airport- Arc de Triomphe terminal, is a *building* with Air France offices, restrooms, waiting rooms, and a restaurant. It is also a reliable source of taxis.
- Downstairs (underground) are Métro and RER stations.

Various city buses (RATP) leave the airport and end at Métro stations, but if you're not an old hand at Paris, follow signs to the Air France buses.

An unmanned train goes directly from Orly to the city.

Shuttles
Roomy 8-seater mini-buses are a great way to get to the city, but usually you have to order them ahead of time. They're super for getting to the air port, and much less expensive than taxis:
-Airport Connection, tel 33 1 44 18 36 02
-Airport Shuttle, tel 33 1 45 38 55 72
(Inside France, drop the 33 and add a 0 before the 1.)

Buses go directly from both airports to Disneyland Paris.

Timed lights (minuteries)
Hall lights are timed in most apartment houses and hotels. They stay on usually for two minutes. Look for a glowing button at each landing and push it. BE SURE YOU'RE NOT RINGING SOMEONE'S DOORBELL.
One evening, after working late in Brittany, Devonshire designer Eve Heard, on her way upstairs to her room, rang the doorbells on every floor of her hotel instead of the hall lights. A lot of sleepy hotel guests came to their doors.

Door codes
Usually composed of three numbers and a letter which you push on a small rectangular plaque in the door jamb of the front door of the house. You can't see the numbers in the dark. You press one of the numbers and a faint light comes on. People over 50 need their glasses to see them. If you don't know the code, try pressing a single button at the top or the bottom of the numbers plaque.
Sometimes the code only comes on at night, which means a concierge is on day time duty.

Street listings
Many streets are named for generals, colonels, doctors, cardinals, commandants, and so forth. In your street directory, look for the street under the first letter of the title, not the name. If the street is named after someone without a title, look under the letter of the first name, not the family name.

Building floors
All over Europe, the ground floor has a special name. The numbers start with the upper floors, so that the first floor is what Americans call the second floor.In France, the ground floor is called the *rez de chaussée* (RC or 0 on elevator buttons).

Changing dollar bills
The best rate for dollar bills is to be found not at a bank or post office, but at certain small money-changing shops which don't charge a commission. You have to be careful to check the rate before handing over your dollar bills. One of the best is in the 6th arrondissement, on the rue Grégoire-de-Tours, between the rue des Quatre-Vents and the Boulevard St.-Germain.

Tipping
These are the people to tip: waiters, taxi drivers, hairdressers, hotel or restaurant car-parkers *(voituriers)*, postal package-deliverers, cloakroom attendants, and your regular butcher if he does something special for you, like

plucking a pheasant or preparing a platter of cold cuts. Also your garage owner, when you feel like it, and service people.

Waiters
An extra 5% or 10% of the bill. Never mind the *service compris* (service included). It doesn't go to the waiter, but to the management to make up for high VAT (value added tax). Americans are known for assuming that *service compris* means just that, and leaving nothing. Things are never so simple in France.

Hairdressers and *Barbers*
10 francs to the person who washes your hair, another 10 to the person who "dresses" it.

Taxis
10% of the bill if you were satisfied. Two francs if you were more or less satisfied. Nothing if you were unsatisfied. This is what French people tell me. But taxi drivers themselves tell me they really don't expect anything, nor do they grunt unpleasantly when not tipped.

Hotel Voituriers
20 to 100 francs, depending on the price of the hotel and its clientele (nouveau-riche or not).

Restaurant Voituriers
20 francs.

Postal Deliverers
20 francs if they make an extra effort (carrying boxes a long way, for instance).

Other Vendors
nothing.

Les Etrennes (special obligatory annual contributions)
The ritual all over France is to give a Christmas-New Year's "present" to certain people obliged to serve you during the year: your concierge and the local firemen, postmen and chimney sweeps: 50 to 100 francs.

City Firemen, Garbage Collectors, etc.,
If they do something special for you: from 20 to 50 francs, depending on how special and how long it takes.

Service People (*electricians, plumbers,* etc.)
After doing their job: a bottle of beer (usually refused) and 20 francs.

For more on the Magic Words, French smiles and their perception of space and time, see *French or Foe?*, chapters 1-3.

Chapter Two

Enjoying Your Hotel Stay

Where is it? Why? How Many Stars?
Hotel Surprises

L'hôtel de charme idéal conserve quelques éloquents témoignages du passé, comme un bel escalier de pierre, des plafonds à poutres, de hautes fenêtres donnant sur un jardin... des chambres joliment décorées d'élégants tissus, de gravures et de quelques meubles anciens... et n'hésite pas à offrir à ses salles de bains le meilleur du modernisme....

(The ideal hotel of charm has saved some eloquent traces of the past, a beautiful stone stairway, beamed ceilings, high windows onto a garden... rooms prettily decorated with elegant fabrics, with engravings and with a few pieces of antique furniture... and the best of modern bathrooms...)

Tatiana de Beaumont, *Guide de Charme*

Savoir-Flair Tip No. 8:
Don't get lost: Put a post-it in your passport with your hotel's address

Of the 1,464 hotels in Paris, 47 are Grand Hotels. Right, there is usually a third word to the name. But there are two at different addresses called the Grand Hôtel Moderne and two others at different addresses called the Grand Hôtel de l'Europe. There is a Grand Hôtel Univers Nord and a Grand Hôtel de l'Univers Nord. I couldn't find the very popular Jeanne d'Arc Hôtel in the phone book because the friend who was staying there didn't tell me its full name was Grand Hôtel de Jeanne d'Arc. The Grand Hôtel Inter-Continental on the rue Scribe, the grandest and the best known of the 47 Grand Hotels, is usually known simply as the Grand Hôtel. If you tell a friend to phone you at the Grand Hôtel, that is a call you easily might not get. On the other hand, if you tell them you're at the Hôtel Inter-Continental (on the rue de Castiglione), they might call you at the Grand Hôtel.

Hotels have similar and sometimes identical names also in other cities in France. The most popular hotel names, besides the Grand Hôtel, are the Hôtel de la Paix, Hôtel Central, Hôtel Moderne and Hôtel de la Gare.

If your hotel was booked by a travel agent or a tour director -- or your spouse -- maybe you haven't paid much attention to its name, or for that matter, its address. Then, if you go out for a little walk alone....

Susan Rosenberg, Brentano's buyer in Paris, tells of a distraught traveler who burst into Brentano's in that state I call EFTN (Extremely Frazzled Tourist Nerves), totally lost. Brentano's is on the Avenue de l'Opéra. This central area is thick with hotels dating from its days of splendor as center of the Belle Epoque (the 1890's) and the Années Folles (the wild 1920's).

"She couldn't find her hotel," said Susan. "She had no idea what the address was. She could only remember the name -- one of those names that lots of hotels have. But, luckily, there was only one of them around here and we found it for her."

Way beyond EFTN and close to a total hysterical collapse was a beautiful young Londoner who stumbled into the Left Bank bookstore-haven for English-speaking foreigners, the Village Voice, on the rue Princesse. She didn't speak French, didn't know the name of her hotel, and hadn't the least idea where it was, except that she'd been walking away from it for what seemed like hours. Odile Hellier, the Village Voice proprietor and her assistant, Aude Samarut, sat her down and tried to comfort her for about two hours. Figuring out her hotel was more difficult.

"She was totally traumatized," said Odile. "Not only did she not know where she lived or how to find her husband, but she was without any kind of document, credit card or cash."

Aude took her out to lunch and finally she was able to talk. She had been supposed to meet her husband in front of the Cathedral Notre Dame. But her alarm clock didn't go off and she arrived there very late. Her husband was no longer there. She'd walked to the Cathedral. She couldn't remember how, but said it hadn't been far from the hotel. So there was one clue.

"We noticed she had curious tattoos on her fingers and asked about them, because we knew there was a tattoo store on the rue de Rivoli," Odile continued. "It turned out that she'd noticed a tattoo shop as she walked by. We figured it had to be that one. So we phoned all the hotels anywhere near the rue de Rivoli and that shop -- and found the right one."

Julie Winn, a savvy Paris veteran you will meet again in later chapters, was walking along the Avenue Victor-Hugo near her apartment in the 16th arrondissement when she came across a girl in tears sitting on a bench opposite a hotel, wailing, "Doesn't anyone speak English?" Several French people were trying to help her.

"She said that this was the address of her hotel," Julie said, "but it wasn't her hotel. She had walked up and down the length of the Avenue Victor-Hugo twice, looking for it."

It turned out that her hotel was indeed on the Avenue Victor-Hugo - - but not in Paris. In Neuilly. Neuilly is a nearby suburb. Julie drove her back.

Tour directors often don't tell their clients that their hotel is not really in Paris, but a suburb. As in the next story.

Savoir-Flair Tip No. 9:
Check before reserving that your Paris hotel's zip code starts with 75

A young American couple I met on the bus to Paris from the airport, thrilled at this first visit to the city of dreams, told me they were staying in a hotel at La Défense. Their travel agent had agreed that it was very expensive, but assured them that it would be worth it to be near the all the fabulous restaurants of Paris, and all the museums and shops.

Fine. Except that La Défense is not in Paris, and is an office conglomeration of skyscrapers about half an hour by express Métro from the Paris museums, restaurants and shops and everything else they wanted to see, and empty in the evenings. The postal address of La Défense is Paris-La Défense so it sounds as if it's in Paris, but it's not. The clue is the postal zip code: 92072. All zip numbers beginning with a number in the 90's are in the suburbs, including Neuilly. The zips of all Paris arrondissements begin with 75. I hope that couple gave themselves a chance to love Paris by spending their first day looking for another hotel.

Where?

Where your hotel is located is too important to leave up to your travel agent. Before reserving, find out everything you can from a friend who has been to Paris, from books, whatever.

Left Bank or Right Bank (of the Seine)?

Paris is a city of many villages on a river. The river is a mystical presence, felt everywhere. The city draws on the river for poetry, romance, commerce and transportation. The pull of the river in the city's psyche is so strong that the streets are all numbered according to its flow. Streets running parallel to the river start in the east and progress as they go west, like the river widening as it winds its way to the Atlantic. The numbering of streets going north and south begins on the river banks, the odd numbers on the left.

Part of the city's mythical appeal is the way the river undulates through it, dividing the city in two sections as distinct from each other as an orange and an apple. No Parisian could confuse the Left Bank with the Right Bank, any more than they would mistake the shapes or the feelings of the river's central islands, the Ile Saint-Louis and the Ile de la Cité.

To a Parisian, the Right Bank means banking, industry, commerce, museums and fashion, plus the varied charms of the Marais, while the Left Bank means culture, schools and scholars, intellectuals, publishing and old-family aristocrats, plus the government.

The super-elegant, super-formal 1st, 8th or 16th arrondissements of the Right Bank, with the 2d and 17th as runners-up, are the hotel haunts of the fairly rich, the very rich, tourists on a spending spree or business foreigners in Paris to check out the 3-star chefs and ransack Hermès. This is where to go for French style. Everywhere. In store windows, on the women passing by on the street. High heels and scarves at 9:30 am. The big bucks of fashion and finance share the Faubourg Saint-Honoré with the Elysée Palace (office-residence of the President of the Republic, with his 506 civilian employees, 446 military personnel, and six chefs), the palaces of the Interior Ministry and of the embassies of the United States, Britain and Japan, and the power clubs of the political and social French elites.

The Right Bank also draws budget backpackers. While the Place des Vosges, a project of Henry IV he inaugurated in 1605, is still very royal for royal resources, much of the surrounding Marais (4th arrondissement) is a lively place for young people squeaking through, and for gays. Here is where to find some of the least expensive hotels and youth hostels, and some of the oldest houses and palaces and some of the city's greatest charm, with winding streets, rickety ancient stairways and tiny family restaurants. The rue des Martyrs, in the 9th, is one of the most exuberant in all of Paris. The 18th, 19th and 20th are hopping these days, and not just with Montmartre, Pigalle and the Flea Market. They're multicultural, multi-color and multi-interesting.

The Left Bank of the 5th, 6th, 7th and 14th arrondissements is less obvious, more secretive. It's here that travelers look for memory, exploring slowly. The Left Bank is the seat of the literati, the scientists, the *"intellos"* (intellectuals), left-wing philosophers, movie stars and the anti-monarchy, as well as of old money, government, aristocracy and some of the most sought-after and elusive, not to say wildly expensive, real estate. This is where French students become Pasteurs and Sartres, and where young foreigners, having underestimated the costs of everything (an affliction of all of us), are taken in free for the night by George Whitman, proprietor of the Shakespeare & Company Bookstore, opposite Notre Dame. George took over the name and the welcoming atmosphere, if not the actual location, from a legend, Sylvia Beach, and has become one himself. The Left Bank is where future Hemingways and Prousts, Rothkos, Van Goghs and Picassos wrestle with words and paint. It's where you find medieval streets, Gothic churches, ancient Roman baths and some of the liveliest open markets. Nearby are publishers and bookstores galore, art galeries, antique stores, universities, cafés for philosophers (yes, really) and in the 13th, that outrageous, gigantic folly, the new François Mitterrand Library. The main artery of all of this is the Boulevard Saint-Germain. Just off it in the 7th is the Hôtel Matignon, office-residence of the Prime Minister, and a dozen government ministries attending to the country's needs from the splendid former palaces of *la vieille France*.

La vieille France (ancient nobility) itself, behind high walls hiding its remaining palaces in the 7th, is somewhat still alive and well, discreet and in jeans in the interest of *égalité*, that is to say, anonymity. For if the Louvre, the palace-home of the kings for 700 years on the Right Bank, is the symbol of the 1000-year-old monarchy, the Left Bank is its aristocratic beating heart, presided over by its crown jewel, the golden dome of Les Invalides, the inspiration of the great King Louis XIV and the mausoleum of the great Emperor, Napoleon.

Between the two Banks in the middle of the Seine is the residential island bubbling with community spirit and unequaled in authentic 17th-century Old World grandeur and charm: the Ile Saint-Louis. Nearby on the Ile de la Cité, beyond a little bridge, are two of the world's greatest celebrations of the Divine: the Cathedral of Notre Dame de Paris, and the Sainte-Chapelle.

Savoir-Flair Tip No. 10:
Three stars is a good hotel investment for your Paris delight

Craig Fitchett, a handsome young Princeton graduate, now a real estate broker in Denver, changed hotels after the very first night in Paris. Not because of the location, but because of, well, everything else.

"Best thing I ever did," he said. "We love it here. Where you stay is important -- it should be a place you like. Just walking into the dining room for breakfast can be a part of the richness of your experience in Paris."

Craig and his companion (who didn't want to give her name) switched hotels because the service was "wretched" and the amenities "in terrible shape." They found just what they were looking for, the Hôtel de Noailles on the Right Bank, near the Bourse in the 2d arrondissement.

"Well, we had to pay a little more," he said. "But the difference between a 2- star and a 3- star hotel is amazing. It's worth every centime of the 200 or 300 francs difference."

Savoir-Flair Tip No. 11:
A hotel near a Métro is the best choice for keeping dry

Picking a hotel near a Métro is how you trump the periodic downpours. The Métro is the fastest and the most convenient way to get around, and also very pleasant. (See Chapter 6.)

Savoir-Flair Tip No. 12:
On arrival, be sure it's the right hotel before you pay the taxi

Mary H., from St. Paul, arrived in Paris at night by train from Barcelona and asked the taxi to take her to the Hôtel de Paris, without saying which Hôtel de Paris. The one she wanted was in Montparnasse. He took her to the Hôtel de Paris in Montmartre, which is, well, not elegant at all. The difference in New York would be between the Village and the Bronx. She realized something was wrong, but was exhausted and confused, and too timid to argue. The taxi had left. She didn't speak French and the concierge didn't understand her. She spent her first night in Paris in a tiny, unpleasant room.

Mary's problem was that in Paris there are four hotels called Hôtel de Paris and a fifth called Hôtel Paris Opéra, as well as one called Hôtel Paris Rome. In Montparnasse there is one called Hôtel Paris-Didot as well as the Hôtel de Paris.

Did the taxi take her to the wrong hotel on purpose? Possibly, if he was in the pay of the - er - unsatisfactory hotel. But probably this was the one he was more familiar with, and he took her there in good faith.

What Mary should have done:
• She should have told the taxi driver the name of her hotel and its address firmly.

• She should have added also the closest Métro station.

• If the driver looked dubious, she should have written the name and address on a piece of paper and shown him the location of the hotel on her own map of Paris. A good plan in any case.

• When she arrived at the hotel, she should have checked her reservation with the hotel concierge before paying the taxi fare.

My pickle in Toulouse

Sometimes things are a little more complicated.

When Ralph Doe, the owner of the English Bookshop in Toulouse, invited me there to give a talk and sign books, I was delighted. I'd never been to Toulouse, *la ville rose* (the pink city), deep in southwest France.

I flew in from Paris. Ande, my husband, was to meet me there, driving the two hours from our place near Bergerac. Ralph faxed me the name of the hotel where he'd reserved a room for us, the Hôtel des Beaux-Arts.

A British colleague of Ralph's met me at the airport. He explained that the hotel was in a pedestrian district with automobile access only by taxis. So he dropped me off a block away.

A sign in the small hotel entrance indicated that the concierge was one flight up. I was surprised that there was no elevator. I dragged my suitcase up some narrow, winding stairs, noticing a couple of holes in the

carpet. At the top, between two dark hallways, was a small office with a half-door like a horse's stall, in which sat, slouched over a desk, a small and very sullen-looking man who appeared to be the concierge. When I managed to get his attention, I gave my name. He couldn't find a reservation. I insisted. He made a show of looking through a much-thumbed little notebook. He found nothing. I elaborated. Mr. Doe of the English Bookstore had definitely made a reservation and I had to be at his bookstore in 20 minutes. Please show me my room. He shrugged and gave me a key. Up another staircase, he said. No, no elevator. I asked him if he could help with my suitcase. No. He couldn't leave his desk.

The room was dark. It had one small window. It was barely large enough for one straight chair and two narrow single beds steeply sloping in the middle. The single bedside lamp had a bulb of 25 watts. The walls were bare and peeling in places. In the bathroom were somehow squeezed a wash basin, a W.C. and a shower -- no room for any of the stuff in my toilette case.

I told myself I had been in worse places. Yes, but that was a long time ago when I was about 20. I made excuses for everybody. This was the only terrible room in the hotel and I had it only because they had lost Ralph Doe's reservation. Or Ralph's bookstore was hard up and I must be graceful. Or this was the provinces and what could you expect. Or something.

I worried about Ande. It was definitely not his kind of hotel room.

It was a cold February day. There was no heat in the room. I unpacked and grabbed a taxi for the bookstore. Ande arrived after my talk. We chatted about his trip and then, my heart sinking, I asked him if he'd found the hotel.

"And the room?" I said. "You weren't horrifed?"

"No, why? It's a perfectly nice room."

Ralph Doe was pleased with the turnout for the talk and the book sales. He invited us with some others for dinner and in due course we piled into his car for the ride back to the hotel. He drew up in front of a palace with pillars and its own circular driveway, next to a fine bridge over the wide lovely Gironde. Ande started to get out.

"But this isn't the hotel," I said.

Ande and Ralph looked at me strangely. "Indeed, this is the hotel," said Ralph.

"Well, that's interesting," I said. "It's not where my clothes are."

This was the Hôtel des Beaux-Arts. My clothes, it developed, were at the Hôtel des Arts.

Savoir-Flair Tip No. 13:
Turn every assumption over three times in a foreign country

In due course, after paying off the grumpy concierge in the Hôtel des Arts, I entered the room which Ralph had very generously reserved. I think it was the most beautiful hotel room I've ever stayed in, anywhere. It was a spacious corner room, with a window overlooking the river. I remember the sumptuous silky red and white bedspread, the thick carpet, the chaise longue, the handsome pictures on the walls. And the bathroom. Ballroom-sized, with terry cotton bathrobes and slippers, and walls of mirrors. You could really see what you looked like (unfortunately).

I fumed at my outrageous stupidity for having believed for one moment the other hotel was the one Ralph had booked for me.

Ande soothed me. "But think how much worse it would have been if you had started out here... and had to move to the other one."

What I should have done:

• Before I left Paris, I should have gotten hold of a map of Toulouse and located my hotel.

• Once arrived at the first hotel, at the very least I should have checked the name against Ralph's fax!

I had assumed that the friend of Ralph's knew where he was taking me. It never occurred to me that he'd made a mistake, as it might have had I been taken to the wrong hotel by a taxi. The Briton probably had never been to the Hôtel des Arts, hadn't lived long enough in Toulouse to know the difference, or even that there were two hotels with similar names.

Hotels come in all sizes and possibilities. If you're at the Ritz or the Bristol or the Plaza Athénée, their 4-star *luxe* in Paris will put you in heaven. You may have to hock your jewelry, but you will get your money's worth. All the frills, all the comfort, and the French *je ne sais quoi* touch. Nice pictures on the wall, good frames. Elegant bedspread. The room will be big, the ceilings high, the television large, the bar well stocked, the shelves and hangers plentiful, the bathroom vast with golden mixing faucets, and totally equipped down to hair dryer and slippers, the service a dream -- including porters -- and the food sublime.

Obviously the stars below 4-star *luxe* have less luxury and fewer hangers and closet space, but they may have a great deal of charm and the hotel personnel may be cozier. If they're not, move out. There are plenty of Paris hotels in all categories with charming personnel. Hotel receptionists, concierges and clerks are wonderfully professional. Helpful, brisk, polite and genuine. I love their manners. I like their reserve. I like the bonds that grow slowly if you go back to the same place faithfully, not even regularly. As with shopkeepers and restaurants, the thing to do is to shop around until you find a hotel that suits you and keep going back, like Robert Vitale below. You don't have to be a big tipper, you don't have to show off, you don't have to be young, beautiful, famous or rich. Politeness and soft voices help.

Faithful attendance is the key. My treasured college friend, the late Hannah Green, came to France with her husband Jack Wesley once every year or two for 15 years while Hannah was writing a book about Sainte Foy of Conques, stopping off in Paris for a night or two on their way to the Aveyron. They always stayed at the Hôtel du Palais Bourbon, a charming and reasonable hotel on the rue de Bourgogne. The hotel always had a room for them. This same treatment extends to me, their friend. Recently during the soccer World Cup, when Paris was bursting, they found a room at the last minute for my brother.

Savoir-Flair Tip No. 14:
Check out the telephone before you need it

One thing hotel clerks can be pretty dense about is an unusual need like itemizing business calls. Callback (the system of using a U.S.-based company rather than France Télécom for long-distance calls) and other telephone cards have sweetened the pain of hotel telephone overcharges, but French hotel phoning retains a mysterious logic all its own.

Tom McTigue, the Boeing executive-culture detective mentioned in the Introduction, found this sign on the door in his hotel room:

EN CAS D'URGENCE
FAITES LE NUMERO 43.25.61.69
(In case of emergency, phone this number.)

The phone was on the bedtable. You couldn't see the sign from the bed. Tom decided to try it out. He imagined a fire.

"There I am," said Tom, "coughing smoke, my sheets ablaze, or perhaps having a heart attack. I somehow get to the door, read the number and heroically keep it in my head as I stagger back to the bed. I dial the number. Then -- and this really happened -- a recording tells me, in French, 'All phone calls in France now require a 10-digit number. Please hang up and dial the proper 10-digit number.'

"Of course! Except that -- even if I somehow happen to know what the 10-digit number might be -- by now the hotel has burned down."

Savoir-Flair Tip No. 15:
Before reserving, phone from home to check room service

Many hotels don't have room service. If they do, enjoy it. Tip if you feel like it. They don't seem to expect it.

Savoir-Flair Tip No. 16:
Bring your own strong light bulbs

The French have different eyes. They see in the dark. Hence, a 25-watt bulb in the one bedside lamp is customary. If you're in a 4-star, it might have as much as 40 watts.

Robert Vitale, Director of International Education at Miami-Dade Community College is a true travel warrior. He comes armed.

"I visit Paris four or five times a year," he wrote to me in a letter, "and the moment I arrive in my hotel -- in the same room and in the same hotel where I've been going for 35 years -- I replace the 25-watt bulbs with the 60-watt bulbs I bought at the Monoprix years ago. They live in my suitcase between trips. I wouldn't dream of leaving them permanently installed, lest I be *grondé* (scolded) by the *réception* on my next visit. In fact, I always carry four bulbs in my suitcase -- two for myself, and two others in case an American traveling companion stays at the same hotel. They are always grateful."

The French use two kinds of light bulbs. The American screw-in type is called a *vis*. You might not need to deal with the other kind, exclusively (I think) French, which is called a *baïonnette*. You push it into the socket all the way and then turn it slightly until it clicks in place. Often it just doesn't. These bulbs can be cranky, for Americans. The French love them and have no trouble.

The only light in a simple hotel room in rural France is likely to be a bare bulb hanging by a cord from the ceiling. You've seen them in old French movies with Jean Gabin. It adds to the sense of adventure. This bulb will surely be a *baïonnette* of 25 -- maybe 15 -- watts, too high up for you to reach and, anyway, difficult to extract. *Baïonnettes* are like that.

Savoir-Flair Tip No. 17:
Don't plug in appliances made for 110 volts without a transformer

French current is 220 volts. Don't plug anything in that's made for 110 volts: it will explode.

Savoir-Flair Tip No. 18:
Wheelchair-users: call the hotel before reserving and ask about the steps

Winnie Hawkes, a writer and activist from Vermont, had polio as a child and walks a little, but less and less as she gets older, though her mind goes faster than ever. She and John, her husband, love France. They met there in 1949 and arrived in Paris in October 1999 to celebrate this 50th anniversary. At their hotel, the Lutetia on the Left Bank, despite assurances to the contrary, Winnie found that to get from her room to the dining room, she would have to take the service elevator and wheel around on the street to its one entrance without steps.

Last summer, Tom McTigue took a group of 15 Americans no longer in their twenties around the Dordogne, in southwest France. They hadn't listened to his pleas to pack lightly. In Sarlat, the hotel had an elevator, *bien sûr*. However, it was not only very small and started half a floor up from the rez-de-chaussée, but it stopped between floors. They had to throw their luggage down to the desired floor.

Savoir-Flair Tip No. 19:
Hall lights go out; look for a glowing switch button

French electricity is expensive. When you get off the elevator in the dark, be calm and look around for a slightly luminous orange glow on the wall at roughly eye height, at the beginning and end of each corridor. Go for it. That's the light switch. It's timed. Get your door open -- fast -- before it goes off.

Savoir-Flair Tip No. 20:
Door keys turn the opposite way

Door openers are often keys, rarely plastic.

"I found the light switch but no matter what I did with the key -- a normal, metal key -- the door wouldn't open," said Ron B., a doctor from Cincinnati. "It was the first day of my first trip to France and I was too intimidated by everything I'd heard about the French to go down and raise hell with the concierge. I checked that the key had the same number as the door. I tried some more. While I was fussing with it, the hall light went out. I groped around in the dark for the switch. I found it and started over again. The light went out again.

"Just then someone -- a Frenchman -- came out of a room down the hall and turned it on. He saw my plight and opened the door for me. He explained that keys in France turn in the opposite direction from what we're used to. Doors open the wrong way, too. By the way, the Frenchman who helped me was very pleasant. They all were, my whole trip."

More Hotel Savoir-Flair Tips

Elevators/Lifts

Push the RC (rez-de-chaussée) or O button for the ground floor. Push 1 for the second floor, 2 for the third floor, and so on. ES means *entresol*, or between two floors, the mezzanine. SS means *sous-sol*, underground.

Apart from the charm, these are some of the conditions you might find in under-4-star *luxe* hotels.

Size

Much, much smaller.

No matter what you're paying, the room may be a squeeze.

What it looks like

Dee Hine, of CNN, said she arrived in her perfectly nice 3-star hotel on the Left

Bank in Paris and was checking in at the Reception when an American woman got out of the elevator and shouted at the concierge from halfway across the lobby. "My room doesn't look anything like the picture in your brochure!" she screamed. "It's ugly and tiny -- I want another room! I want my money back!"

Hotel rooms hardly ever resemble the brochures very closely. If you're uneasy, ask about the colors and the dimensions when you're reserving, and above all, ask if the room has a bathroom and if so, is it with a shower or bathtub.

Porters

A vanishing breed.

This same woman looked around and saw her suitcases still on a luggage rack and had a fit. "Why hasn't the bellhop brought up my suitcases? What is taking him so long?" she raged.

Adults in France are supposed to know everything, therefore they know that they're expected to be able to carry their luggage.

Room numbers

Random. Room 506 might be on the 8th floor. Room 18 might be be on the second floor, which is the first floor for Europeans.

Bathrooms (see Chapter 3)

French 4-star *luxe* hotel rooms and bathrooms are possibly the most glorious in the world. I'm thinking above all of that wonderful one in the Hôtel des Beaux-Arts in Toulouse. Until about 1970, hotels under 4-stars *luxe* didn't automatically provide bathrooms. Showers and *les toilettes* were in the hallway. So, later they had to be built into the rooms, somehow, which means that the bath rooms as well as the rooms are likely to be smaller than you expect. Low-budget hotel rooms still don't have them. There may be a special extra 20-franc charge for a shower in the hallway.

Telephones

Since 1997, two extra digits precede the old numbers in France, first a zero and then the number of the region. The country is divided into five regions, starting with Paris and the Ile de France at 01. The numbers of the other regions proceed clockwise in French logic around Paris from the northwest (02) to northeast (03) to southeast (04) to southwest (05). For all mobile phones, the code is 06.

A few suggestions of pleasant, reasonable hotels

3-star hotels

Hôtel Bourgogne et Montana, 3 rue de Bourgogne, 75007 Paris, 01 45 51 20 22
Hôtel de Noailles, 9 rue de la Michodière, 75002 Paris, 01 47 42 92 90
Hôtel Massenet, 5 rue Massenet, 75016 Paris, 01 45 24 43 03
Hôtel-Résidence Saint Christophe, 17 rue Lacépède, 75005 Paris, 01 43 31 81 54

Hôtel Delambre, 35 rue Delambre, 75014 Paris, 01 43 20 66 31
Hôtel de L'Elysée, 12 rue des Saussaies, 75008 Paris, 01 42 65 29 25
Hôtel Résidence Lord Byron, 5 rue Chateaubriand, 75008 Paris, 01 43 59 89 98
Hôtel Royal Opéra, 5 rue Castellane, 75008 Paris, 01 42 66 14 44

2-star hotels
Grand Hôtel Jeanne d'Arc, 3 rue Jarente, 75004 Paris, 01 48 87 62 11
Hôtel du Palais Bourbon, 49 rue de Bourgogne, 75007 Paris, 01 44 11 30 70
Hôtel du Champ-de-Mars, 7 rue du Champ-de-Mars, 75007 Paris, 01 45 51 52 30
Hôtel La Serre, 24 bis rue Cler, 75007 Paris, 01 47 05 52 33
Hôtel des 3 Collèges, 16 rue Cujas, 75005 Paris, 01 43 54 67 30
Hôtel de l'Espérance, 15 rue Pascal, 75005 Paris, 01 47 07 10 99

Independent hotel
Hôtel du Dragon, 36 rue du Dragon, 75006 Paris, 01 45 48 51 05. Closed in August. No elevator. Telephone in room. TV downstairs in sitting room that looks like granny's parlor. Old piano, silk flowers, pink dragonflies on walls.

These hotels were all mentioned by friends. I was glad to see that most of them are described in detail in the wonderful guide quoted at the beginning of this chapter, with color photos and all the information about the hotel rooms and location.

For youth hostels, write or call:
Auberge de Jeunesse, Centre National
(also called the Fédération Unie des Auberges de Jeunesse):
27 rue Pajol, 75018 Paris
tel. 01 44 89 87 27 fax 01 44 89 87 10

(If calling from abroad, dial first 33, the country prefix for France, and then drop the 0 before the 1.)

Chapter Three

Enjoying French Bathrooms

Soap Talk Can Be Insulting
Les Toilettes are Also Full of Surprises

Le vécé souvent s'illumine dès qu'on ferme le verrou, d'une façon magique. D'autres fois, c'est un bouton qu'il faut tourner: le cabinet replonge alors dans l'obscurité au bout d'un certain temps, ce qui amuse beaucoup les enfants....

(The light of the W.C. in a café goes on magically as soon as one locks the door. Or there is a button that you have to turn: after a certain amount of time the loo plunges back into darkness, which children find very entertaining....)

Alain Schifres, *Les Parisiens*

Savoir-Flair Tip No. 21:
Don't expect French bathrooms to be like home

The French came late to the charm of bathrooms. You get the impression that hotel bathrooms, in particular, are a begrudged concession to the American and Germanic penchant for serious plumbing. The French heart is not in it.

The French have a special relationship to water. Water is a life-giving natural resource to be handled respectfully. They sail on it solo across the Atlantic or around the world. They're champions at this. They drink it, if it's bottled from a special spring. But taking frequent baths in it is complicated. It's expensive, it's wasteful, and it could be bad for you. For a long time it was considered sinful or perhaps poisonous.

Careless American over-consumption of water is not popular with French in-laws. "When we stay with my husband's parents, my mother-in-law feels the water boiler every day to see the water level," said Evelyn Byrne, a former Peace Corps director, in one of my seminars. "If it sinks too low, she asks me to take fewer showers."

French author Sylvie Couturié points out that French people have always lived with a consciousness of the water levels in their wells and springs. If there was a drought, the water levels sank ominously.

"Water is the source of life," she says. "No water -- no life. So of course we don't like to see it wasted. If the water in a well gets too low, then the well goes dry, so of course we use less water when we see the well levels sinking."

In the countryside, water in much of France until the 1950's was drawn by a hand pump from wells. For a bath, someone had to draw up several pails full and then lug the full pails across the courtyard and upstairs, maybe two flights of stairs. Whether the water-lugger was a servant or the farmer himself, it was not a coveted job. It was worse in the cities. Until the 20th century, you bought your water from water carriers, who were at the bottom of the social totem pole. As for washing clothes and linen, the water for it was a community resource. The women of the village rubbed their washing on stones in the local *lavoir*, or public wash-house. I saw them doing this an hour from Paris in Normandy in 1980. Some women still do in Eymet, in the Dordogne.

"Of course," says Sylvie Couturié. "Water is very expensive." Like many other French people in the country, she still uses only her own water from her well at her country farm, pumped electrically now.

In the last 30 years or so, the French have been getting used to having running water, and plenty of it. If they're not taking baths every day, they have sound historical reasons for their aversion to it.

In the Middle Ages, bathing was therapeutic and considered spiritually and physically cleansing. But then in 1347, the Plague hit Marseilles and moved north. One-third of the population died. People thought they were infected by the water. They accused the lepers, the Jews and the vagabonds of having poisoned the wells, the springs, the rivers. They decided that hot water was particularly dangerous; it opened the pores and let in the Plague. Instead of bathing, people took a "dry bath" (*toilette sèche*). Rubbing their skin was supposed to make them clean. People, even rich people, didn't change their shirts. Often they possessed only one. Things must have been pretty high, or ripe, or whichever euphemism you like. But people's noses were used to this. Rich people used a lot of perfume.

In the 17th century a bath was sometimes prescribed for illness, but was considered so debilitating that the patient was kept in bed for a week afterwards. In the 19th century, taking a bath was considered 1) bad for your health (see below about the evolution of the bidet) and 2) sinful. Bathing was what they did in brothels. Friends of mine in a French Sacré Coeur (Catholic) boarding school 40 years ago were forced to bathe with a nightgown on, in order not to be able to observe their own nakedness. Inexpensive housing projects built in the 1920's often had only a communal bathroom in the hall for several apartments. Au pair girls in Paris even now, in the 2000's, when occupying maids' rooms on the top floors, have only a W.C. down the hall and no shower or bathing facilities.

French people carry all this around in their subconscious. Despite modern plumbing and hygiene, the problem of hauling water and the bad effects of bathing are alive and well in the French spirit. The French daily *Le Figaro* (November 1998) reported a French government survey concluding that 53 percent of French people fail to take a daily bath or shower. The British press, always gleeful at an excuse to bash France, had a field day. *The Independent:* "French do not wash -- official." *The Express:* "Don't sniff, the French really do shun the shower," and the *Daily Mail:* "France, the land where soap is everlasting."

You see the same spirit in the decidedly anti-washing colloquial vocabulary of the language. Soap is bad news. *Recevoir* or *prendre un savon* (literally, to receive or take a soap) means to be reprimanded.

When the EDF, the state electric company, was found to be negligent in the application of safety regulations for transporting nuclear waste and in the maintenance of its nuclear reactors, it was reprimanded by André-Claude Lacoste, director of the DSIN, a state watchdog for nuclear safety. This is the two-inch headline about it in *Le Figaro* (March 16, 1999):

Un gros savon pour EDF

(A big soap for the EDF)

Passer un shampooing (to hand out a shampoo) means a *punition* (punishment).

Then there is the French cultural resistance to deodorants. While Americans recoil from what they call B.O., lots of French men and French women find that it's natural and not unpleasant. For many, the smell of perspiration is a sensual come-on. You will hear some of them say that Americans have de-humanized their world, antisepticizing it to the point of total bland and boring non-smell, except for ketchup. The French are keen on olfactory richness of all kinds. Just walk down any Paris street and count the smells -- good and bad. Who developed perfume into a mega-bucks industry? Which country has the most expert "noses" in the wine business?

Thus it is that bathrooms, like vacuum cleaners, have never stirred the French imagination, except negatively. You can't avoid them, but who wants to spend time dreaming about them. Aesthetically, forget it, is the general idea.

Hotel bathrooms

Hotels didn't have private bathtubs until the Ritz led the way, opening in 1898. Bathrooms in expensive French hotels now leave nothing to be desired. They are vast, magnificent, functional and full of light and delightful details.

While bathrooms in less expensive hotels may not be anything to marvel at aesthetically, you probably won't have to put up with anything distasteful or non-functional. It's unlikely, but you may have a few little surprises:

• *Showers*

There might not be a shower curtain. As for showerheads, they may seem to be designed to keep the water in rather than to let it out. Well, it saves water. Don't let a dismal little drizzle depress you. Getting wet is the point.

• *The Bidet*

The bidet was invented in France in the 18th century for the free souls who found washing pleasant and healthy, and because washing after intimate relations was considered a reliable form of birth control. (You've heard the old joke that a bidet is not to wash babies in, but to wash them out.) Made for the court, which dubbed it the "confidant of ladies," it was often a superbly crafted deluxe object for the king's mistresses, the basin in porcelain or silver resting on four delicately carved wooden feet.

However, the Church, anti-contraception, was anti-bidet. Priests were to tell their flocks that bathing, particularly intimate washing was dangerous to their health. While the really pious came down with numerous unpleasant sores and diseases, most French people understood that this was nonsense. But with the French Revolution, sex was in disgrace; bidets were seen by reformers as symbols of lasciviousness and depravity. Then under the Directoire, sex came galloping back, and bidets along with it. Later, Napoleon, a real hygiene convert who brushed his teeth every day, rehabilitated bathing and took small portable bidets with him on military campaigns. He ordered his officers to do likewise.

Now that bathtubs and showers are in, as well as contraceptives, including the Pill sold legally (since 1974), is the end of the bidet finally approaching?

- *Bathtub Handles*
Not always where you need them.
- *The W.C.*

Putting all the plumbing fixtures in the same space, Americans think, makes good structural sense. The French, however, like the Japanese, spiritually resist this. For them, the bathroom, if it has any justification at all, is for bathing -- washing -- purifying -- getting clean. So, what is that object for eliminating waste -- dirt -- doing in a place for getting clean? Thus the W.C. is often separate from the rest of bathroom. In the simpler hotels, the bedroom may adjoin a shower and wash basin, but the W.C. is likely to be down the hall. In the 4-star *luxe* hotels, it will have its own solid separate door.

- *Washcloths:*
Considered personal. French people are expected to bring their own. Their version of a washcloth is called a *gant de toilette*, or a "glove," that you can put your hand inside. Monoprix stores have them.
- *Other Accessories*
The shower caps, shampoos, creams, soaps, bath gels, sewing kits, etc. are great, if provided. This is uncertain, under 4-star-*luxe*. If you bring your own hair dryer or iron, be sure they work on French current (220 volts). French plugs are different too; try to bring your own adaptor.

Savoir-Flair Tip No. 22:
Les toilettes means both the ladies' room and the men's room

In French, *les toilettes* means both the room (the *cabinet*) and the toilet itself. It's the same for men and for women. It's a curious word and difficult to get used to, because it's in the plural, even if you're in an apartment where there is clearly just one such fixture.

You can also say "W.C.," but *les toilettes* is the best, and good under all circumstances (*a passe-partout*). You **cannot** use *les chiottes*. No foreigner can, and a Frenchman is *very* careful about when he uses it.

S'il vous plaît (please), *où sont les toilettes?* is how you ask the way to the men's room or the ladies' room in a public place. One evening at the Ritz, Columnist Art Buchwald asked the way to the men's room and was directed to a stag party given by the Duke of Windsor.

La toilette, in the singular, is the washstand, or the table with all a woman's cosmetics, pins, figures, perfumes, etc. on it. *Faire sa toilette* is to wash and dress. *Sa toilette* is a woman's whole getup.

A curious feature of French *toilettes* is that whether in a café, a restaurant or a theatre, there are no drinking fountains anywhere near. No water coolers. Also not in railroad or Métro stations or airports. However, many Paris squares have fountains with drinkable water (*eau potable*) gushing out of them. Parisians fill up jugs with it and carry it home.

Savoir-Flair Tip No. 23:
A shop not serving food doesn't have public *toilettes*

Except for the ones on the sidewalk (described below), public *toilettes* are available only in a place offering food. Stores without a food counter -- shoestores, dress stores, hardware stores, etc. -- don't have them, anyway not for you. Department stores do, because they serve food.

Savoir-Flair Tip No. 24:
Nevertheless, they'll take care of you in an emergency

French people take natural things naturally. If you have an emergency in a shoe store or some other non-eating place, the sales personnel will find you a W.C. It may be at the end of an alley with a key, tiny and cold, but you're home free.

Savoir-Flair Tip No. 25:
In a café, you're expected to order something before visiting the W.C.

If you want to use *les toilettes* in a café, order a cup of coffee, or at least something. If you're a daily customer, well, then it's all right to go straight to *les toilettes* once in a while without buying anything -- but don't make a habit of it.

Sometimes you may need a 2-franc coin to open the door. Even places that seem drastically down-market have reassuringly clean and well-equipped *toilettes*. At a tiny Italian pizzeria on the Place de l'Odéon opposite the Horses Tavern, where they give you a plastic tray and a plastic cup for your wine, the *toilettes* is not only clean, but has a washing possibility *next* to the loo in the same room, very rare in France, and in the adjoining washroom, soap, water that runs, and a *clean* cloth towel.

Savoir-Flair Tip No. 26:
Don't worry about sudden darkness; *les toilettes* lights are timed, too

You may look in vain outside and inside the W.C. for a light switch. This means that the light goes on automatically. Inside the *cabinet*, the light may go out while you're using it. The darkness is total, but don't panic. A different system is at work. A previous occupant switched it on and the timer is only now turning it off. If there is no glowing orange light switch inside the *cabinet*, there will be one in the next room. Just open the door and grope.

Savoir-Flair Tip No. 27:
If you're a woman, ignore a man peeing in front of you

Please don't freak out if I tell you that in many cafés and several department stores, the whole affair is unisex. The French just aren't as uptight about all this as "Anglo-Saxons" are.

Inez W., still shrieking at the memory: "I went to the loo in that restaurant -- and there was a man -- with his back to me, but still! -- using the urinal!"

Diana G. asked what the protocol was in this case. The answer is, just breeze on into the W.C. compartment. It will have a door. It's not unusual for café-restaurants in outlying districts of Paris to have this sort of an arrangement. As the urinals are not enclosed, women on their way to the "ladies" can see men from the back or side peeing into the urinals.

American men are also sensitive about this. Mark Brosamer, a history teacher from Chicago, e-mailed me of his distress during a recent trip to Paris:

> I went down in the Métro, it's sort of unisex down there. Anyway, there's this woman taking the money, FF 2.70. And she's facing the men's urinals. I thought, how am I going to go, with her back there? And the more I thought, the less I could concentrate on my "business" at hand. Why, in this bathroom in the middle of Paris, was there a woman sitting at a folding table just behind me, collecting money in a little tin dish? And why, in this wealthy, magnificent city, do they need 2 francs and 70 centimes from every hapless pedestrian caught between their home toilet and the one at the office?
>
> Staring at the wall, trying to let nature take its course, I was gripped by a kind of stage fright. Was she looking at me? Who is this woman, this robust "Madame Pipi" who looks like my Aunt Frances from Las Vegas? Is she some kind of professional pervert, put on the municipal payroll to humiliate American tourists? She was so close that I fantasized about turning around quickly and sending her back a few steps, table buckling, coins flying... Instead I stared more severely at the wall.
>
> When I finally finished, I arranged myself as discreetly as possible (forgoing several customary gestures of men urinating alone or among other men) and stood motionless for a moment. Then, in one fluid motion, like an owl hunting a mouse, I snapped my head around, hoping to catch her in her lascivious occupation: a pair of frightened eyes, a weasel caught in a truck's headlights. She was not looking at me. She was reading a book.

Savoir-Flair Tip No. 28:
If it's a W.C. "à la Turque," jump before you flush

In the provinces, and also in Paris's outlying districts, there are still quite a few cafés and restaurants which offer you a round porcelain hole in the floor of the *cabinet*, the system known as Turkish. This arrangement still has its faithful: easier to clean, etc. If you're good at squatting, fine. Even so, there is a technique involved. You have to flush and jump, or else your feet will be in a puddle. If the door opens inside, well, you're in trouble, unless the *cabinet* is bigger than most.

• *Drying your hands*

Some cafés and restaurants still provide real paper in a nice old-fashioned dispenser with a handle that you crank around to release the next bit. I bless them and wish them a clear ride to heaven.

Tom McTigue had lunch at a restaurant in Bergerac and later visited *les toilettes*. He washed his hands. He looked around for paper towels. He found only an electric dryer, the kind that comes on automatically when you put your hands under it. The dryer was placed very high on the wall, almost at the ceiling. In order to trigger the mechanism, he had to raise his arms over his head. The result was that the water on his wet hands trickled down his arms and dripped off his elbows.

Tom, an engineer, studied this phenomenon. "I thought maybe it was deliberately placed that high," he said, "in order to draw off the excess from your hands to your elbows, where it would drip onto the floor and hence increase the speed of drying your hands. Sort of unusual, but you never know.

"Then I noted that the electrical outlet mounted on the wall was almost at ceiling level. The electrical cord on the hand dryer was rather short. So this hand dryer must have been installed not by an electrician but by a carpenter. He simply moved it up the wall until the short cord would fit into the electrical outlet. Inventive, logical, and useless."

The public *toilettes* on the sidewalk

The oblong spaceship-looking W.C.s on the sidewalk are a little, well, daunting. Dave Barry put it like this in his syndicated column: "Paris has high-tech public-pay toilets on the streets that look as though, if you went into one, you might get beamed up to the Mother Ship."

I decided to be brave and check one out. The side where you insert your two francs didn't open. I kept pushing what looked like a door, and then began banging it, until a member of the CRS (the riot police) in battle gear appeared from nowhere. He thoughtfully advised me that the door was around on the end. Still dubious, I asked about the sign saying that children under 10 were not permitted to use it. He explained that sometimes, when you're inside, the door doesn't open. Hmm. Would the CRS agent hear me banging from the inside? I abandoned the project.

Later I heard that Dave Barry's reaction was right on. A seven-year-old girl died in one of these. Not clear why, something to do with the automatic flushing and her lack of weight.

Note: At least one of Paris's famous green Vespasiennes, or *pissotières* (sidewalk urinals) still exists near the Place d'Italie.

Savoir-Flair Tip No. 29:
Shut the W.C. door in a private house, if you want to be invited back

The only acceptable position for a bathroom and/or a W.C. door in houses all over Europe is shut. When in use and when not in use. Leaving it open is a cultural taboo, like blowing your nose in your napkin.

Chapter Four

Enjoying Walking in Paris

Parisian Solicitude
Safety Crossing Streets

... a walk about Paris will provide lessons in history, in beauty and in the point of Life.

Thomas Jefferson

Savoir-Flair Tip No. 30:
Look lost, and Parisians will stop and help you with directions

You've arrived. You've settled into your hotel and are ready to venture out. Please, this first day, *walk...* with the *Plan de Paris par Arrondissements* in your pocket and your umbrella in hand, even if the sky is pure blue. You never know. It's a good idea to take your passport (or a photocopy), but please, please, don't take your camera. Just take your time... to *look.*

Paris is a place to see on foot, cobblestone by uneven, softly colored cobblestone, square by breathtaking square, bridge by dazzling bridge, palace by splendid palace, church by soaring church. In one day, taking time to look around you at the passing scene, you can drop in and out of 2000 years of human endeavors at living, loving, dreaming, ruling, battling, worshipping, dying, by human beings who were particularly gifted for beauty and determinedly seeking it. Their handprints and footprints may give you a different sense of why you're here and who you are... as Jefferson suggests above.

Tip No. 30 demands two of the French Magic Words, even if you don't speak French. As you approach someone, map in hand, say, before

you point to it, *"Excusez-moi, monsieur..."*
Believe me, the moment Parisians understand that you need help, they help. Britons, particularly, need to be reminded of this, as I found out when John Dunn, popular English MC of the "The John Dunn Program" (BBC), did me the honor of interviewing me live from London, and said this:
"Now Polly, you know it's true that the French hate foreigners. I mean, if you stand on a street corner in Paris with your map out, the French will cross to the other side of the street in order not to help!"
No, no. Big horrible Anglo-French misunderstanding.
Craig Fitchett, the real-estate broker from Denver mentioned in Chapter 2, came to Paris after a week in London with his lovely companion on their first visit to France, without a word of French. I met them outside the Musée d'Orsay sitting on a stone curb barrier, watching the happenings of the street comedians and the crowds going by.
"We love it here!" said Craig. "People are so lively and warm. We have tourist written all over us, with our Fodor, camera and backpacks, and when we get the map out, someone always comes up to us and asks if they can help. People here are delighted to talk to you, they say hello everywhere... I wish I could really talk to them. It's the first time I've really wanted to learn a foreign language."
If Parisians don't stop, it's because of their discretion. If a foreigner has a map, it would be insulting to imply that he can't read it.

Muggings? What muggings?
As for safety, muggings or street violence in Paris are rare. At night you can walk or take the Métro without worrying about footsteps behind you.
The Marquise d'Andigné was a 7th arrondissement *monument historique* by the time she died in her late seventies around 1990. She was known for her huge diamond and sapphire pendant earrings and her strident voice in the courtyard of her *palais* on the rue de Varenne, just opposite the Prime Minister's office-residence. She loved those earrings, and she rather loved shrieking at her unruly foreign tenants. In her later years she was very bent and so tiny and thin that she was hardly there at all, apart from her voice and her upswept hairdo of voluminous snow-white hair. From the moment she rose in the morning until she turned in at night, she wore those drop earrings, bright as headlights for spotting her on her frequent walks around the neighborhood with her little

dachshund... mugger bait if I ever saw it. But, after an active day of courtyard shrieking, she died peacefully in her sleep, the earrings in place. If I were you, however, I'd leave my Cartier glasses at home. I know two women who have had them torn off while walking along a Paris sidewalk.

Crossing Paris streets

Walking in Paris. Well, the traffic lights are different, the drivers are different, the police are different, and so are the unwritten rules. Since most French pedestrians are also drivers, and vice versa, they know what to expect from each other and how the system works. You, the foreigner, might not. French drivers stopped at a red light are like race horses at the starting gate, champing at the bit. When the light turns, they're off. The definition of a second, in Paris, is the moment between when the light turns green and the car behind you blows his horn.

Anne-Elisabeth Moutet, a French journalist, wrote about this for the Internet:

> There you are, strolling down the Champs-Elysées, enjoying the view and already regretting the two McDonald's restaurants that mar the gloriously Parisian alignment of shops, cinemas and cafés. You decide to cross the avenue. Just as the light turns red for the traffic, a taxi zips past, missing you by millimeters. Still in shock, you are relieved to see that a uniformed policeman, a *flic*, has witnessed the scene. Surely he will stop the cab and fine it?
>
> However, you are the one who is in the wrong. "*Mais enfin, madame,*" the *flic* admonishes you, "*il faut être plus prudent!*" (Madame, you should be more careful!)
>
> The policeman had taken in several essential details of which you were completely unaware. One, the light was only *turning* red. There is a grace period of a few microseconds, nowhere written in the road code, but understood by all, allowing drivers (who drive at a smarter clip in France than in any other Western nation, save Italy) to keep their momentum so as not to "miss the light."
>
> Just to make life even more complicated, this period varies according to a policeman's mood, the time of year, the weather, the result of the elections. It really does, and everybody takes (usually successful) gambles on it every day.

Savoir-Flair Tip No. 31:
Don't cross without a light without a sign from the driver

If you're crossing without a traffic light on the zebra stripes (a row of white lines from sidewalk to sidewalk to aid pedestrians), it can happen that an approaching driver seems to be looking you in the eye -- but you're not sure. You hesitate and he makes a hand sign or flashes his lights at you. That means he's letting you cross. If he ignores you, wait.

Savoir-Flair Tip No. 32:
Cross certain streets only with other pedestrians

The Pont de la Concorde is a brutally congested Right Bank-Left Bank link over the Seine. For a pedestrian to reach it from the Place de la Concorde, or vice versa, means crossing the Quai des Tuileries, an artery leading to the Right Bank Expressway on the Seine. This is the DEFINITIVE PEDESTRIAN CHALLENGE in Paris. There is a traffic light, but no pedestrian signal. The zebra stripes are like makeup on an old woman: cosmetic and without effect. When the traffic light is red for the Quai and green for cars on or approaching the bridge, it is theoretically green also for pedestrians. However, instantly on green, these drivers roar into your crossing turning right from the bridge, and turning left from the Place, flowing into it steadily bumper to bumper, until the light turns green for the Quai. Then in a wink, the Quai traffic zooms into your crossing until the light turns again. Again the bridge and Place traffic get to your crossing before you. And so forth. I've seen knots of pedestrians with bulging eyes waiting for four lights before plunging ahead.

The thing to do is take a cue from little old ladies. Rent a cane from a pharmacy. The second the traffic light turns green for the bridge and the Concorde, wave the cane and charge.

Even for returning Parisians...

Paris street crossings are just as tricky for French people living abroad as for foreigners, says Chrystel Hug, author of *The Politics of Sexual Morality in Ireland* and former director of the French Cultural Center in Edinburgh.

"You get used to the British cars stopping from far away when they see you on the zebra stripes," she said recently on a visit to Paris. "They just don't, here. I almost got run over at a roundabout yesterday."

Savoir-Flair Tip No. 33:
Don't cross the street at a light until all the traffic has _stopped_

Ten years in Paris have made Susan Rosenberg extremely traffic-wary. She warns most of all against motorcycles. "I came within two feet of being killed last night," she said. "I was crossing a street in center city on the zebra stripes. I had the green light for pedestrians. All the traffic was stopped. But when I was halfway across the street, a motorcycle came roaring out of nowhere. He snaked between the cars going about 80 miles an hour, and went through the red light without slowing down in the slightest."

So now for our walk, beginning on the Left Bank in the Latin Quarter, so-called partly because the Romans settled it in the third century A.D., but mostly because Latin was the only common language of the scholars trooping to this trendy hot spot from all over Europe, beginning in the 12th century. Latin was the language of Sorbonne professors and students until the French Revolution in 1789. This is where you find medieval streets and buildings. The 15th-century houses are narrow and tall with topsy-turvy roofs as if you could do a better job yourself, but you couldn't. They were built without machines, the measurements being rather vague -- a man's thigh -- which is why they're all different, engaging, full of secrets.

Let's meet at the Café Les Deux Magots at the Place Saint-Germain-des-Prés, across from the church. The coffee costs twice as much as it does anywhere else (think of it as rent for a special space), and the café isn't *in* with the literary lights of Paris anymore (too many tourists invaded it, see Chapter 10) but where else do you have a grandstand seat for beholding one of the most stirring steeples in Christendom? It was built before 1014. The portico and the church are much later; churches built on this spot have been successively burned or destroyed since the fifth century. But think of it, this tower has been standing here already for almost 1,000 years, each stone fashioned by human hands and placed one on top of the other by other human hands, in reverence and awe of God. They, these honey-colored stones, glow with the faith of those hands, and with their memories year after year, century after century, of the monks, crusaders and knights gathering in the square and then worshipping in the chapel next door before going off to war; of the crowds milling around the square when it was a famous medieval fairground in the 12th and 13th centuries, and the crowds today. This tower isn't just old, it isn't just serene. The only remaining Romanesque monument in Paris, it stands its ground firmly and not a little sternly, a beacon from the Age of Faith. No wonder that Jean-Paul Sartre, full of wonder at it, created Existentialism sitting right here.

We'll contemplate this steeple for a while, sipping our (wildly expensive) coffee... then stroll down the Boulevard Saint-Germain for a few blocks, as far as the Boulevard Saint-Michel (the "Boul' Mich"). Have a good look at the 15th-century-Gothic Cluny Museum of medieval art behind the trees on the southeast corner, built on the remains of Roman baths. Inside are the mysterious tapestries of "The Lady and the Unicorn," sisters to the ones in the Cloisters museum on Riverside Drive in New York.

Just after this crossing, take a left on the rue de la Harpe. Wind around on medieval streets towards the Seine until you get to the Church of Saint-Julien-le-Pauvre. Built in the 12th century on the remains of a church of the 5th century, this solid little church, early Gothic with a Romanesque barrel vault, is one of the three oldest in Paris. The liturgy is Greek Melchite, or Roman Catholic but Eastern Orthodox in feeling, with its bigger-than-life-size icons of Orthodox warrior saints on gold back-grounds, the ritual opening and closing of the doors to the altar, the chants of the choir. And clouds and clouds of incense. The services are always crowded.

But the centuries have not been kind to this Gothic pearl, stirring the late American-French author Julian Green to write in *Paris* that the church is so badly cared for that "it is difficult for us to appreciate that one of the loveliest ceremonies of the Middle Ages was held in a place that our spiritual poverty has brought so low... we catch only a feeble glimpse of the way it was when... fifty monks filled its vaults with the sound of their chanting... This could be the spot where Dante knelt, between these green-stained walls that look as if an ocean has draped them with its algae; this was where the visionary hailed the invisible, and he later recalled the narrow Paris street where his meditation had enjoyed a moment's respite on its journey toward the abysses of the inner world."

Oldest Tree in Paris

Inside the garden of Saint-Julien-le-Pauvre is Paris's very oldest tree, a Robinia, a "false acacia" or a sort of locust tree, planted in 1601 in the reign of Henry IV. It's not very big or tall and is extremely odd-looking, partly because tender efforts to keep it alive include wooden planks supporting it and cement encasing the trunk. Bent with age as well it might be, it yaws to one side like the Leaning Tower of Pisa. This little garden, with its medieval echoes and struggling Robinia, is the place for the overwhelming view just across the Seine of that 12th-century colossus on the Ile de la Cité, the Cathedral of Notre Dame de Paris, which was badly hurt by the Christmas Night (1999) tempest. Begun in 1163, Notre Dame still thunders with Romanesque massiveness as well as early Gothic striving to the heavens, its vaults so high they had to be bolstered by some of the first flying buttresses. In honor of the new millennium, Notre Dame presents a scrubbed, clean face to its faithful crowds.

This walk may seem a little heavy on churches until you remember that God, personified by the Church, controlled the mind and soul of France from the fall of Rome in the fifth century until the Renaissance in the 16th century. Theology was what the students studied at the Sorbonne; other subjects had to be approved by the clergy and usually weren't; and the only buildings built to last were to the glory of God. The French monarchy wrestled with the papal chains for centuries, but it took François I to wrangle some ecclesiastical distance from Rome in 1518 with his Concordat.

Now let's cross to the Ile de la Cité, the island seat of power shared by the medieval rivals, the kings in the royal palace (now the law courts) and the cardinals in Notre Dame. We won't take the bridge in front of us, the Pont au Double, but the next bridge eastward upriver, the Pont de l'Archevêché.

The Most Moving Memorial

At the end of the Pont de l'Archevêché, a sign on a post says, "Monument aux Déportés, 1940-1945," pointing to the right. This is the memorial to the 200,000 French political prisoners, including 74,000 Jews, killed in Nazi concentration camps during the Second World War. Designed by Georges Henri Pingusson, inaugurated by Général de Gaulle in 1962, it galvanized the future architect of the Vietnam memorial in Washington.

Travelers often miss it. Most guidebooks ignore it. Once, after I'd been living Paris for four years, a friend, the late Jack Stewart, a former *New York Times* editor, asked me if I'd seen it. I admitted I'd never heard of it. "Go!" he bellowed. "Go the moment you get back! It's important! It's the most moving thing in Paris. And it's *now*, it's us, it's the 20th century. Don't forget!"

You enter through a little gate to the very tip of the Ile, the Square de l'Ile de France, a quiet, cheerful garden with clipped yew trees, cherry trees and rose bushes, and a large weeping willow. Why not sit down on one of the garden benches, and think for a while about the 200,000 deported martyrs. You can't see any sign of the monument yet, only the river, the buildings of the Ile Saint-Louis to the north and of the Left Bank to the south. After a moment, you notice letters written in the red of blood on a low wall in front of you:

Martyrs Français de la Guerre, 1940-1945

Now go down the steps in the stone wall ahead. The steps are narrow and get narrower and deeper as you descend. Below, you're in an enclosed courtyard with stone walls rising 40 feet to open sky. Thick iron bars of a grate about two feet high and three feet wide are set low in the wall ahead. High black spikes with sharp triangular metal blades ascend in a portcullis effect from the iron grate to the height of the wall. Through the bars of the grate you can perceive a patch of water. Can it be the Seine? It feels like Alcatraz. The city has vanished.

To the left between two slabs of stone, you can see a space just wide enough to pass through. I'll let you enter alone, discover the cells and read for yourself the poetry engraved on the walls to the French people who died at Auschwitz, Mauthausen, Dachau and all the others. Beyond, along the sides of a deep cavern housing the long black tomb of the Unknown Déporté, are 200,000 small bits of backlit glass.

A visit to Hell calls for a strong dose of the Divine. Just two blocks from here is one of the world's sacred glories: the Sainte-Chapelle, the shrine conceived by France's royal saint, Louis IX, to house his holy relics (now in Notre Dame). Saint Louis had bought Jesus's Crown of Thorns and several Nails of the True Cross from the Emperor of Byzantium. They cost three times as much as the construction of the chapel.

But first, lunch. You need strength. Walk around the Cathedral on the north side, down rue du Cloître-Notre-Dame. The Vieux Bistrot is right there at no. 14. Real Parisians love this restaurant. The waiters, if not really the food -- at least not when I was there recently for the first time -- are sure to bring you back pleasantly to the post-Nazi world. They love to banter.

To get to the Sainte-Chapelle from there after lunch, cross the square in front of Notre Dame and turn right at the first cross street, the rue de la Cité, for one block to the Marché aux Fleurs (the Flower Market). If you're lucky and it's springtime, late April or early May, about 30 tall trees in the midst of the market will be in bloom with lavender-colored flowers. The French florist I asked said these were paulownia trees, unknown in Europe until someone brought them from North America. Some American ladies passing by said they were cottonwood trees, and that there were lots of them in the American South.

Cross the Flower Market. The Sainte-Chapelle is on the next street, the Boulevard du Palais, just inside the courtyard of the former palace of Saint Louis, now the law courts of the Palais de Justice but still with its royal gilt entrance gate. So many travelers flock to the sublime Chapel that this gate is no longer the way in (although it is still the way out). The entrance is now 50 feet to the left.

After the turnstile, you cross the courtyard ahead and there, on the right, emerges the tall thin hymn built in 33 months, just 80 years after Notre Dame. It's called Radiant Gothic, but how can you name it? It seems to be entirely made of air, the stained glass windows floating to the sky, held up by -- nothing. No flying buttresses keep the walls in place; the masonry of the slender piers seems hardly to be there. I've decided it's held up by angels.

You enter the lower chapel and take a high, steep spiral stone stairway to the upper story, the King's chapel, once connected to Saint Louis's chambers in the palace. This is where the holy relics were venerated.

Entering it, you are transported into another dimension. The walls, a staggering 50 feet high of stained glass -- the thin piers between them hardly visible -- enclose this tall space which is proportionally extremely narrow, so that the reds, golds, blues, greens and mauves of the windows blaze in an unearthly holy glow.

It takes your breath away. There are chairs. You can sit to contemplate the 1,134 religious scenes depicted in the windows, 720 of them originals, the oldest in France. You can look at them as long as you like -- look especially for the Last Supper -- and think about this: that twice, citizens of the same country that created it almost succeeded in burning this Chapel to the ground: the first time during the ferocious rampage known as the French Revolution in 1789, and the second time during another uprising called the Commune in 1871, when petrol was poured on it, the match not lit only for lack of time. It was desecrated. No masses have been celebrated there since. Now, it is a concert hall. Unconsciously you give thanks that these fragile walls still stand, as great a miracle as their creation 800 years ago.

When you're ready, go back down the spiral stairs to the lower level, out and around, to exit by the royal gate. There, turn right, pass by the Sainte-Chapelle's entrance and turn right again on the Quai des Orfèvres walking along the side of the Palais de Justice until you come to the Pont Neuf.

At the bridge, have a long look at the bronze equestrian statue of Henri IV. You can tell from the proudly pacing horse, the regal posture and the noble head, as well as from the statue's eminent position on the city's oldest bridge -- which he himself ordered -- on the island symbolizing government power, that this was the king the French loved most. He ruled for 20 years until assassinated in 1610. Known as the Vert Galant, he was the grandfather of Louis XIV. That he was a lusty bon vivant who fathered 54 bastards is part of what he is remembered for; but above all he reigns in his country's memory as the leader of the Protestants who became a Catholic king ("Paris is well worth a mass," he said) and issued the Edict of Nantes, his signature, and above all, his stature ending the religious wars of the 16th century. Protestants were transformed into honorable citizens after almost 100 years of royally authorized persecution.

Crossing the bridge to the Left Bank, go to the right along the Seine on the Quai des Grands Augustins to the Pont des Arts. This footbridge is as wide as a small drawing room, which it feels like -- an outdoor salon -- furnished with bushes, trees and benches. Here, the British art historian, Sir Kenneth Clark, began his 12-part BBC television series "Civilization."

"On this bridge," he said, "how many pilgrims from America, from

Henry James downwards, have paused and breathed in the aroma of a long-established culture, and felt themselves to be at the very center of civilization?"

Ahead of you to the east you can just see the steeple of the Sainte-Chapelle behind the Palais de Justice. On your left is the Louvre, the palace built during 700 years by successions of kings to house themselves and their treasures. On your right is the Institut de France, Cardinal Mazarin's legacy to France, built with his final bequest. Designed by Le Vau on the orders of Louis XIV, it houses the five academies, including the Académie Française. Its dome, together with the dome of the Invalides, are masterpieces of the reign.

Now for a special treat off the beaten tourist track, inside the Institut: the library of Mazarin, Louis XIV's statesman, diplomat and prime minister, his mentor and probably his stepfather as well, who was in a class by himself in brilliance, cunning, ingeniousness and greed, all of which are on magnificent display in this collection of books and works of art. The entrance to the Institut is on the left as you face the dome. Under the arch (*la voûte*) you'll see a small door quietly marked "Bibliothèque Mazarine" in small letters, where you leave your passport as deposit while you visit the library upstairs. You reach it by entering the courtyard and mounting the steps on the left side. Two flights up, half way around the landing, open the only door, and there you are, in the library, one of those 17th century rooms unequaled in felicitous proportions. The ceiling is 25 feet high. Daylight floods in from twelve 16-paned French windows dividing fluted and carved bookcases to the ceiling, stuffed with Byzantine manuscripts, drawings by Leonardo, Bouchardon, etc. and original scores written by Mozart, as well as medieval manuscripts and ancient leather-bound volumes. Don't forget to retrieve your passport on way out.

Savoir-Flair Tip No. 34:
Get your museum pass at a Métro station (or before leaving home)

Finally the Place Vendôme, another glory of Louis XIV's reign. Back over the Pont des Arts, left along the Seine one block, then right, passing the Pyramid of the Louvre, and the lines -- endless, in the summer -- of tourists waiting without tickets. (When you want to go to the Louvre, buy yours at a Métro station and go in without waiting, at one of the other entrances listed below.) Please, as we go by the Pyramid, reflect on its geometrical straight lines of cold glass. Do they enhance or insult the honey-colored stone curves of the royal palace, built, as it was, in a continuity of style by succeeding architects over 700 years? Or is the Pyramid a Masonic symbol... mocking the Monarchy?

Whatever, I. M. Pei, the architect, has long been obsessed with pyramids and triangles, as you know from the National Gallery in Washington, so let's move on, through the arches on the other side of the garden, to the rue de Rivoli. Turn left for three blocks, then turn right on the rue de Castiglione. Two more short blocks... and here you are at the Place Vendôme, originally known as the Place Louis XIV.

Mansart designed it to celebrate this King as only he knew how. Arches ring the square and giant orders of pilasters soar up to its steeply pitched roofs, epitomizing, according to the Guide Michelin, "the full majesty of 17th-century design, a square of unequaled harmony and rhythm of line, material and design." A bronze equestrian statue of the King as a Roman emperor reigned in the center until Revolutionary mobs wrecked it. A few years later, it was Napoleon's turn to hail France as the new Rome. He ordered that column imitating Trajan's and put himself dressed as Caesar on top. The column was cast from trophy cannons, 1250 of them, dragged back from the battlefields of Austerlitz by his victorious *Grande Armée*. Napoleon-Caesar was in turn toppled after Waterloo. Luckier than Louis XIV, he's back, a copy of the original.

The Hotel Ritz is at No. 15, its bar, "liberated" by Hemingway in 1944, as charming as ever, its piano already playing quietly. Do go in. You've earned a glass of champagne, at the very least. And after that, you might want another one at the "Hemingway Bar" on the other side of the Ritz. Art Buchwald, Mary Blume, Diane Johnson, other writers and past and present members of the English and American press in Paris met there at the end of 1999 for an evening of Hemingway nostalgia.

Savoir-Flair Visiting Tips for Your Walk

Museum Pass

• A special Museums and Monuments Pass (Carte Musées et Monuments) gets you into 65 of Paris's 100 museums, including the Louvre and the Château of Versailles, without waiting in line. You can buy this pass at Métro stations, in the museums themselves, or from travel agents before leaving home. It's a glossy, handy little museum booklet full of information about opening days and hours, plus a description of the contents of the museums.

• It costs FF 80, FF 160 or FF 240 for 1, 3 and 5 days respectively.

• Without a pass, you can get Sunday discounts at many museums.

Le Louvre (*tel.* 01 40 20 53 17)

There is often no wait (and no ticket or pass required) at the entrance via the Carrousel du Louvre shopping area at 174 rue de Rivoli. You can buy your ticket once in the museum. Three other entrances with a pass or ticket required, but no wait, are: 1) the rue de Rivoli side of the Arc du Carrousel, 2) on the rue de Rivoli opposite the Métro station Palais Royal and 3) at the Porte des Lions entrance of the museum on the Seine.

• *Opening times*

Daily, including Sundays and holidays, except Tuesday. And sometimes, strikes (*grèves*). The first Sunday of the month is free, as in all national museums.

• *Hours*

9 am to 6 pm except: Wednesday, all departments, open 9 am to 9:45 pm
Monday: only the Richelieu wing is open late, to 9:45 pm

• *Entrance fees*

FF 45 for all adults without passes. No discounts for seniors or students. Free under age 18.

• *Disabled visitors*

Wheelchairs are available from the Information Desk. Call 01 40 20 53 17.

PLEASE HELP
I am on deadline

Le
LOUVRE

practicalities

open 9am to 8pm Thurs-Sun
9am to 10 pm Mon & Wed

closed Monday, mostly

They gave up!

- *Parking*

Off the avenue du Général Lemonnier, under the Tuileries Gardens.

Le Monument aux Déportés
- *Fee::* none
- *Opening times*: Daily   April-September: 10 - 12, 2 pm - 7 pm
                             October-March: 10 - 12, 2 pm - 5 pm

La Sainte-Chapelle (tel. 01 43 45 30 09)
- *Fee:* FF 35, no discounts.
- *Opening times* : Daily   April to September: 9:30 am - 6:00 pm
                             October to March: 9:30 - 5:00 pm

Mazarin Library (Bibliothèque Mazarine)
- *Fee:* none
- *Opening hours:* Daily 9:30 - 6:00 pm,

Le Vieux Bistrot, the restaurant mentioned above:
    14 rue du Cloître-Notre-Dame, 75004 Paris, tel 01 43 35 57 07

Chapter Five

Enjoying Speaking French

Useful French Bluff Words
Good French-Bad French

In these days of free trade and rapid traveling, of constant and friendly intercourse between Great Britain, America and France, all persons advancing the smallest pretension to a liberal education have more or less studied French; but many perceive, when they set foot on the soil of France, that they have also more or less failed, from want of contact with French people, to acquire that practical acquaintance with the language, which, whether one wishes to establish friendly or commercial relations, or simply to enjoy the sights of the French Metropolis, becomes an absolute necessity.

*The Diamond Guide for the Stranger in Paris,*1870

Savoir-Flair Tip No. 35:
Expecting all French people to speak English is insulting

Things have changed in the 130 years since the *Diamond Guide* above was written. Many educated people have not studied French, and many more French people speak English now than then. For foreigners, therefore, if you're in France for only a short time, speaking it *fluently* is not an "absolute necessity" either in "establishing friendly or commercial relations" or in "enjoying the sights." However, mastering the formulas of politeness, never mind the pronunciation, will make the French happy -- and you more comfortable.

I had lunch with a group of young executives on leave from their companies, who were visiting Paris as part of their Georgia Tech MBA program. They were still in shock that everyone in Paris didn't speak English.

"Before you leave the U.S., people tell you, 'Oh yes, everyone speaks English in France,'" said Scott Lambert (IXL). "So it never occurs to you that not speaking French can be perceived as rude or as having an attitude. I've found that if you at least start with a few simple words in French like, *'Parlez-vous anglais, s'il vous plaît?'* (Do you speak English, please?), it shows respect and breaks the ice. Even if you say it in English, it helps."

Savoir-Flair Tip No. 36:
Five expressions of politeness are essential with all French people

Joseph Mon (AT&T), born in Argentina, was careful to pack at least the courtesy words. "You can get by nicely if you use them all day," he said. "But next time I come, it will be for longer, with a lot more words."

Here they are, with pronunciation more or less phonetically:

hello, how do you do, sir, madam, miss	*bonjour, monsieur; bonjour, madame,* *bonjour, mademoiselle* (bohjoor, m'syeu, bohjoor, mahdahm, bohjour, mahdemwahzell)
thank you	*merci* (mairsee)
please	*s'il vous plaît* (seal voo play)
excuse me	*excusez-moi* (excusay-mwah)
good evening, sir, madam	*bonsoir, madame, bonsoir monsieur* (bohswahr; mahdahm, bohswahr m'syeu)
goodbye, sir, madam	*au revoir, madame, au revoir, monsieur* (oh revwahr mahdahm, oh revvahar, m'syeu)

With these words, and only these, you can dress like Batman and walk down the sidewalk on your hands and French people will love you. It's **important** to add the *monsieur* -- *"Bonjour, monsieur"* -- to all males over 12 . Add *madame* (my lady) for all women. *Mademoiselle* is for girls over 12 and for *very* young women.

Many Anglophones have shaved off extra time from everything, including the seconds for saying hello to ticket agents, store clerks, grocers, etc. As noted in Chapter 1, in France, saying hello comes first. Eve François, assistant buyer at the W.H.Smith bookstore in Paris: "I see many

Americans coming to buy books, and it is really shocking for us that they so often don't say hello, even in English, before they ask a question or give a book to the cashier."

Ellen Sugarman, of Miami, an investigative reporter and author, was refused service when she asked for a *Herald Tribune* at a sidewalk kiosk in Paris without saying hello first.

"I'm always telling people they have to say *'bonjour'* in France, but I was tired, in a hurry, and simply forgot," said Ellen later. "The news dealer looked at me sternly and said, *'Bonjour, madame!'* without making any motions of giving me the newspaper. He was right -- and I was awfully embarrassed. So I said *'Bonjour, monsieur'* -- and he gave me my *Herald*."

The politeness words will save you in an emergency. Never mind that they take time to say. It takes even more time if you insult someone by leaving them out, and he corrects you.

Jill Benjamin, an artist from Cleveland, took the RER C train at Invalides one day when she was late for a meeting. This train, due every 15 minutes, finally came after she'd been waiting for 20 minutes. She tried her best to jam her way in with the crowds, but the doors closed just in front of her. She called to a conductor in the car: *"Monsieur, ouvrez les portes!"* (Sir, open the doors!)

"He opened the doors," said Jill, "and while I stood on the platform, he lectured me that I should have said *'s'il vous plaît!'* (please!) Wasting more time! He let me on -- but I was so upset at having upset him that I missed my stop!"

Savoir-Flair Tip No. 37:
Don't feel embarrassed if you master only the politeness expressions

You may have heard that the French are "arrogant" and "stuffy" if you speak it badly. This is 300% wrong. It is the please, hello, thank you and so forth that matter. They are beguiled by your effort to speak their language.

Chuck Darrow is a financial adviser from Syracuse, N.Y. He spent three years in Paris with his wife, Jackie, from 1989 to 1992. They came back for a visit in 1998. I invited them to tea and asked them to tell me how they found Paris now.

"Rainy, as usual," Chuck smiled. "Wouldn't have it any other way."

Yes, but besides the rain?

"They remember us! It's so nice!"

The Darrows are quiet, careful Americans. Chuck managed to speak some French. Jackie tried but had a hard time with it. She would smile and ask, very modestly, *"Excusez-moi, mais je ne parle pas français"* (I'm sorry but I don't speak French).

"When we moved back home, everyone said, 'How did you stand living among the French? Aren't they just awful people?'" said Jackie. "And we told everyone we could that this terrible image of the French is dead wrong. They're wonderful. We loved it here."

Despite the rain beating down, they stopped in at their old haunts.

"I used to go to a hairdresser on the rue de Bourgogne, Jean Daniel," said Jackie. "He was wonderful with hair -- this was my big weekly splurge. I didn't speak French and he didn't speak English, but with smiles and sign language we managed to get along very well. I stopped by to say hello yesterday and thought he wouldn't remember me after six years -- but do you know, when he saw me come in the door, his face lit up with the most beautiful smile. He said right away, in French, that his English wasn't any better, and I said, neither was my French. So we laughed and had a lovely time."

I asked them what their advice would be to foreign travelers here.

"Speak French!" they both said right away. "It's not true that they're cross if you don't speak it right. It makes all the difference that you try. *Even three words.* It shows respect, and that you appreciate them. Respect is what it's all about."

Non-Ugly Americans are Appreciated

The distress and hurt feelings of French people when foreigners come into a store and just point and grunt, without even saying hello, without even a whisper of French, is something you don't hear about too often.

Jim Bond is an executive recruiter from Hartford, Connecticut, with cousins in Quebec. He loves speaking French with them and works at improving it by visits to French-speaking places. He e-mailed this about a recent vacation in Martinique:

> While I was brousing in a shop next to the marina, two American women were very brusquely looking through the clothing racks, periodically firing questions in English at the obviously flustered French saleswoman behind the counter. Not that my French is great, but eager to do my bit to keep down the "Ugly American" image, I offered to translate. The two women declined and soon left.

> I then began to do my best to speak with the Frenchwoman. I told her of my partly French-Canadian lineage and of my love for French culture and language.
>
> She poured out her soul to me. The proprietor of the store had told her not to worry about her lack of English; few Americans traveled to Martinique, he said. But those Americans who did come to her store virtually never could speak French and, to make matters worse, rarely bought anything, etc. etc.
>
> The next day I stopped by to say hello. The French saleswoman greeted me warmly. She told me of having gone home that evening and saying to her husband: "Today there was an American monsieur who came into the store and he was SO nice that he made up for all of the others!"

You can't master French in a total-immersion course of two weeks. However, many are the fruits of mastering it even a little, as Mia Cunningham discovered. For 11 years, at a school in Cincinnati run by Belgian nuns, Mia had French lessons five days a week that hardly left a trace. Marrying Jim changed things. Jim and Mia traveled a lot, often to France. When Jim drew a three-month assignment in Paris, Mia decided that her dream 50th-birthday present would be a total-immersion course in French. Her walk to the language school from their hotel took her by Ladurée, the famous tea room, twice a day, Mia told me, "with its irresistible almond croissants." She soon became an almond-croissant addict. One day she mentioned them in class.

"The class went crazy," she said. "They insisted on my bringing them some. This required careful planning. I worried about saying the wrong thing in the shop or looking like a stupid American turning up in class empty-handed."

She decided to check out almond-croissant procedures a day ahead. She entered the shop at 8:45 am the day before ordering them, just as the employees were filling the display cases. Mia asked her carefully rehearsed question: *"Est-ce que les croissants aux amandes sont prêts à cette heure?"* (Are the almond croissants available at this time of day?)

A shake of the head. *"Mais non, madame."*

Mia tried wording the question a little differently, just to be sure: *"Alors, on ne peut pas en acheter huit ou neuf à cette heure?"* (Then, one can't buy eight or nine of them at this time of day?)

"Non, madame."

Okay, she thought, let's wrap this thing up with the definitive question and answer: *"A quelle heure sont-ils prêts normalement?"* (What time are they normally available?)

"A huit heures et demie, madame." (At 8:30.)

What craziness is this, Mia thought. The croissants you can't buy at 8:45 are normally ready at 8:30? Then, in shock, she realized that all the employees were laughing at her. She left the shop in a misery of embarrassment, sure she was being given "the Parisian runaround."

When she told her story to some other students before class, a German classmate cleared it up: "It's just a language confusion!" he told her. *"A cette heure* (at this time) sounds just like *à sept heures* (at seven o'clock)."

Mia laughed. "Since that day of my 50th-birthday French lessons, I haven't been afraid of trying to say anything to anybody in French," she said.

Now an engineer with Lafarge Aluminates, Richard Cory started out his adult life as a U.S. naval officer. When his ship came into port at Marseilles and docked at the French Naval Station, he found out how delighted French people are with even few words of a foreigner's French.

"We were invited to the Naval Station command for lunch," he said. "I had some schoolboy French, but only remembered the few words in my Berlitz phrase book. However, my pronunciation had no hint of an American accent. When the French officers asked me a simple question in English, 'How many brothers and sisters do you have?' I gave them a simple answer in French. This really got them excited. *'Vous parlez très bien le français!* You speak very good French! Please, let's continue in French!'" they said. "I couldn't convince them that these were about the only words I had!"

Savoir-Flair Tip No. 38:
You can bluff with certain words

The French language would never have become French without the rigidly centralized school system. Basques would have kept to Basque, Bretons to Breton, Alsatians to their peculiar Franco-German dialect, and so forth. French is taught all over France the same way and with the same intensity.

The United States, the country of immigrants, never imagined a centralized program of English taught in schools. Wave after wave of immigrants from all over the world have brought their own color to American English, and have played with it as they pleased. They devised

short cuts and discovered ways of bluffing. A French friend told me one day that you can cross the United States with just these three expressions and Americans will congratulate you on your perfect English:
- If you look at it that way
- You've got a point there
- Is that so?

In French it's not quite that easy, but there are a few fillers which sound impressively native. You can say, *"Ah bon?"* (Really?) in a slightly surprised, pensive way, if you want to sound as if you understood, without committing yourself to, let's say, the extermination of bullfrogs.

If you do more or less understand but can't formulate an appropriate response, just fix your interlocutor with an intense look, nodding your head, and repeat a series of very fast yeses: *"Oui! oui oui -- oui oui - oui oui oui! "* I once had a French neighbor who did this all the time. It was her way of being charming and non-committal.

If you think it's safe to ask for a fuller explanation without being obliged, later, to say much yourself, here are some expressions that sound awfully French:
- *Ça veut dire quoi, ça?* (That means what?)
- *Ça rime avec quoi?* (That rhymes with what?)
- *C'est à dire...* (That is to say...) if said pensively, questioningly, serves more or less the same purpose.
- If you want to agree in a very French way, then you say, *"C'est exact"* or *"Tout à fait"* (Absolutely) or *"D'accord"* (Agreed).
- You can also say knowingly, *"C'est clair"* (that's clear), which doesn't mean necessarily that you agree, but that you heard and understood.
- If you're ordering something from a merchant, insert a *petit* (little) before everything and you're onto real French. It has nothing to do with size: *"un petit croissant," "un petit kilo de pommes"* (a little kilo of apples).

A *petit* inserted before an element of time --- *une petite minute, une petite heure, une petite semaine,* may mean that, regretfully, it will take longer, and maybe much longer, than a minute, or an hour, or a week. Whoever says it knows you're in a rush, and is doing her best. However, it can also mean less than a minute or an hour. It's one of the nice French ambiguities that shows you're really an old hand at the language.
- Another technique to make you sound very French is to talk in opposite negatives: you say the opposite of what you mean, but in the negative. It's stronger, has much more punch than anything in the affirmative.

Dubbed in French, this is what Bill Pullman, playing the President of the United States in the movie "Independence Day," says to the computer genius who saved the world from the Aliens: *"C'est pas mal."* (That's not bad.) In other words, the highest praise.

"C'est pas désagréable." (It's not disagreeable) means it's very pleasant.

"Elle n'est pas laide" (She's not ugly) means she's beautiful.

"Elle n'est pas mince" (She's not thin) means she's really, really fat.

When you're exasperated at someone's slowness, you grind your teeth and say, *"Il n'est vraiment pas pressé."* (He's really not in a hurry.) Don't tell a French civil servant this to his face, however. He'll be furious and stop doing it altogether, or just be even slower.

"C'est pas terrible" is a heaven-sent phrase if you don't know whether it's prudent to be positive or negative. *Terrible* can be either. Which means there is a big ambiguity problem with *"pas terrible"* if someone says it to you. Does he mean awful, as in English, or wonderful? Your clues must be in the context or in the expression on his face.

• A favorite for almost anything is *c'est normal,* and one that moves me each time when a French person says it after going far out of his way to do a favor or to help someone, as in the opening pages of Chapter 1. You thank him and inevitably he says, "It's normal" when, in another country, it wouldn't be normal at all. I heard about a down-and-out American student who couldn't pay for his food and was fed, for nothing, every day for months by the bistro next door. I went to see the owner to check this out, and he said, "But of course, madame. *C'est normal."* This is when you remember that Médecins du Monde (Doctors of the World) and Médecins Sans Frontières (Doctors Without Borders) are French, as well as Restos du Coeur (Restaurants of the Heart) which serve meals to the needy, of food left over from restaurants and supermarkets.

Savoir-Flair Tip No. 39:
English Words of 3 syllables are very likely the same in French

Jack Anderson, a partner at Ernst and Young, has been living in France for 15 years and speaks mostly French with his French Pied-Noir wife. He said that when he figured out that most words in English with more than three syllables were the same in French, bluffing his way in French turned into a fun game.

"Take what we're doing now -- conversation," he said. "Exactly the same word. Simple!"

Jack is right. Premonition, semestre, meditation, permanence, perfection, signification, department, abandon, religion, perseverance are all useful French words. There are about 5,000 of these shared words of Latin origin. However, *attention!* Some of them don't mean the same thing. They're called *faux amis* (false friends). For instance, *déception* means disappointment. *

Savoir-Flair Tip No. 40:
When learning French, avoid certain gaffes

In French, some of the stumbling blocks for foreigners:

• A reflexive verb (one with a *se*) means something different from the same verb without it.

• The meaning of a word is often transformed by its context or position in the sentence. For instance, whether you put the word *bien* before or after *vouloir* changes a polite request into a demand. *Aimer* (to love) means to like if that little word *bien* follows it. (See Chapter 12.)

• Some words change their meaning with just a slight twist: a noun can mean something totally different when it becomes a verb.

Here are a few expressions to be wary of:

1. The infinitive of the verb for calling someone *tu*, the intimate form of "you," is *"tutoyer."* *"Tu peux me tutoyer"* means literally,"Thou canst call me thou."

• *Tuer*: to kill.

Rhoderic Bannatyne, a British financial consultant transferred to France, found it stilted and cold to call his very young French secretary *vous*. He didn't speak much French yet. So one day, in the interest of being friendly, he said to her, *"Tu peux me tuer, si vous voulez. "* (You can kill me if you like.)

2. *Un baiser*, the noun: a kiss.

• *Baiser*, the verb: to f...

After their wedding in Haverford, Pennsylvania, Priscilla Weld Grosjean and her bridegroom, a Belgian, left on their honeymoon on the Queen Elizabeth. A group of Belgian businessmen were on board who knew Priscilla's husband slightly.

"Thinking they were being hospitable, they invited us to their table," she said. "We felt obliged to join them. I was very confident about my schoolgirl French, so when they asked if I was sad to leave my country, I

---

* see *Faux Amis & Key Words*, by Philip Thody & Howard Evans, Athlone, G.B., 1995

replied gaily, *"Pas du tout! Tous mes amis sont venus à bord me baiser une dernière fois!"* (Not at all! All my friends came on board to f... me one last time!)

3. *La règle, les règles:* the rule, the rules.

• *Avoir ses règles:* to have one's menstrual period.

Newell Wright, from Provo, Utah, is assistant professor of marketing at James Madison University in Virginia. Like all Mormon men, he spent two years as a missionary abroad after college. Newell's post was Paris. He loved it and worked hard on his French.

"As missionaries, we had a lot of rules to follow," he said. "For example, we couldn't call home except on Christmas and Mother's Day; we couldn't date, play basketball, read newspapers or watch TV; we were expected to study French for two hours a day and Gospel topics for another two; get up at 6:00 am and go to bed at 10:30, proselytize for 60 hours per week, etc. We even had a handbook we kept with us with all the missionary rules.

"One of the rules was that, for insurance reasons, no one could ride in our car except other missionaries. Well, one day, a French woman wanted us to give her a ride home. We politely explained that we couldn't do that. She persisted. Finally, exasperated, I said something like, *"Je ne peux pas vous ramener chez vous parce que j'ai mes règles."* (I can't take you home because I have my period.)

The French woman cracked up and told him that she certainly didn't want to interfere with his *règles*.

4. *Femelle*: female

However, while female and *femelle* both mean female, female means "relating to the sex that bears young or produces eggs," while *femelle* means only female animal; in particular, a cow elephant or a hen bird.

Richard Cory, the American engineer of the Naval Station anecdote above, was learning to speak French when he joined Lafarge Aluminates, a French multinational. One day he told a French colleague that he had a telephone message. He thought he was saying, "A woman called you." What he said was, *"Une femelle vous a téléphoné."* (A cow elephant telephoned you.)

Richard was disconcerted by the weird look on his colleague's face. The caller was his colleague's wife.

5. *Se sentir*, to feel. *Je me sens bien* means I feel well.

• *Sentir:* to smell. *Le parfum sent bon.* (The perfume smells good.)

Lynn and Russell Kelley, both young lawyers, hit Paris about 10 years ago from California. Instead of practicing law, Lynn opted for time at home with her new baby. In addition, she studied French with a private teacher, joined the board of the American Library and honed her skills as a Paris hostess *à la française*. In due course she was invited to her first elegant French dinner party, a triumph for a foreigner. The other guests were charming, the men attractive and subtly flirtatious, the conversation brilliant, the food delectable.

Lynn was having a great time until she used a trap phrase her teacher hadn't warned her about. Trying to tell the Frenchman on her right how well she felt, said, *"Je sens bon."* (I smell good.) He looked at her strangely for a moment and then burst into laughter.

Manners and the French language

Mastery of the French language and speaking *comme il faut* (correctly) is a concern of educated French people, as it has been since the founding of the Académie Française in 1635. At the top of their grammar horror list is the expression *aller au coiffeur*, instead of *aller chez le coiffeur*, *aller au boucher* instead of *chez le boucher*, and so forth.

Another top horror is the crucial difference between playing a game (golf, bridge) or a musical instrument. *On joue au golf* but *on joue du piano*. It hurts their ears when that preposition isn't right. If you're mixed up, say it in English.

The crowning ear-pain is of making a liaison in Les Halles, so that it sounds like Layzhall. The two words have to be clearly separated; the " h" of Halles is mute: "Lay Al."

When you get into the language a bit, you realize how much language and good manners are involved with each other. Practically all the words in English concerned with etiquette (a French word), and with behavior and the tricky art of entertaining, are simply taken over from French: faux pas, gaffe, comme il faut, savoir-faire, reception, RSVP. (See Chapter 17 on business entertaining.)

Being *comme il faut* in France means you are *bien élevé*, which means a whole cluster of radiant qualities: that you speak correctly and are well-brought-up, well-educated, have exquisite manners, know how to hold your knife and fork, are mindful of others and have "culture" in the full-blown French sense of that all-important word.

Calling a person *mal* élevé, the opposite of *bien* élevé, is one of the worst insults in the French language. On television I saw a minister of the

French government, a woman, driven to this extremity by an insulting journalist. *"Mais, monsieur, vous êtes mal élevé!"* she said. The journalist shrank into his seat and was not heard from again.

Savoir-Flair Tip No. 41:
Learn good French for good manners

If you're going to learn French, you might as well learn distinguished, as opposed to undistinguished or incorrect French.

Distinguished French	**Inappropriate or wrong French**
Bonjour, monsieur Bonjour, madame *(say hello with a handshake* *to each person individually)*	Bonjour messieurs-dames
Bonjour, monsieur	Bonjour, monsieur Dupont Bonjour, monsieur Yves
Bonjour, madame	Bonjour, madame la Comtesse
Au revoir, madame (goodbye, madame) *(say goodbye, with a handshake* *and an au revoir, madame, to* *each person)*	Au revoir, mesdames
Au revoir, monsieur *(to several, same as above)*	Au revoir, messieurs
Comment va votre femme? (How is your wife?) *(to friends, people of the same class)*	Comment va votre dame?
Comment va votre épouse? (How is your wife?) *(to tradespeople, people of a* *different class)*	
Comment va votre mari (husband)? *(to friends, people of the same class)*	Comment va Monsieur Dupont?

Comment va votre époux (husband)?
(to tradespeople, people of a different class)

Monsieur et Madame Dupont	Monsieur Dupont et sa dame
When being introduced: a man can say *"mes hommages"* to a lady and *"Bonjour, monsieur"* to a man It's fine for both a man and a woman to say, simply *"Bonjour, monsieur"* or *"Bonjour, madame."*	Never say *"Enchanté"* by itself.
Je vais chez le coiffeur, chez le dentiste (I'm going to the barber, to the dentist)	Je vais au coiffeur, je vais au dentiste (*bad grammar*)
Excusez-moi, je vous prie de m'excuser	Je m'excuse, faites excuses, excusez
(Nothing!)	Bon appétit
(Nothing!)	A la vôtre
Pardon?	Quoi? Comment?
Prendre un verre (*to have a drink*)	Prendre l'apéritif
A votre santé *(before sipping your apéritif)*	Au plaisir *(never never!)*
Je vous en prie	De rien, à votre service

What does that mean, good manners in France? Sometimes, for the sake of good manners, you have to sacrifice distinguished French.

Philippe Berend, young French entrepreneur and author, put it like this: "Good manners are whatever makes others comfortable. While you would normally never say *'Bon appétit'* yourself, if your table companion says it, respond with a cheerful *'Bon appétit'* of your own."

Chapter Six

Enjoying Paris on Wheels and Water

The Métro, Taxis, The RER, Buses, The Batobus, Driving, Cycling, Rollerblading

Invalides (Lignes 8, 13 et RER)
Henri IV puis Richelieu s'étaient déjà préoccupés de la situation des blessés de guerre...
l'Hôtel Royal des Invalides fut construit selon le souhait de Louis XIV, appuyé par Louvois, à partir de 1671, et terminé cinq ans plus tard en 1676... cet hôpital-hospice pouvait recueillir jusqu'à 7,000 invalides, d'où son nom.

(Henri IV, then Richelieu, had already been concerned about the situation of soldiers wounded in battle... The Royal Hotel of the Invalides was built according to the wishes of Louis XIV, supported by Louvois, from 1671 to 1676.... and could house up to 7,000 wounded soldiers, wherefore its name.)

Gérard Roland, *Stations de Métro*

The Métro

Savoir-Flair Tip No. 42:
To board, you have to open the door yourself

You have to hand it to the French for fantasy: they have now perfumed the Métro. Well, what would you expect for a 100th celebration of the most convenient, fastest, smoothest and most comfortable subway in the world? It's also probably the cleanest -- the ceilings look as if they were scrubbed yesterday -- and the quietest. The no. 1 line -- the oldest, laid in 1900 -- has rubber tires. So do nos. 8 and 14. As for comfort, the new cars have soft blue and gray cushions, plenty of standing and knee-room and free circulation between the cars.

And yes, it's true, the Métro even smells good! The RATP, the Paris regional transportation authority, decided to act on some of the complaints of its passengers and is now dumping one and a half tons a month of a perfume it christened "Madeleine" (after its smelliest station) into its cleaning products.

The RATP undertook this project with the thoroughness French government projects are known for. It took five years of R&D, screening 500 scents, testing four of them in eight stations and polling 5,000 commuters about their preferences before "Madeleine" triumphed, trailing aromas, say the RATP agents, of "countryside, woods, flowers and fruit."

"We had to find a smell that was sweet rather than violent, that lingered for two weeks and that suggested a feeling of cleanliness and well-being rather than of filthiness being covered up," said the Métro director, Jacques Rapoport, at the Invalides station during "Madeleine's" inauguration.

The Métro's customers, five million daily commuters of the Ile de France, have 370 sweet-smelling stations to choose from on 14 different lines, running over 200 kilometers (124 miles) of track. No point in Paris is more than 500 meters (550 yards) from a Métro station. Some people, like me, for instance, are lucky enough to live close to three of them.

No. 14 is the latest in high-tech innovation, just opened in 1999. No driver. The cars are sleek, comfortable, streamlined: designer cars, just the elegance *à la française* you'd dream of for a subway. The doors are automatic. The stations are splendid halls of marble and glass. A wall of automatic glass doors on the platform separates you from the tracks. It runs between the Madeleine station and the new Mitterrand Library (Bibliothèque Nationale de France).

Two of the older stations feature artwork on the platforms. The copies of statues and paintings at the Louvre station rival the originals. Murals on the platforms of the Hôtel de Ville (City Hall) station depict the history of this vast palace, the official seat of the city government. It was here that Louis XVI kissed the Revolutionary tricolor cockade in 1789, that Napoleon III proclaimed himself emperor in 1851, and here that General de Gaulle's famous tenor boomed out, *"Paris! Paris outragé! Paris brisé! Paris martyrisé! Mais Paris libéré! Libéré par lui-même... "* (Paris! Paris violated! Paris broken! Paris martyrized! But Paris liberated! Liberated by itself....)

The murals show the fairs and the executions on the square in front of the Hôtel de Ville, known until 1830 as the Place de Grève. Rent was high for windows looking onto it when bourgeois and commoners were hanged, gentlemen beheaded by the axe or the sword, witches and heretics burnt at the stake and murderers ground to pieces on the wheel.

Métro maps are given out free at the ticket windows. All guidebooks include them, as well. It's a good idea to have one on you all the time.

The logic of the Métro is directional. Each of the 14 lines runs between two fixed points, or terminuses, which give the line its double name. The key is first to find on a map which station is nearest the address you're heading for, then to check the names of the terminuses of that station's line, and finally to figure out which terminus is the direction you'll be going in, and follow signs to that terminus. If you forgot to check, and, once on the train, notice you're going in the wrong direction, you can get off at the next stop and go back without paying again. Just be sure you don't go through the exit doors, but stay in the station, simply going up and down staircases.

Two lines, no. 7 and no. 3, split in two directions on their southern route, so that they have two end-stations. You can check the name of the terminus on backlit panels on the side and the front of each car.

The number of each of the 14 lines is also posted with the terminus signs, but Parisians rarely bother about them.

If you change lines, follow the black-on-orange *correspondance* signs with both your terminus on it and the line's number, to get to the connecting train.

Métro trains always arrive in the station from the left. But -- *attention!* -- RER and SNCF trains might come from the left or the right.

When the train arrives in the station, the doors don't open automatically, except on no. 14. There will be a button to push, or a handle. From inside the car, you have also have to open it yourself to get out.

Almost all the Métro stations have electronic ticket distributors now, freeing you from the ticket agents. That is, if you can figure out which ticket you want from all the maps and charts on the station walls. For instance, there are combined Métro-museum passes and nifty-sounding *formules* for various routes and zones. I try to unravel the zones at the end of this section.

Métro Savoir-Flair Tip No. 43:
The ticket agents prefer just one question at a time

Lee Ordway, an English "cast member" at Disneyland Paris asked a ticket agent in English about the best deal for commuting to Marne-la-Vallée every day. Then she asked if there were a reduction for people under 25.

"She slammed her window down!" said Lee. "Refused to answer!

Can you imagine?"

For tired ticket agents in April, when Paris starts to fill up with the 70 million foreign visitors arriving in France every year, answering questions asked in English can be the *goutte qui fait déborder le vase* (the drop that makes the vase overflow).

Trudy and Richard DeWeese, New York photographers in Paris taking photos for their book on Paris dogs, overheard two of these tourists with their own ears at the Opéra Métro station.

"We were in the ticket line behind this elderly American couple who kept asking the agent all these questions in English about things like where they could get tickets to the Opéra and the visiting hours of Versailles," said Trudy. "The agent was nice but totally bewildered, she didn't understand anything. It turned out the Americans didn't know it was a Métro station, didn't know what the Métro was, and thought this was a sort of tourist office."

The DeWeeses patted them on the back, told them a few essentials and sent them to the Tourist Office, 127 Avenue des Champs Elysées, near the Etoile.

Métro manners
Savoir-Flair Tip No. 44:
If you're not going to give to a begging vagrant, don't look at him

Jay B., an accountant with DuPont, and his wife Mary, had been in their rented house in Neuilly for a week when they went to Paris's most completely stocked department-hardware store, the BHV (Bazar de l'Hôtel de Ville) pronounced "Bay-Ash-Vay," for various household necessities. Determined to take the Métro back to Neuilly "for the real feel of Paris," they entered it piled high with hangers, umbrellas, frames, pots and a toaster.

Soon their car was visited by a vagrant. Jay and Mary felt sorry for him, but reaching into their pockets for some change was impossible. They looked at him sorrowfully and gestured with their heads towards their encumbrances.

The man spat in Mary's face.

• *what Jay and Mary did wrong:*

They made eye contact with him, but didn't give anything.

In the Métro halls, the street artists playing an instrument and the silent beggars squatting by the wall are stationary. You can ignore them or not, drop or not drop a franc in their cap as you walk by. Inside a Métro car, it's they who move around, clamoring for your attention. You're in the concert hall for these musicians -- and you had free entry, so maybe you'd like to contribute? The ones carrying a weekly newspaper they edited themselves will first impress you in a booming voice with the hardships of life -- which they always precede with the Magic Words -- and since you are their readership, suggest your buying it for 10 francs? It's graceful to give the francs even if you decline the paper.

Most of these streets artists and vagrants (please don't call them beggars) have an above subsistence-level income from the State. It is understood that you can't give to all of them: up to you to choose whom you'll sponsor. The rule is that you don't look at the ones you don't give to. They don't want your pity. They want your money. If you look at them with a commiserating oh-I-just-wish-I-could-help look on your face and then give nothing, this is when they might spit.

Savoir-Flair Tip No. 45:
For women: on the Métro, keep your eyes on your book or expect a kiss

If you're a woman under 85, don't look *any* man on the Métro in the eye unless... well, I mean, unless you're looking for new acquaintances. If you're under 25, they might kiss you right then and there. It happened to Elizabeth K., a Medill School of Journalism student. You see a lot of kissing all over Paris. It's not known as the City of Love for nothing.

Swift help from strangers

I have an unreliable knee, and have a way of falling down on the sidewalk or on the street. Instantly there are people rushing to help me up. Last week on a Métro platform, I put some coins in a fiddler's basket and landed flat on my back. Three people, two men and a woman helped me up right away and inquired after my condition. I was fine, I said, thanking them. Another woman came up and advised me to sit down until the train came. "You took quite a fall," she said. "It is bad for the nerves and you must calm them."

More Métro Savoir-Flair tips

• *Tickets*

After inserting your ticket in the turnstile, you have to retrieve it to get through the barrier ahead. Keep it handy. You may be fined without it. RATP inspectors don't care what your story is. You could be a deaf half-naked headhunter from Borneo carrying a spear, if you don't have a ticket, you pay. These are among the few hard hearts in France.

• *Hours*

The first train is at 5:30 am. The last train leaves the end of the line at 12:30 am.

• *Zones*

1-2 are Paris; 3 is near suburbs, including Saint-Denis, La Défense, Le Bourget Airport; 5 is the other airports, Disneyland Paris, Versailles. There isn't any 4. But there's an 8 for the medieval town of Provins, though no RATP train goes there. This is one of the French Mysteries I collect.

• *Maps*

Don't forget to get one at the Métro ticket window (*un plan du Métro*).

Taxis

There is much to rejoice about in Paris taxis. They're reliable. They're relatively inexpensive. The drivers get out of the car to stow your luggage (which costs extra, per piece, but not always, depending on the mood of your cab driver).

Perhaps more than in other big cities, they're intent listeners (to you as well as to the radio) and can give you new angles on the local scene. Also, they are on the whole meticulously honest (see slight reservations about this further on) and go to great lengths to return wallets, cameras, etc. left in their cab. (See Chapter 11.) That there are no separations between the front and back seats is not only a help to conversation, but also an indication that you can walk around Paris streets most of the time without looking over your shoulder. The few women taxi drivers I've come across say they run into no danger. (These women are not to be tangled with; they might scream at you if your suitcase is heavy.)

Otherwise, enjoying taxis in Paris is another of the French ballets which has to do with:

- knowing the steps, and what the drivers expect of you
- remembering that French taxi drivers are a touchy lot
- being alert, but not *expecting* to be cheated

Savoir-Flair Tip No. 46:
Be polite and respectful until you have a good reason not to be

Like New York taxis, Paris taxi drivers often don't know their streets perfectly, even if they're French. Or they're tired and confused at the end of the day, and take you by what is clearly not a direct route. It doesn't necessarily mean they're out to gyp you.

Recently I took one from the Gare Montparnasse to my apartment on the rue de Bellechasse. At the Boulevard des Invalides I suggested he turn left, but he said firmly his way was better, via the rue de Grenelle. I thought, well, he sounds so definite... but as he drove along I realized that his route was really *way* out of the way. I said so. But he said, *"Mais non, madame.* I am a Parisian and I know the way." Finally, I insisted that he turn left on the Boulevard Raspail. Which he then did. At our door, I asked for a receipt.

He shook his head. *"C'est gratuit, madame. Je me suis trompé."* (It's free, madame. I made a mistake.)

Savoir-Flair Tip No. 47:
Don't expect to hail a cruising taxi; find a taxi stand

Harriet Holt, visiting Paris with her daughter on a Stanford University tour after her 50th Wellesley reunion:

"I was standing on the Boulevard Saint-Germain in the rain for at least 15 minutes, desperately trying to hail a taxi," she said. "Several went by, occupied, or with their roof lights low -- on the way to another client, I suppose. And then a French woman way on the other side of the boulevard, loaded down with groceries, went to the trouble of crossing that wide street to tell me that taxis don't cruise in Paris, that I should find a taxi stand and wait there."

Taxi stands are at major intersections and sometimes in the middle of the street. They're indicated with a large blue sign saying Taxi, and at the head of the rank, *Tête de Station*. You have to take the first in line.

Very often the taxi stands are empty. The best way is to call a radio taxi from your hotel. The flagfall (*prise en charge*) is 13 francs, but in this case, the meter starts running from the moment of your call. It might say 30 francs by the time it gets to you.

It's illegal for a taxi to pick you within 50 meters of a taxi stand. Don't they ever do it anyway? A driver I asked shrugged Gallically. "*Oh, vous savez, madame, s'il n'y a pas de flic....*" (Well, you know, if there's no policeman around....)

Taxi scams

A cruising taxi might be a bogus taxi. The driver might have been expelled from his company, or retired. In which case, you're without recourse if, for instance, he takes you miles out of your way or has his meter on the wrong rate. Nor can he be relied on to bring you whatever you forgot in the cab, as the genuine taxis inevitably do.

Another reason against hailing one is that he might have had his meter running for some time before you got in. This could double or triple the fare. The *Wall Street Journal* ran a four-column story about taxi scams recently (November, 1999), mostly about this "arming the meter," cautioning its readers that if you ask for a receipt, the driver may hand you a fake one from a supply bulging out of the glove pocket.

If you do find one cruising, I wouldn't worry too much. Julie Winn has been hailing taxis for 10 years and says she has never had a problem. My experience with Paris taxis has also been just fine.

Fake cassettes

It's possible that even if you phone a bona-fide radio taxi, you could be taken for an unwelcome ride by an ingenious cabbie. A French businessman had a good laugh telling me about being driven miles and miles out of the way around a miles-long gridlock traffic jam which was announced on the driver's radio. When his company's auditing department saw this colossal bill on his expense account, they freaked out. And checked up on the Paris traffic that day. It was perfectly fluid. The taxi driver had taped reports of a real traffic jam and played the cassette, pretending it was his radio.

Savoir-Flair Tip No. 48:
Hop in the taxi, greet him, and only then tell him your destination

Wherever you find the cab, get in before you tell the driver where you're going. Right away, say, *"Bonjour, monsieur."* If you don't greet them politely, they'll either scold you or be ostentatiously grumpy for the whole ride.

"I was scolded by a taxi driver because I didn't say *'bonjour'* when I got in the cab," said Laurie Perry, a lawyer with Microsoft in Paris. "Then he scolded me for my horrible French. He was very blunt about it. I tried to explain that I work in English all day and it is very difficult! It's frustrating if a stranger corrects you, and isn't tactful about it. But he's right, I should have said *'Bonjour, monsieur.'*

After you've said *"Bonjour, monsieur,"* tell him where you're going. If you tell him before you get in, he might consider the ride too short to bother with and refuse to take you. Legally he has to, but, in practice... well, he knows you probably won't complain to the address in black letters on the sticker of the left rear window: Préfecture de Police. (See the address below.)

After a flight from Alaska via New York to Charles de Gaulle Airport, Mary Ann Rabeau, the cheery grandmother from Anchorage mentioned in the Introduction, took an Air France bus with her traveling companion and friend, Louise Henceroth, age 77, from the airport to the Porte Maillot terminus, next to the Hotel Concorde Lafayette. Three taxis were waiting at the nearby taxi rank. Mary Ann made the mistake of saying her destination before getting in.

"The first one refused to take us to our hotel in Neuilly, and then the other two also refused to take us," said Mary Ann a few days later. "How were we supposed to get there -- walk, three kilometers? with our luggage? We managed to find another taxi stand, and there, a taxi took pity on us. Otherwise, everyone has been lovely to us. People always get up on the Métro to give us a seat."

Ande, my husband, is hard to shock, but I managed it recently when I told him what happened to me at the Arc de Triomphe bus terminus, also after a transatlantic flight to Charles de Gaulle airport. I saw three taxis lined up across the street from the bus stop. Leaving two suitcases on the sidewalk next to the bus, I hurried with my carry-on bag to grab the first taxi. The driver got out of the cab to stow it. I told him I had two more suitcases across the street. He made no move to come with me. Piqued, tired from the flight, I lugged the second suitcase across the street and remarked, *"D'habitude, on m'aide avec mes valises."* (Usually, one helps with my luggage.) He didn't budge. I went to collect the third one. When I came back, there was no sign of the taxi. My carry-on bag and the other suitcase had been dumped in the middle of the street.

If the driver refuses to take you even if you do get in the cab before telling him where you're going, then please follow the example of Julie Winn. In spite of being a woman, beautiful, charming and speaking excellent French, this is what happened:

"I explained to the driver that I knew it was a very short trip, but this was an emergency," she said. "My neighbor across the hall had gone away, leaving her three children in charge of the au pair. The au pair got sick and had to go to the hospital, so there I was, taking care of those three, plus my own small ones and I had to go to the pharmacy for one of the children -- and the driver wouldn't take me! Another day a taxi swore at me because I didn't have change. So I wrote two complaints -- and I was later informed that one of them had to pay a fine of FF 2,000 francs and the other was fined *and* had to stop driving for five days."

Savoir-Flair Tip No. 49:
In the rain or at dinner time, the Métro will get you there faster

You'd think that the 14,900 Paris taxis could also cope with rain, but believe me, if it's raining, the radio taxis hardly ever answer and the taxi stands are empty. Better call the taxi the day before. If you're in a hotel, your concierge has a special taxi pal. If not, you have to go to a taxi stand and wait. The queue will be long. You'll wait something like half an hour. This is when Parisians revert to their Gaulois past, taking on both each other and the Romans (any foreigners around). Even young women like Judy S. and Allison M., students at Medill School of Journalism of Northwestern University, are likely to be lost in the shuffle.

"We'd been tramping around museums all afternoon and were exhausted," Judy said. "After the Musée d'Orsay, we joined the taxi queue at the rue de Solférino. The line was endless. We waited for about 25 minutes. At last, it was our turn -- and when the taxi drove up, the woman behind me practically knocked us over to jump in first. When the next taxi came, same thing -- but it was a man who bumped us out of the way!"

What they did wrong and should have done:
• They shouldn't have spoken English together, demonstrating to any veteran Parisian taxi-grabber that they were pushovers. Line-jumping,

particularly in a taxi line in the rain, is a popular sport here. Like movie and post office queues, taxi lines are not *"noble."* *Noble* lines are opera and theatre queues. French people don't jump these. Waiting for a taxi behind foreigners, a French person would reason that it's hard enough to get a taxi in the rain without all these foreigners horning in.

• Having made this mistake, they should have stood there with defiant body language, elbows out, and been on the alert to jump in the next cab the first possible instant. Standing in line at post offices is a good warm-up for this.

Taxis at pre-dinner and dinner time

Even if it's not raining, it's practically impossible to get a taxi between 7:15 and 9 pm, unless you have subscribed to a special service (see Taxi Tips, below). If you're in a hotel, fine. As usual, your concierge will come through. Otherwise, plan to take a bus or the Métro.

Savoir-Flair Tip No. 50:
Insist on your own address of a nightclub, or expect to be cheated

The French Tourist Office has tall piles of letters from Anglophones, who stopped in for a drink at a night club suggested by their cab driver, stayed for two, and were given a huge bill for a couple of whiskeys.

Savoir-Flair Tip No. 51:
Only charm will get your group a fourth seat in a taxi

Taxis don't have to accept a fare in the front seat. Often they reserve it for their dog. If they do accept a fourth person, they can charge extra. If you're a family of four -- or five -- this is your chance to practice PPO (Persistent Personal Operating). That is, being terribly polite and throwing yourself on their mercy. Julie Winn is a master at it: "The fourth person counts as an adult only. I've squeezed in four children plus myself many times, with no extra charge. Also, if you ask the driver politely if he will accept a fourth person, in front by him, he will probably say yes. I've never had one refuse yet."

If he doesn't charge you extra for extra people, you should tip more.

More Taxi Savoir-Flair Tips
Roof lights

The taxi is free only if the wide white roof light saying Taxi Parisien is lit. If one or more of the three little lights under it are lit, either the taxi has a passenger inside or is on call.

Rates

In use A , B or C, depends on the zone and the time of day. Night rates click in between 8:00 pm and 6:30 am
- white = rate A: daytime, inside the Blvd Périphérique, Monday to Saturday
- orange = rate B, at night, trips to the suburbs during the day, Sundays and holidays
- blue = rate C, for trips to the suburbs, 7 pm to 7 am

Extra charges

On the rear left window of all bona fide taxis, you can discern black letters telling you the number of the taxi, the address of the complaints office, and the amount of the extra charge for:
- rail station and airport pickups
- heavy suitcases, unwieldy packages (This depends on the taxi; often I am not charged extra)
- 4th person or an animal (see Tip No. 51)

Radio taxis
- Taxi Bleu: 01 49 36 10 10
- Alpha Taxi: 01 45 85 85 85
- Taxi-radio Etoile: 01 42 70 41 41

Airport shuttle
- Airport Shuttle: 01 45 38 55 72 (less expensive, excellent in my experience)
- Airport Connection: 01 44 18 36 02

Taxi subscriptions

If you're staying a while, you can avoid the taxi-panics between 7 pm and 9:30 pm; when it rains, and the first day of vacation periods. These three taxi companies give you a subscription. The system may be different -- either a lump yearly sum and the meter price, or no lump sum and a higher meter price:
- G7 (pronounced Jay Set): 01 47 39 47 39
- Taxi Bleu Privilégié: 01 49 36 10 10
- artaxi: 01 42 03 50 50

Tips

Usually between 2 FF and 5FF but not obligatory. See Chapter 1 at the end, under *tipping*.

Complaints:

Service de Taxis

Préfecture de Police

36 rue des Morillons

75015 Paris

The RER

The RER, pronounced "air-uh-air" (Réseau Express Régional) is the system of four lines of fast suburban trains (known as RER A B C or D) that take you to places like Versailles, Marne-la-Vallée (Disneyland Paris), Orly Airport and Charles de Gaulle Airport.

Inside the Périphérique, the boulevard circling the city, RER stations are often in Métro stations, only deeper. If you're transferring from a Métro to an RER, for instance at Saint-Michel, where you can catch the RER to Charles de Gaulle Airport, you'll have a long way with lots of stairs to navigate with your luggage. Better take a taxi directly to an RER station.

A Métro ticket will take you to any RER station within the Périphérique, but farther than that, you'll need to buy a special ticket. Hang onto it. You can't get out of the station at the other end without it.

Savoir-Flair Tip No. 52:
Be sure you know the *name* of your train

Unlike the Métro, where all the trains arriving on the same platform go to the same terminus (except for lines 7 and 3 mentioned above), RER trains coming in on the same platform split off to different routes. The RER train-recognition system is by words of four letters, some of them names, like SARA, others just a jumble of letters. The RER C train that ends on the Rive Gauche near the Château in Versailles, for instance, is called VICK. The electronic monitors on the platform tell you the time the next trains are due, what stations they stop at, when they're approaching the station and when they're actually in the station. The names of the trains are on the electronic monitors and on the front of the first car of the train.

Savoir-Flair Tip No. 53:
Be sure the white light next to your station is lit on the monitor

Only if the white light is lit next to a station's name on the platform monitor will the incoming train stop there. Unlike the Métro trains, which stop at all the stations on their line, some RER trains are locals and some are express. All the possible stations on that route are listed on the monitor. But the train will not stop at a station not lit.

Some stations, like Saint-Michel for the C trains, don't have these helpful monitors on the platform. There will only be a sign -- one -- on the wall, noting the stops of the next train, but without its name. You have to find the name from the timetable chart above. This sign often doesn't change for the next train until it's practically in the station. If you're not standing in front of this sign, there is ONLY ONE WAY to know if the train approaching is yours, which is checking the 4-letter name on the front of the first car of the train.

RER lines are run not by the RATP, which runs the Métro, but by the SNCF, the French railway system. Knowing this can make a difference during a public transit strike.

Buses

It took Anne Harris, a Canadian and longtime Paris friend, to convert me from Métro to bus. Each time she and Russell, her husband, came for dinner on the no. 69, she'd comment on how beautiful the early evening light was on the Seine, on the Conciergerie -- on Notre Dame!

With the bus routes in different colors on your *petit parisien* guide and your pocket-sized *Plan de Paris* with a list of all the stops on each bus route, it's possible to figure out the bus you want. Be sure to note the one-way streets on their route. Paris buses are scheduled to go all over Paris every few minutes, but they can be held up in traffic, demonstrations, whatever.

Bus drivers are endlessly patient. If you missed your stop, they'll make a special stop for you. If you're running to a bus stop and they're just leaving, they stop and let you on if you look pathetic and charming, and even if you don't. And they have change for a ticket!

But like most Frenchmen, they have their pride. Tread softly. Particularly as, lately, bus drivers are often harassed, sometimes violently, in the racially agitated suburbs. Roller-bladers and cyclists are hard for them to keep track of.

Savoir-Flair Tip No. 54:
If you phone immediately for lost property, you might get it back

If you leave something on the bus and call the terminus of that route right away, you have a 90% chance of getting it back. Call 08 36 68 77 14 to find out the number of the bus terminus for that route. (See Chapter 11.)

Savoir-Flair Tip No. 55:
Check the time intervals between buses on the chart at the bus stop

Most bus stops have shelter now, with seats, and charts of the bus routes concerned on the wall, and below, other charts showing the frequency of the buses, the first and last buses of that route and whether they go on Sundays. If your bus is more than five minutes late, ask the driver of another bus if there is a problem. A few days ago, an 83 told us he couldn't take his usual route on the Boulevard Raspail because a car was burning in the middle of a street on his route. He had to make a detour without knowing the area, so his French passengers guided him. He courteously stopped wherever they wanted.

Another time, when I'd had a 20-minute wait for a 94, I greeted the driver warmly and asked him if he'd had trouble? He looked surprised. He showed me his watch, and his timetable. "I am exactly on time," he said.

"Maybe, but I've been waiting for 20 minutes," I said.

Now he looked angry. A woman in the front seat came to my rescue. "I also waited for 20 minutes," she said.

At the next stop, another woman boarded and complained at how long she had waited. The driver was now upset. He looked stumped. Finally he had the answer. "The bus before me must have been early," he said.

More Bus Savoir-Flair tips

Bus tickets

• If you have a pass, just flash it at the driver as you get on.

• Otherwise, buy a block of 10 Métro tickets from the nearest Métro station or at a Tabac. Buying a *carnet* of 10 for FF 54 (as of Jan 3, 2000) reduces the cost of each ticket.

• Insert one ticket in the punching machine behind the driver when you get on. When it comes out, keep it with you till you get off.

• If you forgot to buy Métro tickets, you can buy a bus ticket from the driver. It costs not quite double a Métro ticket.

• If you want to transfer to another bus or to the Métro, it costs another ticket. (Inside the Métro itself, you can ride all day on one ticket, transferring to other lines as often as you like.)

Getting off

• To be sure the bus stops at your stop, push the red button -- sometimes it's green -- near the exit. It will light up letters in red above the driver: *arrêt demandé*. Sometimes the door doesn't open, and someone calls to the driver, *"La PORTE, s'il vous plaît!"*

The Batobus

From mid-April to October, the best fun for getting around town, and at FF 12 a ticket the best sightseeing deal, is the Seine shuttle known as the Batobus, operated by Les Bateaux Parisiens. It runs every 35 minutes, from 10:00 am to 7 pm, and stops at the Eiffel Tower, the Musée d'Orsay, the

Louvre (on the opposite bank), near Notre Dame and near the Hôtel de Ville.

Driving a Car in Paris

The English and the Germans hate driving in Paris. The Spanish and the Italians love it. Americans, keen on challenge and risk, love it too. Usually not right away. Rob Chelseth is a tall American from St. Paul, Michigan, who had had about 30 years' experience in driving when he arrived in Paris, age 46.

Savoir-Flair Tip No. 56:
Driving in Paris means rewiring your brain's reflexes

"For six months I held both hands tightly on the wheel in a tense grip, totally focused on what the other cars were doing," he said. "No playing with the radio. No winding the window up or down. Your U.S. reflexes are no good here. You have to rewire the circuiting.

"You don't know what they're going to do. Turn left from the right-hand lane? Or vice versa? Or come at you full steam ahead from the right, from a much smaller road, without stopping? They make out because they have a sort of symbiosis with each other about what they're all going to do. After a while, I did too. But... it took a while."

And then, Rob began to love it. "When I'd been here a year," Rob added, "a Frenchman was driving with me and gave me the greatest compliment. He said, in a tone of wonder, 'You drive just like someone who lives here.'"

Savoir-Flair Tip No. 57:
Get used to Paris drivers before joining the Etoile traffic

The good news is that French drivers are skillful and have split-second reflexes. Just watch them at the Etoile, where cars from 12 main streets zoom in, whiz around the Arc de Triomphe pellmell in a non-stop free for all -- no traffic lights -- and zoom out against the cars zooming in. Foreigners without previous Paris driving practice get paralyzed in a middle lane. They inch along in gridlock, going around maybe five times before they dare exit.

For Rob Chelseth, the Etoile is the definitive driver's challenge: "Now I love it. I anticipate, just like them. I look it over, scope it out, see where the competition is, who has a bent right fender, and then I take off.

It's a great contest. But you better strap on your helmet. When a Frenchman is at the wheel, it's war. Americans get very upset at this. They can easily sink into psychological difficulties and work themselves into a jam. They tell themselves that the French are crazy, their mental health is all screwed up. But that's not it. It's that it's different here. A man in his car in France is a cavalry charger on his horse 100 years ago."

Foreign passengers being driven around the Etoile for the first time either faint or exult. John Rudder, an African-American interior designer from Chicago, driven around it his second day in Paris by a friend, was ecstatic. "I LOVED IT!" he told me. "What a crazy place! And no horns honking! No accidents! Just everyone going bonkers! I demanded that my friend take me around again, twice more."

Savoir-Flair Tip No. 58:
The car coming from the right has the right of way

Not all Paris cross streets have a stop sign or traffic light. In this case, the car coming from the right has priority. This *priorité à droite* takes getting used to and I recommend doing so, in the interests of staying alive. See Chapter 19 for a detailed report on it.

Buses always have priority and take it very aggressively. And the on-ramp on the Boulevard Périphérique has priority over the right lane.

Savoir-Flair Tip No. 59:
The priority is for those inside roundabouts, supposedly

A journalist with *Le Figaro* noticed that some roundabouts in Paris had *priorité à droite*, and some didn't. He asked the police about it. They said it was a mystery to them, too. See Chapter 19 for more on roundabouts.

Motoring Parisians have observed that, whatever the law is, at the roundabouts at the Etoile, the Trocadéro, the Porte Maillot, etc. the priority is to the right, to the people entering.

Even if a sign at the roundabouts says that the priority is not for drivers entering, many people assume that it is. In other words, you're on your own.

Savoir-Flair Tip No. 60:
On expressways, drive aggressively or you'll be tailgated

Rob Chelseth pointed out the "vocabulary of honking" in Paris. "One toot if you're lax at the traffic light. Two toots if you're in his way. Three toots and leaning on the horn if he's really annoyed. On the expressway, if you don't drive aggressively enough, then they tailgate you. This makes Anglophones boil over indignantly. We have to learn not to be John Law. Easy does it."

Savoir-Flair Tip No. 61:
Navigate in Paris by monuments

Rob added, "Also, you have to learn to navigate differently in Paris. In the States you learn names and numbers of the streets. In Paris, the streets change their names every few feet. So you navigate by landmarks. There always is one -- the Eiffel Tower, the golden dome of the Invalides, the Arc de Triomphe. When you're near your destination is the time to get out the map."

The sign posting is excellent in Paris. In the provinces it's... well, it's different. See Chapter 18. Also for information about U.S. drivers' licenses, etc.

More Driving Savoir-Flair Tips for Motorists

Card for the parking meters: at a Tabac.

Parking on a street with a towaway sign

You have about 10 minutes grace. Taking more than that is dangerous. In addition to the inconvenience and the hassle of finding the nearest police station (*Commissariat de Police*) to discover the whereabouts of the car, your fine comes to about 900 francs total, if you get the car the same day. More if you wait until the next day. Each day adds on.

Seatbelts

Obligatory, even if lots of Parisians don't use it. The police are more likely to stop you for this than for speeding.

Honking

It's illegal, unless you're in danger. In danger of being late for an appointment doesn't count (unless you can dress it up excitingly for a policeman).

Addressing a policeman

Always say *"monsieur l'agent."* For all other men in France, *"monsieur"* is correct.

Documents you ought to have with you all the time

Your passport or your French I.D. card, driver's license, car ownership papers (*carte grise*) and insurance proof (*carte verte*).

Not stopping at a traffic light (brûler un feu)

Can be fined from FF 1500 to FF 3,000. Cars might run red lights exiting roundabouts, as mentioned in Chapter 4. I never saw one stopped by a policeman (*un flic*, in street language).

Fuel (essence)

See Chapter 19 for details about the different types of fuel at the pumps.

• In Paris, service stations may be a pump or two on the curb. They're indicated on Michelin scale maps of the city.

•A few Paris self-service stations with many pumps are open every day 24 hours a day:

1) in the 7th arrondissement at 6 Boulevard Raspail
2) underground at the Esplanade des Invalides (7th)
3) in the 3d arrondissement at 42 rue de Beaubourg

For one nearer you, look in the yellow pages under *Stations Service*.

Paris by Bicycle

Even if you're in Paris only a short time, why not bicycle? You can rent one in the train stations and lots of other places listed at the end of the chapter, along with indications of how you can have one delivered to your hotel. It's fun, it's exercise, it's a great way to see the city.

Above all, for Paris cyclists, our time has come. The Mayor loves us. *Le Figaro* magazine ran a full-page color photo of him in *tenue de vélo* (cycling gear) leaning against his mauve bicycle, which matched his mauve turtle-necked sweater, trousers and wind breaker.

Until recently, we cyclists have been the transport pariah. No part of the street or sidewalk belonged to us. Trucks thundered down on us, buses skimmed by within an inch, cars cut us off at intersections.

Mayor Tiberi is changing all this. He has ordained that highways along the Seine are reserved for cyclists Friday evenings and Sunday afternoons. He has promised the Association des Cyclistes 150 kilometers of bicycle lanes by the end of the year 2000. Lanes on the *right* of streets, to be sure. In two years, he has already put 126 kilometers of lanes in place, on the right; real lanes, many with one-foot high cement dividers to scare off trespassing motorists.

Trespassers on our lanes are actually being fined by attentive policemen. In 1998, 5500 traffic violation tickets were handed out to these 4-wheeled trespassers.

Bus drivers are being given training seminars in polite manners to cyclists. Part of the program is for the bus drivers to ride a bike in the city themselves, and see how they like it, each of them, when a bus roars by him with about an inch to spare. We're even promised care for our lungs. Buses running on diesel are gradually going to be replaced with non-polluting, possibly electrically powered buses.

It's enough to make a city cyclist dangerously dizzy with joy. And on top of this, the Mayor inaugurated an annual *Fête du Vélo et du Piéton* (Festival of the Bicycle and the Pedestrian). It's part of his "Politics in Favor of the Bicycle." The fourth Festival was on March 19, 2000. The Mayor invited all Parisian cyclists with or without a bicycle to come to breakfast (free), to borrow (for free) a bicycle if they didn't own one, and set off on a (free) specially arranged car-free tour of one of four areas of Paris.

In addition, the RATP announced that Métro line No. 1 has now opened its doors to cyclists with their bicycles all day -- on Sundays. It concedes a slight problem. During the ride you have to hold the bicycle in the air with two hands.

Savoir-Flair Tip No. 62:
Don't turn from the middle lane of an avenue without a traffic light

I did, once, from the center of the Champs Elysées, and don't recommend it. Nothing broken, but almost. Two weeks on my back. The cars behind going at Formula One speeds just didn't have enough space to stop in time from my arm signal.

Savoir-Flair Tip No. 63:
Watch out for doors of parked cars opening suddenly in front of you

A study by the City of Paris in 1997 showed that, of accidents caused by non-cyclists to cyclists, 14% were caused by parked-car doors opening suddenly.

Savoir-Flair Tip No. 64:
Watch out for cars cutting you off at traffic lights

When the traffic light turns green, wait for the car on your left. It might cut you off turning to the right. Cars suddenly changing direction was the reason for 15% of the accidents by non-cyclists to cyclists in that 1997 study.

Savoir-Flair Tip No. 65:
A helmet is advisable but not obligatory

Legally, pedal reflectors and a bell, plus, after dark, a white or yellow front light and a red back light are required for bikes.

I've never worn a helmet in 30 years of cycling in Paris. However, lots of specialists advise it.

Savoir-Flair Tip No. 66:
Police may be indulgent, but respecting traffic regulations is healthier

Remembering and respecting the absolute priority of any vehicle coming from the right, unless there's a traffic light or a stop sign, is another strongly recommended way to remain healthy.

Paris police are usually tender with recalcitrant cyclists. They probably won't fine you for missing or shabby gear, or for cycling on a sidewalk.

However, going through a red light is not popular with them. Don't. It's dangerous for everybody and you'll be fined on the spot, though I've never seen Paris police fine a car for going through a red light. Cars do this a lot. You should be wary of them when you're on a bike.

Going down a one-way street the wrong way is tempting, but may also bring trouble. Two tough policemen have given me a hard time about this. One of them hopped out of a police car and angrily insisted I get off my bike and walk, instantly. The other, elderly and gnarled, wanted to see my passport and threatened to take me to court. But didn't.

Another time, three policemen caught me at this, near where I live. They were standing on a street corner.

"We've been watching you," said one, not aggressively. "The whole length of the street. You know the fine for this? It's 1500 francs."

"*Mais, monsieur l'agent,*" I said, plaintively, "I'm late -- I have to cook my husband's lunch! He'll be angry!"

"Oh," said the policeman, "does he beat you?"

"Well... not often," I said.

All three policeman cracked up and I cycled on.

That's one way to handle it. Not that I recommend it. The policemen have to be in a relaxed mood for it to work. There is a surer method, which is pulling a French fit, but your French has to be fast and your tone indignant. Dominique Lacoste, very French, is a master at this.

"If a *flic* stops me on my bike going the wrong way on a one-way street, I simply scream at him furiously," she said. "I ask him if he hasn't anything better to do than stopping women on a bicycle. Why doesn't he go out to the suburbs and arrest some real criminals? Then they sort of shrivel up and look meek."

Savoir-Flair Tip No. 67:
Watch out for motorcycles jumping the gun at a red light

Motorcycles often zoom forward from a traffic light when it's red for the other street, but not yet green for them. If you're on a bike, watch them.

Savoir-Flair Tip No. 68:
Cycling around the Etoile is suicidal

If French motorists (particularly men) are usually polite and solicitous of cyclists, at the Etoile with those 12 converging streets, it's a different matter. Their own survival is at stake. **They have no time to think about yours.**

Jean Henceroth, a banker with Chase Manhattan in Paris, was at the top of the Champs Elysées, waiting for a light to change, when she saw a cyclist trespassing this basic rule of common sense. A man on a bicycle, followed by his *dog*, a setter, plunged into the Etoile traffic near where she was standing.

"When I saw that man on a *bicycle* -- with a *dog* -- entering the Etoile, I was horrified," said Jean. "I was sure the man or the dog or both would be killed. I had to wait to see what happened. The cars went crazy. Horns honked, brakes screeched. The man and the dog went around the whole circle and then turned into the Champs Elysées again, near where I was standing. I had to find out if this was a bet or what, so I went up and asked him. It turned out he was Dutch. He said that this was just something he had always wanted to do. He had been training his dog for a year in Amsterdam."

Savoir-Flair Tip No. 69:
A mask helps against breathing problems from pollution

Paris is getting more and more polluted. A mask is a good idea if you have any kind of breathing problem. The French Institut National de la Consommation (Consumers' Institute) tested six different kinds of masks and only okayed one, the Respro mask. It's English and filters 85 % of diesel exhaust.

More City Cyclist Savoir-Flair Tips

Fédération Française de Cyclotourisme:

   8 rue Jean-Marie Jégo, 75013 Paris,

   tel 33 1 44 16 88 88

Bicycle rentals

   • The RATP rentals offer probably the lowest rates. They have four sites.

   Headquarters: Maison Roue Libre, 95 bis, rue Rambuteau, 75001 Paris

- Bike 'n Roller
    137, rue Saint Dominique, 75007 Paris -Métro Ecole Militaire
    tel. 33 1 44 18 30 39
    6, rue Saint-Julien-Le-Pauvre, 75005 Paris, Métro Saint-Michel
    tel. 33 1 44 07 35 89

Bicycle tours in Paris
    All of the above, plus:
    - The mairies (town halls) of the arrondissements have city bicycle
        maps available.
    - The Hôtel de Ville has put out a map for trips just outside the city limits, *"100
        kilomètres pour vivre à Paris à vélo"* (100 km for living in Paris on your
        bicycle). For example, one for 32 kilometers along the Marne River,
        starting at Joinville le Pont.

Bicycle rental delivery to your hotel :
    - Paris on Wheels, tel. 33 6 80 66 95 58 (delivery within the hour)

Biking vocabulary: see Chapter 20: "Country Biking."

Rollerblading: For tips, see Savoir-Flair Cyclist Tips above

Everybody's doing it. You see them all over, gracefully skating the
streets of Paris. It's almost a show, and it's new and joyful. Young and not
so young, Parisians are rollerblading, lots of them in dark suits and ties,
holding a briefcase.

In Paris, 3.5 million rollerblade skates were sold in 1998. The
phenomenon has hit cities all over France: from Rennes to Marseille, from
Lille to Bordeaux. The Hôtel de Ville tried to fight it and then, reasonably,
decided to join it. Police were put on rollerblades to chase criminals. In
1998 Mayor Tiberi instituted "ParisRoller" meetings: rollerblading outings
on Friday evenings on streets cleared of traffic and also on Sundays, for
rollerbladers skating along the Seine.

And by the way, for ice skaters there's a huge skating rink in the
winter on the Place de l'Hôtel de Ville.

More Rollerbladers Savoir-Flair Tips

Rollerblade renters:
    - Bike 'n Roller
    137, rue Saint Dominique, 75007 Paris -Métro Ecole Militaire
    tel. 33 1 44 18 30 39

6, rue Saint-Julien-Le-Pauvre, 75005 Paris, Métro Saint-Michel
tel. 33 1 44 07 35 89
• FranScoop
47, rue Servan, 75011 Paris, Métro St. Maur

Information about organised rollerblade activities:
•ParisRoller
6 Impasse Baudran, tel 33 1 45 88 23 43,
E-mail:ParisRoller@bigfoot.com,
Web site: www.bigfoot.com/pari.roller

Chapter Seven

Enjoying French Dogs

City Hall's Wars Against Dog Poop
Dogs are Different in France

Je chante le chien crotté, le chien pauvre, le chien sans domicile, le chien flâneur, le chien saltimbanque, le chien dont l'instinct, comme celui du pauvre, du bohémien et de l'historien, est merveilleusement aiguillonné par la nécessité, cette si bonne mère, cette vraie patronne de l'intelligence!

(I sing to the muddy dog, the poor dog, the homeless dog, the wandering dog, the acrobatic dog, whose instinct, like that of the bum, the gypsy and the historian, is marvelously stimulated by necessity, that excellent mother, that real patron of intelligence!)

Charles Baudelaire

Savoir-Flair Tip no. 70:
The French not only love dogs but love others who love dogs

Paris isn't just a city with dogs, it's the city *of* dogs, 200,000 of them, more per person than in any other city. Paris is where dogs enter restaurants, head held high, and jump up on a chair next to their owner. The city with a dog cemetery. The city with taxi drivers holding the front seat for their dog, and where café owners let their German shepherds lie across the entrance mat. Climb over them if you can.

The pre-eminent dazzle of dogs is clear from the language: *avoir du chien*, which means literally "to have dog," is the supreme compliment every French woman aspires to. She can be old and/or ugly, if she *a du chien*, if she "has dog" she has nothing to worry about. She is very, very

101

sexually appealing. Only a woman can have dog.

Yes, but the *sidewalks*, you say....

Shelly Betz, a beautiful African-American trailing her Minnesota Mining (3M) husband, brought her golden retriever, Ganymede, to Paris. At first she was upset by the sidewalks, and then....

"All the dog poop really unnerved me, but I wasn't going to say so," she said. "And then I went into a restaurant -- and there was this cocker spaniel sitting beside me at the next table! I did a double take, I can tell you. So I thought well, maybe I can take Ganymede the next time I go out? I told myself this was crazy, he's much too big, but I thought... I'll try. He hates being left in the apartment alone. He yowls and drives the neighbors crazy. So next night out, I arrive at the restaurant -- a really expensive elegant place -- with this enormous dog -- and I'm thinking I'm going to be bounced -- and what do you know? The maitre d' pats Ganymede and asks me what he wants for dinner! I thought Americans had a fixation on dogs, but these French have us beat by a long shot."

Don and Lynda Horowitz, of San Francisco, came to Paris with Queenie, a tiny Yorkshire terrier. Don walks Queenie while Lynda is at the Ritz cooking school.*

"I've met four or five neighbors walking dogs on the Avenue Foch," said Don. "People in bars talk to Queenie. She had a crush on a Scottie, so I got to know the Scottie owner -- and through him met other people. One day in the park I met a lady with another Yorkshire called Gizmo. Gizmo and Queenie hit it off -- and then the woman said, 'Oh, so this is the famous Queenie! I've heard all about her. She is the famous American dog in the neighborhood!'"

Henry Haley, a financial controller at Lafarge now back in the U.S., went for many walks in the Tuileries with his white-haired Pekinese, Gloria. Gloria was always very popular. One evening, Henry found a dinner invitation in his letter box, "To the owner of Gloria."

Hervé de Charrette, former Foreign Minister of France, walks his black female Labrador regularly on the Champ-de-Mars. A fervent dog lover, he's honorary president of the Association of Friends of the Dogs of the Champ-de-Mars.

"Having a dog is a perfect way to meet people," he told *Le Figaro*

---

*Lynda loves the Ritz cooking school. She says the ingredients are fresh, the kitchens immaculate, the teaching exciting and the administration responsive, unlike the Cordon Bleu cooking school, which, under new management, she says is "money-grasping, filthy dirty, uses tired ingredients and lacks any interest in the cooking students."

(Nov 6, 1998). "While the dogs are sniffing each other up and down, their owners can talk. It's amusing, because around this area, people know each other by the names of their dogs... and you know, dogs give a great deal of pleasure. They're attentive, sensitive and have many more feelings than people imagine. I would say even that a good dog can talk. But that depends also on his master.... "

If you happen to be a dog skeptic, then Parisians will quote Homer to prove what you're missing, which is that dogs are smarter about a lot of things than people. It was Ulysses's dog, after all, who was the only one in his household who recognized him after his 20-year Odyssey away from home.

Yes, but the sidewalks?

Well, the City of Paris declared war on the dog-pooped sidewalks in 1978. Things had gotten really out of hand. Parisians in the 70's were zigzagging about the sidewalks as if they were playing hopscotch, looking in vain for a spot without a dog *crotte* on it. Sidewalks (*trottoirs*) were called *crottoirs*. Blind people stayed home. Parisians were outraged. Tourists were disgusted.

Savoir-Flair Tip No. 71:
Don't complain -- it's better than it was !

Now it's better, really. Much better. Yet despite zillions of francs spent

year after year since then to change dog habits, Parisians are still outraged and tourists are still disgusted.

"I find it staggering, it blows my mind, all that dog shit," said Alistair Ironside, an English banker.

Foreign media play up to the outrage. In the American movie "Prêt-à-Porter," by Robert Altman, the principal character slips on it four times. The BBC TV series "Highlander," on French television M6 every evening in the fall of 1998, took place in Paris for many of the episodes. "You could tell it was actually filmed in Paris, and not because of the nice shot of Notre Dame," said Newell Wright, the professor we met in Chapter 5. "The protagonist, Duncan McLeod, was walking down the sidewalk, and there was dog poop all over it."

"When I first got here," said Salem Eway, one of Newell's juniors abroad, "I wondered why everyone was walking with their head down. Then I found out that you better have your head down and watch carefully where you put your feet.... or... squoosh!"

Why on earth, if war was declared, haven't the sidewalks been *really* cleaned up in all this time?

Savoir-Flair Tip no. 72:
French solutions take time: *patientez*!

Well, you can see that the position of City Hall has been delicate. On the one hand, all those dog owners (who also vote). On the other, the domestic and foreign outrage and 16 tons of *déjections* to clean up *every day*, costing *"les contribuables"* (us taxpayers) about FF 7 a pound, not to mention the 650 or so people hospitalized yearly from accidents officially attributed to the *déjections*. The problem was a little like tobacco and cars. Tobacco isn't healthy, but the government needs to sell its cigarettes; cars pollute the air and make noise, but the government needs the fuel taxes.

So the strategy of the 1978 war was gentle persuasion. A Director of Cleanliness was appointed. He undertook various educational maneuvers to convince dog owners to nudge their *toutous* to perform not on the sidewalk but in the gutters on the street, which are washed down regularly. A 15-second film on television and in movie theaters showed a man on a tree-lined sidewalk pretending not to notice the steaming object just deposited nearby by his *toutou*. A polite child says to him, "Monsieur, you forgot something." On buses and billboards, in subway corridors and shop windows, dogs of various sizes and breedings were pictured politely saying, "I go where I'm told to go." Underneath, a tactful caption added, "Teach him to use the gutter."

Silhouettes of dachshunds in white cement were embedded in the sidewalks, their noses and arrows under them pointing to the gutters. The dogs didn't get it. Neither did their owners. Tourists were confused. One of them remarked to me about how strange it was that, in Paris, there were "all those dachshund graves under the sidewalks."

Tourists stumbling into *crottes* had another misunderstanding that upset the street cleaners, who complained about their mats. You've probably noticed those filthy wet rolled-up mats in the gutters. I had assumed they were part of the trash being cleaned up, but no. The mats are there on purpose. When the gutter water is turned on, the mats are placed in a special way to guide the flow in the desired direction. Suddenly the mats began to be smeared with dog *crottes*. Was somebody so angry at the *crottes* that he was taking it out on the street cleaners? The City made an investigation. It turned out that tourists thought the mats were put there by thoughtful city officials, to clean their shoes after an unlucky encounter.

Gentle persuasion wasn't working. In 1991, the Director of Cleanliness asked the Ministry of Agriculture, the Society for the Protection of Animals, police headquarters and a TV veterinarian for advice. Another campaign was undertaken called Awareness. Ronald Searle, the distinguished British artist, was engaged to draw a *séduisant* message for dog owners. Posters of his delightful cartoon, showing a civic-minded dog owner gracefully sweeping his dog's *crotte* into a dustpan, were plastered on buses and walls all over Paris. Special agents were hired to reason with dog owners. French versions of pooper-scoopers were designed. A cane with a folding spatula at the end was put on sale.

Still no effect. Non-dog owning Parisians were getting more and more fed up. They were writing 3,000 letters of outrage a week to newspapers and City Hall.

So the City gave up on the dog owners and concentrated on cleaning the sidewalks, creating and outfitting 80 small green Vespa-type vehicles with vacuum cleaners attached that scoop up the *déjections* as they whiz along. The locals call them *moto-crottes*. They cost the city of Paris 32 million francs a year, which brought the price of dog dirt on a line with veal, about 37 francs a kilo. The city, understandably, would prefer to do without them.

Savoir-Flair Tip No. 73:
Be careful what you say: Parisians hate it too

In 1998, according to a poll made by the Prefecture de Police, 70% of Parisians continued to find the poop *"insupportable"* or even *"extrêmement insupportable."* More had to be done.

Savoir-Flair Tip No. 74:
City Hall's new cleanliness czar will make a difference

The new cleanliness czar, Patrick Trémège, adjunct to the mayor for environmental matters, is a dedicated anti-*crotte* director. He shifted 50 of his park custodians to dog patrol and has put through a series of new measures: mobile information kiosks to go from arrondissement to arrondissement to sensitize Parisians to urban cleanliness; a seminar educating the city's civil servants on good dog training so that they can advise dog owners appropriately; a team of young counselors to accost dog owners on the spot with advice on good dog manners; creation of several special fenced-in dog *"toilettes"* in various arrondissements; and, most recently (autumn 1999) more posters and movie shorts to be shown all over Paris. They're pretty revolting. Much more vivid and gripping than the gentle suggestions of the '70's pubs. One of them shows a blind man returning home, having speared 8 *crottes* on his cane. Another shows a

child in the park about to play with one.

But what about getting really tough with these civil delinquents? I mean, making them pick up after their dogs, as in other cities? I went to the annex of the Hôtel de Ville to ask Monsieur Trémège.

He told me that he's all for it. But first, for French dog owners to be the tiniest bit willing, you need a really elegant, long, cleverly designed pooper-scooper, like the one he saw in New York in 1974 but no longer available, even as a model. He has City Hall engineers hard at work endeavoring to recreate one.

As for fining recalcitrant dog owners... well, that's full of problems too. Legally, they can be now, up to FF 3000, but in practice, the police say they have better things to do than chase delinquent dogs, and Mr. Trémège's dog patrollers have no legal power to demand identification or make arrests. Also, he says, you have to remember that many of the recalcitrants are elderly, if not very old, perhaps with old dogs. Teaching old people and old dogs new tricks... well... and the old people may be poor, as well. You don't want to make life any more difficult for the elderly poor.

Meanwhile, Parisians continue to be outraged and tourists continue to be disgusted. Mr. Trémège said that these two different cultural reactions were perhaps the key to the problem. French people, inclined to take natural things naturally, are outraged, but not disgusted.

"How can I explain?" he said. "French people are made differently. Seeing it in the street is not so shocking as it is to you."

Chapter Eight

Enjoying Getting Information

It's Spoonfed

To get from A to B in France, you have to stop by C. Which is another way of saying that the French like to go around a subject, not straight into it.

Dr. Michael Zeising, Consultant, Cologne, Germany

Savoir-Flair Tip No. 75:
Think of all possible questions to elicit the answer you need

In a popular French film, *"Le Bonheur est dans le pré"* (Happiness is in the Pasture), Michel Serrault, the French actor, plays an ex-husband who finds a new life with a lady who owns a farm in *la France profonde*, probably the Auvergne. They would like to legalize the situation. The only problem is the lady's husband. He's a shady character, probably a crook. He's been missing for 26 years, but is he dead? Or might he show up and make trouble over the new arrangement?

They question everyone they can think of, including, eventually, the hired farm helper. We have already had glimpses of this wary peasant behind a window, looking dourly out at the farmyard while he eats his lunch in silence.

"When did you last see Monsieur Michel?" they ask.

"About 26 years ago," says the farmhand.

"Where did you see him last?"

"In the well."

"What do you mean, in the well?"

"He fell in the well," says the peasant.

"When did he come out?"

"He didn't come out."

"You mean he's still in there?"

"Far as I know."

Serrault and his adopted wife gasp. "Well -- for goodness sake, why didn't you tell someone?" says Serrault.

"No one asked," says the peasant.

Information is spoon-fed in France. That is, piece by piece, put together yourself, step by step. As in the Sherlock Holmes story, the dog *not* barking was an important piece of evidence.

Perhaps you remember Peter Sellers as Inspector Clouseau when he left out a key step on arriving at an inn. Never mind that the inn was in Austria; it could just as well have been in France. Blocking his way towards the concierge was a large ominous-looking dog.

With a careful look at the dog, Sellers asks, "Does your dog bite?"

"No," says the concierge.

Sellers, reassured, advances. The dog bites him.

"But you said your dog didn't bite!" Sellers howls.

"It's not my dog," says the concierge.

Savoir-Flair Tip No. 76:
Don't expect any information to be volunteered

Foreign executives transferred here go crazy on the subject.

"I find out that one of my reports has a piece of information I've been hunting all over for weeks and he didn't tell me!" is the typical reproach, and one I heard again recently from Paul Salacain, the director the Heidelberg Web Press near Chantilly, mentioned in the Introduction.

"But did you ask him?" I wondered.

"He should have volunteered it."

About eight centuries of habit are behind this information hoarding. During the Inquisition, French Cathars and later, Huguenots (Protestants), found out that speaking in codes might save them from being burned. During the Terror, it could save your neck. Heads fell one day that had been in control the day before. An efficient spy service was a priority of the French kings and above all, of Napoleon. Concierges were felt to be informers. The less anyone knew about you, the better were your chances of surviving. And paying less tax. You had to find out things on your own.

This side of Frenchness has not helped their foreign image.

Newell Wright, the professor of marketing in charge of a group of

James Madison junior-year-abroad students in Paris, asked about the train for Versailles, without specifiying that he wanted to go to the Château. The agent correctly directed him to the platform A. Newell knew something was wrong when his train began crossing the Seine. What he hadn't known was that trains on the A platform of the RER C go to two different stations in Versailles. The train called SLIM goes to the one on the Right Bank, called Versailles Chantiers. The train Newell wanted, which goes to the Left Bank (Versailles Rive Gauche), is called VICK. The ticket agent's information was right, as far as it went.

Had Newell asked, "Which train goes to the Château de Versailles?" or, "Is there more than one Versailles station?" he would have received the clue he needed.

The trouble is, as an English wag put it, "To ask the right question in France, you have to know the answer."

The point is cultural: that France is "high context" and the U.S., the U.K. and Germany are "low context." In high-context nations, often ones with a tradition of a strong police, people spend a lot of time talking to the people they know and trust, so that they know and are expected to know about everything. The agent undoubtedly assumed that if Newell had wanted to go to a specific place in Versailles, he would have said so.

In low-context countries, people congregate less and talk less, and so everything has to be spelled out in documents with rules, regulations, etc.

A low-context business example: A German (low context) fired by a French manager, complains: "But no one told me what to do."

A high-context business example: A Frenchman, bored, quits his job in a German company, saying, "People were always telling me what I already knew."

The ultimate example of France's high-contextedness is the ordinary pink stamp you see all the time with a picture of Marianne, France's symbol. A friend of mine who had just bought some asked me how much they were worth. I looked at him strangely -- after all, he had just bought 20 of them. I said, well, it says on the stamp. Then he said, "That's just the point. It doesn't say anything on the stamp."

I couldn't believe it was true. I'd been sticking that stamp on letters for over 20 years. It's the basic French stamp for letters up to 20 grams, and the only one stocked by the Tabacs. It's valid for France and the EU plus Switzerland. The reason that there's no number on it, nothing indicating its worth is that "everyone" knows that it costs 3 francs.

So, in France, the reason you get an answer only to the exact segment of information you inquired about is the assumption that you know the rest, or you would have asked, and to tell you more would be insulting and a waste of effort.

Savoir-Flair Tip No. 77:
Never assume anything except that you didn't ask all the questions

My trusty Mac PowerBook crashed recently, potentially beaming into Cyberspace forever about 70 e-mails that I'd intended to answer, or file, or both, but hadn't yet and had no record of. I took it to the cowboys ("cowboys" because young, good-looking, smart, quick and cool, very cool) who run the Apple concession nearby. They hooked it up to a special gizmo and were able temporarily to revive everything from the hard drive, but my Eudora post office still was empty. Something was wrong with the *système*, they said. I would have to leave it there overnight to have the software reinstalled. Stéphane, the boss cowboy, the only one who was in on the mysteries of the Eudora program, would *maybe* be able to recuperate my mail.

He said it would be safer to reinstall the *système* in French. Okay? I agreed, assuming I'd get my mail the same way as before, only in French. The next day Stéphane said it had been very difficult but he had managed to rescue my e-mail. Back at our place in the Dordogne, I labored to file the e-mails on a disk. I couldn't find the icon of Eudora, which used to be on my desktop. I looked for it in the hard drive, couldn't find it, eventually found an icon marked *Dossier Eudora* in something called *Dossier Système*. Whenever I had a minute I copied e-mails and pasted them onto a disk by opening the hard drive, clicking the *Dossier Système*, clicking the Eudora folder and then finally clicking the next e-mail. All the clicking seemed to take forever. To shortcut, I decided simply to move the Eudora icon out of the *Dossier Système* onto the desktop, removing an operation. Which I did. And lost everything.

I phoned Stéphane. He let out a yelp of horror. "But you must never touch anything in the *Dossier Système!*" he screeched.

No point whatever in asking him why he hadn't warned me.

Savoir-Flair Tip No. 78:
Always ask three people for any piece of information

French people themselves are not always sure about how to get to any given destination. If they do know they will very often not only tell you, but take you there.

If they don't know, they think they should, so they may tell you anyway. It's a question of face. I went into a map store in the Latin Quarter to find out where the rue Lacépède was. The saleswoman perused her little book of Paris streets (an *indicateur des rues*) and then said categorically, "*Ça n'existe pas.*" (The street doesn't exist). I politely asked if I might look at her *indicateur* for myself. And found it. Apparently she didn't know how to spell it.

Savoir-Flair Tip No. 79:
Figure out all the information you can by yourself with maps

French strangers have often told me frankly they don't know, but not always. On the Métro, realizing I'd forgotten to check on my map which station was closer to Saint-Roch, Tuileries or Palais Royal, I asked three people standing near me. The first was from the provinces. The second was Romanian. The third, French, hesitated and then said Palais Royal.

"Are you sure?" I said, skeptical.

He nodded, but didn't look absolutely sure.

I got off at Palais Royal. Wrong station. It was raining.

Savoir-Flair Tip No. 80:
Like the Métro, RER and SNCF agents can tolerate just one question

Because France is high context, because everyone either knows everything or figures it out himself, Métro, RER and SNCF ticket agents don't expect questions and don't welcome them. Not part of their job. They have enough stress as it is. Foreigners' questions are annoying. The agents figure that maps and schedules are available to be consulted.

Roger Williamson, from Edinburgh, was given not only incomplete but incorrect information. It was a similiar Versailles story, except that he knew there were two Versailles stations. At the Métro station Malakoff-Plateau de Vanves he asked how to go to Versailles Rive Droite (Versailles Right Bank). Any Métro map would have indicated that his route was easy. All he had to do was switch to the RER C5 at the Métro-RER station Invalides. Roger also wanted other information. Was there a ticket reduction for his children? "The very rude clerk sent us to the Gare Saint Lazare to get an SNCF train to Versailles -- as if the RER didn't go there at all -- and told us that no, there was no reduction for children. The only accurate thing he told us was that you could buy tickets to Versailles Rive Droite from the Gare St. Lazare!"

Too many questions. Indeed the SNCF gives a reduction for children (at Saint-Lazare) but the RATP-run Métro (where Roger was asking his questions) does not.

Savoir-Flair Tip No. 81:
The system for street listings is different and demands study

Street maps list streets named for people beginning with their titles (Docteur, Général) or their Christian names. Thus if you're looking for avenue Franklin D. Roosevelt, look under "F" and avenue du Président Kennedy under "P." Streets with a "de" to their name are never listed under "d." If they are called "de la" (lower case "l"), as in rue de la Bienfaisance, look under "B," but if the "l" is capitalized, as in rue de La Baume and rue La Boétie, look under "L."

The system is the same in the telephone book, so that if you're looking for the phone number of a friend whose name is "de la" something, you have to know whether it is spelled "la" or "La." Late on my way to see my friend Marie de La Martinière, I was wildly frustrated not to be able to find her under the M's in the telephone book. Even if I'd known if her "la" was a "La " or not, which I didn't, it would never have occurred to me to look under "L."

Savoir-Flair Tip No. 82:
Patience and preparation: you can triumph at the Préfecture de Police

Too many foreigners want to live in France. The government is obliged to give social security benefits to foreigners with certain permits. The French Social Security system is in the red. Therefore, dedicated as it has been since the great Revolution to the principle of giving asylum to the tortured, it has had to think up ways of discouraging the less tortured from getting visas and residence permits... without transgressing its principles, its laws or the laws of the European Union.

The method favored by the civil servants at the Préfecture de Police, where the papers are issued, is stonewalling. They refuse to give out complete, precise information about which official documents are required for that precious stamped visa or residence permit. The list they do give out is inadequate, in order to keep you coming back for months. The hope is that you will give up.

Don't! You can outfox them, like Gail Chaddock, the star correspondent of the *Christian Science Monitor* in Paris. On her first trip to the Préfecture, she had the usual hours of waiting in line and the usual result, an appointment four months later. At the second visit, after more hours of standing in line, she was scolded for a missing document. And given still another appointment. Someone in the same line then gave her this advice:

"You need a thicker file. More words, more papers. Xerox your telephone bills. Xerox your electric bills. Xerox every document in the house."

"On Visit No. 4," Gail reported in the *Monitor*, "the clerk was visibly shaken when I produced my French tax return, not on the official list. 'Your American tax return,' she fired back. I opened my fat folder, slowly, never breaking eye contact, and slid my 1996 United States tax return across the table."

Chapter Nine

Enjoying French Customer Service

How to Get It
What to Do If You Don't

What I'm seeing in French customer service is a very mixed bag. As a marketing professor, it seems to me there is a whole, untapped segment of the French market to be exploited by offering both good sales and after-sales service. I react badly to poor customer service, and this has been very hard for me to deal with in Paris. So I'm delighted when I run across the merchant who treats me with respect.

Newell Wright, professor of marketing, James Madison Univ.

Savoir-Flair Tip No. 83:
For good service, learn how to *flâner* (stroll, dawdle)

Customer service in France is a state of mind. Look at it this way. Americans generally grow up with this cultural syllogism:

A- Good customer service is helpful in the enjoyment of life.

B- Everyone has a right to enjoy life.

C- Therefore everyone deserves good customer service.

Foreigners, particularly Anglophones, complain about customer service in France. Transferred Anglophone businessmen who have lived in France a few months complain about it. Sometimes they boil over about it. Visiting academics complain about it. Journalists complain about it. I complained about it.

Adrian Leeds, the marketing specialist for www.wfi.fr, a Web site targeting Francophiles in North America, is one of the most articulate Americans about what she feels are French customer service shortcomings. Adrian has lived in Paris with her teenage daughter for almost six years.

She wrote this letter to the H&M department store after a frustrating experience there. It's full of American cultural artifacts. How many can you spot?

Dear Sir or Madam:

The bad service at your Paris store on the rue de Rivoli was so overwhelming today that my daughter and I dropped four bras and three pairs of stockings onto the counter and stormed out. We shop there often, and while we are fairly accustomed to the contrary attitude of the French toward good service, this was well above the line of reason.

As usual, the store was packed. We waited in line for about 15 minutes to try on 16 bras. As each customer was allowed only five items, the fitting room employees agreed to hold the six others for trying on later. We shared one dressing room. Of the 10 bras we tried, we decided to buy four, so my daughter took six back to exchange for the six being held for us. She returned saying that the fitting room clerk told her that to try on the six bras we'd reserved, we'd have to go back to the end of the line. That meant getting dressed and waiting again. The line was long. If we had known this from the beginning, we would have chosen the items to try more carefully; plus, making us wait again obviously served no purpose. Since we were sharing one room, we would have tried them on quickly and probably bought more!

As an American used to friendly helpful service where the customer is always right, I couldn't imagine this was happening. I tried to convince the clerk that the rule was ridiculous. It ended up in a huge and loud argument with your sales personnel. So, you lost the sale and two customers, plus the good feeling I'd always had about H & M. What a shame for all of us.

I just hope my letter helps the next person who comes along and ends up in some silly battle over nothing with a lowly sales clerk at H&M.

Sincerely yours,

Adrian Leeds

The American cultural artifacts in Adrian's letter:
- the customer's right to be right
- the right to save time
- the right to be properly informed
- the right to protest unreasonable rules
- the right to prevail over a sales clerk
- the desire to rectify a situation for the next customer

None of these cultural values are shared by the French.

Adrian is under pressure and works excruciatingly hard. My guess is that she expects her day to be as crammed full of things accomplished as in an American day. This is fatal in France. As Rob Chaddock says in the Conclusion, you can never get through more than half the things on your list for an American day. Time is different in France. You have to jump off the train. Even if you're working. Particularly if you're working.

What could Adrian and her daughter have done to avoid standing in line a second time? At that point, probably nothing. No doubt the signals of impatience and exasperation had already hit their mark. The sales clerk had perhaps felt Adrian's vibes ranking her as "lowly." PPO -- Persistent Personal Operating, throwing herself on the employee's mercy -- could only have worked if she had really jumped off the train, and taken the time to demonstrate respect for the clerk's power over that precious commodity, time; and had tried to win her over with charm, jokes, reasons why they couldn't wait in line again (Adrian's daughter had to be back at school on time, etc.).

The trouble is that the French grow up with a different cultural syllogism:

A- Employees selling wares are used to certain codes to trigger good customer service.

B- Foreign tourists don't always know the codes.

C- Therefore employees don't always give them good customer service.

Simple. The catch is the "certain codes."

Meghan Ducey, an anthropologist from Boston, has been observing the tribal rites of shoppers in Provence for the last 10 years, and comparing them to the ones back in the U.S. "American window shopping," she says, "is a restrained way of describing the ritualistic entering and leaving of many shops, having touched almost every article in each at least once, and having ascertained every price in a sometimes mad frenzy of searching for the Best Deal. Compared to this, French window shopping, or *lèche-vitrines* ('lick-windows'), is more like what happens in a museum or art exhibit, where display windows are admired and critiqued and discussed from a comfortable distance. One enters the shop to enquire about a specific article, often seen in the window. *Lèche-vitrine* is a sensual way of describing the gentle stroll adopted by the French as they walk, both observing the windows of the stores they pass and engaging in conversation."

Shellie Karabell, a veteran television journalist who has covered pretty much of the planet Earth's flora and fauna and is now NBC Paris bureau chief, lives in the Marais (the 3rd arrondissement).

"If you go into a store here, you have to focus on what's happening -- right then and there -- the way the French do," Shellie says. "You have to go at Paris's pace. Not barge into the place aggressively, but say hello, take your time. "

In other words, don't go in with a grin (this seems superficial to the French) but looking pleasant and *relaxed*. Look around the store, or shop. If it's the butcher's, look at what else he's selling besides meat; or at the greengrocer's, what exotic vegetables and fruit are displayed that you never saw before. Don't expect to be waited on immediately (in a hurry) even if no other customer is around, and don't look cross, sigh or purse your lips when you're not (which is rude).

Shellie has had innumerable instances of pure kindness. "I'm not sure what French people are motivated by," she says. "I haven't figured it out yet. But it's not what Americans are motivated by.

"Here's a word you won't hear people using about the French, but it's true: the French are *tender*. I mean... for instance, the florist near where I live. He does magical things with flowers. He always gives me extra ones when I buy some. One day when I went by in the pouring rain without a raincoat or an umbrella, he came running out in the rain with an umbrella for me."

She didn't realize she'd feel as comfortable here as she does.

"If you're alone in a city, this is a good city to be alone in," she says. "You're part of a community. People remember you. They say hello, and take time to say it. It is a protective environment. People notice you, take care of you. I find them wonderful."

Savoir-Flair Tip No. 84:
Always go back to the same café, store, whatever, again and again

Shellie always goes back to the same café, the same merchants, and advises foreigners to do the same, even if they're only visiting for two or three days. Being recognized is the first step towards good French customer service.

Once you feel in your bones that the French are tender, and you go into the store according to her advice, at Paris's pace, like a Parisian, then wonderful things happen to you, like this:

"Near where I live on the rue des Blancs-Manteaux," Shellie said, "there is a building that used to be, probably, a stable. They have exhibitions there, often of local artists. Recently they were showing crafts. One Sunday I walked by a booth with fun-fur vests and jackets. I tried on a short rabbit jacket that I quite liked. The guy looked at me, cocked his head, then rummaged around and handed me a fur hat. 'Here's a hat to go with it,' he said. I wasn't looking for a hat, but when I put it on, he smiled and said, 'You look great!' Then three people standing around looked at me with the hat on and clapped. 'Gorgeous!' they said. The artisan then said, 'If you buy the jacket, I'll give you the hat free.' A fur hat -- free. Try that on for size in New York. I wear it all the time, much more than the jacket."

Savoir-Flair Tip No. 85:
Don't go shopping unless you feel happy

Another thing you realize after living in France for a while is that growing up with the U.S. kind of customer service empowers Americans with the feeling that it's our birthright everywhere. Bad customer service triggers a rage that we feel perfectly justified in letting loose on whomever practices it.

Rage with merchants works sometimes in places where arrogance is aristocratic (Central Europe, for instance). It doesn't work in France.

You have to think of French salespeople as snails without their shell: sensitive. No skin at all. Vulnerable. Reacting to you. And that they're not tethered to customers' receipts. They're free. If you feel a little tense, they will take it personally. Remember, French people grow up having it drummed into them that they should never make a mistake. Which is why they don't accept having made mistakes (because they didn't). Your slightest frown will be an accusation. They do *not* grow up having it drummed into them that if they're salespeople, their mission in life is to smile and sell, sell and smile: to make life delightful for the buyer, to swallow whatever he dishes out. No. And they don't grow up with the example of sales people jumping to serve them, either.

In addition, French people have lives besides their working life. The American expression "get a life" is not applicable in France. The French already have a life. This is one of the reasons foreigners like to come to France: the details of life itself are enhanced. The disagreeable exchange with a salesperson may not be at all because you are a tense, impatient, hurried American but because the vendor's wife left him that morning, or the heat hasn't gone on yet in his building. He came to work cold. The non-working life in France is what counts. No one expects him/her to bottle up pain. French people aren't expected to be happy all the time. It's not in the Constitution. They don't have to put on that brave I'm-just-fine smile.

Savoir-Flair Tip No. 86:
Respect for sales personnel will encourage good service

Selling is not one of the coveted jobs in France. As money is not the declared (or undeclared) supervalue in France, starting out in sales is not an activity that attracts the power people who go to the ENA and the Ecole Polytechnique. Salespeople need your esteem and tenderness more than vendors in money-first countries. In other words, the codes: all the politeness words mentioned in Chapter 5. Refusing to give you what you want unless they find you pleasing or entertaining is one of their few available ways to feel important.

Savoir-Flair Tip No. 87:
For a return, a repair or an exchange, practice PPO

For all the reasons above, no extra service like exchanging, returning or repairing is to be expected, much less taken for granted. These need to be negotiated with all your reserves of charm, patience, good will, humor and imagination. In other words, it's up to you.

And it takes *time*.

This is how French people operate. Many Americans complain that this is "hypocritical" behavior. Not really. When in Rome....

For Christmas, from his sons, Philippe Dubrulle, a French banking executive with the Société Générale, was given a handsome silver cigarette case with an interior lighter. But after three months, the lighter gave out. He took it back to the little store where his sons said they'd bought it. Here is a first-rate illustration of PPO at work:

"Of course, the first step was politeness," he said. "The Magic Words... *'Excusez-moi de vous déranger, madame, mais j'ai un problème.'* I explained the problem, with all possible charm. No dice. Without a blink the saleslady snapped: 'We don't refund or exchange.'

"Mais, madame...' I played my violin. My sons had gone to such trouble to choose the cigarette case. With a lighter. So difficult to find one that was good looking. They had searched everywhere -- and at last they found it, here, in this store. This charming store. It had been a special Christmas, with the whole family together for the first time in a long time.

I poured on the sentiment, adding a few imaginary touches, and then I poured on my respect for her power and authority, and her choice of ending this story in misery or happiness... for a whole family....

"For a long time she stood there shaking her head and frowning. No. Then gradually... I could see her melting. I kept it up. Finally, she said, *"Bon.* I'll send it back to the factory."

"So we both won. Victory for me, and the saleslady had her *divertissement* (entertainment)."

Score: 1 to 1, which is ideal.

Cheers for Carrefour

Sometimes, however, you get nice surprises. Jilly Crane from Swindon returned a high-tech Calor iron to Carrefour one day before its one-year guarantee expired. They were pleased to replace the iron, no PPO necessary, but her model was no longer available. They produced a superior model, a brand new top-of-the-line Calor iron, more expensive by FF 400. Jilly said she couldn't possibly pay that. So they gave it to her.

Now, she won't shop anywhere but at Carrefour for anything.

Savoir-Flair Tip No. 88:
If vendors don't play by the rules, have a strategy

It's true that, sometimes, some salespeople seem to be taking out a special gripe against the world on you. I'm not suggesting that you stand there and let yourself be shot down. But for a strategy to work, you need to be in good form, and to take time. Shari Segall is an elegant marketing professional with Desbordes International, a moving firm. After 15 years in Paris, she has learned French and has learned the system. She loves France, and the French feel it. She gets wonderful service with her calm *"Bonjour, madame,"* her *"Excusez-moi de vous déranger"* and her attitude of time to burn. If there is an unusual problem, she may boil inside, but outside she stays cool, very cool, and spins her strategy.

Among other things, Shari is a knitter. One of her triumphs is having stayed cool negotiating a wool return with Bon Marché.

In her words:

At the Bon Marché I bought more skeins of wool than required by the pattern for my coat -- you never know if you'll want to make the sleeves longer, or add a tassle or something -- and I carefully kept the unused skeins in a safe place. As you may not know if you're not a knitter, it's *globally* understood that unused, untouched skeins will be taken back by the seller, and an appropriate refund given to the buyer. So, very proud of my finished coat, I went back to the Bon Marché and presented my extra skeins to the knitting-counter lady. She looked at me quizzically. I explained. Then she frowned -- and barked at me!

"Which garment did you make?" she snarled.

"The coat in the Pingouin catalogue on page so-&-so," I answered warmly.

"The Pingouin catalogue?" She leapt from her stool, bolted over to the instruction-book racks, grabbed the Pingouin catalogue from its niche and leafed furiously through its pages. Then she bound back to her counter and pointed to a certain line in the instructions manual.

"You see that?" she snapped in her Grand Inquisitor voice. "What does it say? How many skeins of yarn are required for that coat?"

"Yes, but all over the world --" I began.

"*C'est irresponsable!* You shouldn't have bought so many!" Folding her arms over her breast, she added,"What you do with them is your problem."

I couldn't believe it. "You mean -- you won't refund me for them?"

"*Impossible.*"

At this point I leaned over the counter close to her and said that as I understood it, this department store was founded years and years ago by Madame Boucicault, who was known for having introduced to France the concept -- "*if not the practice,*" I added -- of customer service.

"You see that intersection over there?" I pointed to the center of the store where its two main aisles crossed. "I'm going to station myself at that intersection -- with my unreturnable skeins of yarn -- and ask every passing customer what they think of your style of the Boucicault tradition."

As I marched off, the knitting-counter lady screamed, "HALT!" She dragged me back to her counter, wrote out a refund slip, showed me where I could redeem it and plopped herself back onto her stool as if nothing had happened.

Savoir-Flair Tip No. 89:
Other French people will help you to contest unfairness to customers

Sally Murray, now a medical librarian at the University of South Alabama Biomedical Library, used a similar technique with a waiter in a café. Sally is in love with France and has been saving up for her next trip.

As a college student, she visited a friend in Normandy and had one of those "deliriously delightful summers," except for one afternoon when they stopped in at a sidewalk café.

"We ordered two beers on tap," she said. "After we finished, the waiter brought us the bill. We gasped. It was much too big. He explained that it was for two imported American beers, because he 'knew' that this was 'what we really wanted.' We tried to argue, but he insisted and our French wasn't confident enough for advanced dialectics."

Sally and her friend paid and went home feeling gypped. They decided that they'd fallen on the rare stereotype of a waiter out to rip off tourists. They plotted how to beat him at his own game. The next day when the café opened, they planted themselves on the sidewalk next to it. Each time a customer turned up, they politely introduced themselves and explained how that waiter ripped off tourists.

"The waiter was furious and threatened to call the police," Sally said. 'Go ahead, we'd LOVE to talk to the police,' we told him. Then the manager came out. He also threatened us with the police. We said, fine with us.

"All of the people we spoke to were lovely. They told off the waiter and gave him an awful time. We stayed all day! The next day when they opened, we sat down and ordered two beers on tap. We were served quickly. The bill was in the correct amount. We said, thanks -- that's all you had to do in the first place!"

Score: 1-0 for Sally, with a medal for her bloodless revolution

Savoir-Flair Tip No. 90:
Don't judge all French stores by one French store

One thing most Americans agree on is the horrific customer service at La Samaritaine, the department store. Eldon Braun, an advertising executive from San Francisco, boils over describing it: "They advertise that it has everything -- and when you go there, they send you around the whole store on a wild goose chase for something they don't have but won't admit not having. They're disagreeable and treat you like dirt." Like many foreigners, he swears by the BHV (Bazar de l'Hôtel de Ville) "where they really do have everything and the courtesy to guide you to it properly."

Nice Service at Printemps

George and Anne Linn are also from San Francisco. Anne runs the French-American school there. George is with the local housing authority.

The Linns had bad luck. They flew in to Charles De Gaulle Airport and waited for their luggage at the carousel... in vain. United Airlines suggested they phone the next day. Fine. Meanwhile they had nothing to wear.

"We went to Printemps," said George. "Luckily Calvin Klein underwear was on sale. Everything costs double what it does in the States -- but the important thing was that everyone was so NICE at Printemps. There were big signs everywhere saying 'If you find it cheaper somewhere else, we'll make up the difference' and 'If you change your mind, we'll take it back.'

Galeries Lafayette was a different story. Everything was a problem. The Linns were told that they'd find the clothes they were looking for on the second floor. There, they were sent impatiently up to the next floor. They didn't know that the American "second floor" is the first floor for the French, who don't count the ground floor (rez-de-chaussée).

"The two stores are very different," George said. "Galeries Lafayette is crowded, like a bargain basement, and the people indifferent or downright unpleasant, impatient and nasty. At Printemps there were fewer people, the sales people were nice, they seemed to welcome our business."

United Airlines eventually found their luggage, so a lot of the things they bought they didn't need any more.

"We tried to take something back to Galeries Lafayette," said Linn, "and you can't imagine the fuss they made. Very rude! While it went smooth as butter at Printemps."

Mixed bag of customer service

The American expert on French customer service is undoubtedly Newell Wright, quoted at the beginning of the chapter. He specializes in unsatisfied consumer behavior and contributes regularly to the Journal of Consumer Satisfaction, Dissatisfaction and Complaining Behavior.

In Paris with his family to shepherd a group of juniors abroad, Newell went after customer service with a microscope whenever he bought something, or tried to. He had unpleasant problems buying his dryer, a TV and a VCR. "Some service encounters made me want to scream," he said, "but others were very encouraging." Newell had both good and bad experiences with Darty, the chain specializing in household appliances. One day his apartment oven stopped working. He changed all the fuses; it still didn't work. He called Darty and in short order, a technician stopped by the house. Apparently Newell's son, when trying to reset the clock, accidently set the time to zero, effectively making it impossible to work. The technician fixed the problem in 15 seconds.

Newell was upset. "*Zut, alors*, 400 francs for that!" he exclaimed.

The technician then suggested that he call Darty and cancel the visit. He would never tell them he stopped by, he said.

Newell marveled at the "wonderfully charming and helpful" business people in the French provinces. He had consistently good customer service outside of Paris.

"I bought a very expensive cuckoo clock in Strasbourg," he said, "from a merchant who spent 45 minutes with me explaining all the intricate details of cuckoo clocks, and why one of them was the best for me, given my budget. He laughed with me, and was generally thrilled that I was speaking good French to him. I ended up spending 1,500 francs.

"He even invited me and the whole family in for hot chocolate, and told me to come back whenever we were in Strasbourg. Which we did, a few days later, to get some more items, and check on a second cuckoo clock for my Dad.

"He then told us all about the winter festival in Strasbourg that begins on November 26, and again invited us back. He said that there is a French saying, *"Jamais deux sans trois,"* (never two without three) which meant that since we'd seen each other twice, we must see each other three times. You know what? We're planning on going back for that festival, and we WILL visit this merchant again, and buy more of his souvenirs. Perhaps even a cuckoo clock for my wife's brother. Now THAT is customer service."

Savoir-Flair Tip No. 91:
Think of buying something as a challenging sport

Shopping in Paris is a challenging sport. You have to train for a sport. Dress carefully: the French respond to elegance. Think of Shellie Karabell, strolling, perceiving the French as *tender*. Breathe deeply before going into a store. Tell yourself that the store people are wonderful and you are wonderful. Don't touch anything. Pretend that the salespeople are important for your promotion or your spouse's promotion, or your daughter's invitation to a party. Charm them. Then, enjoy.

Chapter Ten

Enjoying the Local Scene

General Shopping Hints
Post Office, Barber-Hairdresser, Movies, Markets, etc.

Until you have wasted time in a city, you cannot pretend to know it well. The soul of a big city is not to be grasped so easily; in order to make contact with it, you have to have been bored, you have to have suffered a bit in those places that contain it. Anyone can get hold of a guide and tick off all the monuments, but within the very confines of Paris there is another city as difficult of access as Timbuktu once was. I call it a secret city, because foreigners never enter it, and I am tempted to call it sacred, because its sufferings make it dearer to us.

Julian Green, of the Académie Française

Savoir-Flair Tip No. 92:
French vendors remember regular customers years later

Chuck Darrow, the financial adviser we met in Chapter 5, looking for special coffee, finally found a little boutique on the rue de Bourgogne (7th), where an ageless lady for years and years has been selling dozens of varieties of tea and coffee for people who have special tastes.

"French coffee is just too strong for me," said Chuck, on his recent visit to Paris. "So I wanted to make it at home, freshly ground by this lady. She grinds it according to how strong you want it. At first she gave me number 2 or 3, but this was still much too strong! Eventually we worked our way up to grind No. 13, which is *treize* in French. After that, every time I came in the door, she said, '*Bonjour, Monsieur Treize!*'

"This morning, after six years, I entered the store again to see how she was, and immediately her face lit up and she said, '*Bonjour, Monsieur Treize!*'"

Savoir-Flair Tip No. 93:
You'll be acknowledged by the vendor when it's your turn

High on foreigners' complaints list in France is not being acknowledged by a salesperson when they line up to buy something. This is another of those reverse-politenesses of the French. If they acknowledge you, they consider that they're being rude to the person they're waiting on. When it's your turn, they'll give you their full attention, too.

Savoir-Flair Tip No. 94:
You can fight line-jumpers if you want to

Julie Winn's solution, if someone cuts in front of you:
"If you say loudly, 'C'EST A MOI!' (it's my turn) fast enough, they always answer, '*Mais bien sûr!*'" If someone cuts in the line far ahead of her, Julie has a different technique: "When I yell at a line-jumper, they invariably say, '*Faut pas vous énerver!*' (You shouldn't lose your temper!) as if it's *my* problem. Recently I've discovered that if you retort, '*Les gens énervants disent toujours ça!*' (Aggravating people always say that!) it shuts them up and makes them behave."

The Post Office

An English friend of mine used to say that if she were given the choice between being executed by firing squad or going to a Paris post office, she'd take the firing squad any time.

But Paris post offices have changed! In the last two years, even with the Paris agents, the wind is changing.

For about four years I'd been going to the post office on the rue de Grenelle every day. Almost always I dealt with the same agent. He's a little bald, about 35, not very tall, very quick and *very* impatient. I always smiled and said, "*Bonjour, monsieur.*" There was no response, not even the suggestion of a smile. I ordered stamps or a "diligo" (the post office packaging for France), adding "*s'il vous plaît.*" When he gave me the diligo, I said, "*merci, monsieur*" and then I said it again when he gave me my change. Transaction ended, I said, "*au revoir, monsieur,*" and cocked my ear for a response. Nothing.

Usually, getting together my various marketing letters, correspondance, book shipments and so forth took all day until the last minute before the post office closed at 7 pm. I cycled over and rushed in about 10 minutes to 7:00, and just managed to slide everything under the window to this agent before another agent at the door cranked down the iron curtain. Often by the time I'd made my transactions the curtain was already down, and had to be cranked up again.

One day, however, I managed to get my correspondence and book packages ready earlier. It was about 6:30 when I said, *"Bonjour, monsieur"* to the slightly balding agent.

He looked at me in shock. "But, Madame, you are early tonight!"

"Comment? What?" I said, taken aback. He really seemed to be speaking to me as if he'd maybe seen me before.

"Yes! Look what time it is!" he said, glancing around at the clock. "Usually when you come, I know it's time to go home!"

I burst out laughing. What a surprise! I was not only recognized, my habits were noted. Then he laughed! We laughed together. It was a sweet moment. Now, every time I've been back since, that agent always sparkles at me. If I'm at a different *guichet* (window), he catches my eye with a twinkle. One time I showed up at noon, and he made great big eyes, as if to say, Oh no! Impossible! And when I left he said, *"A ce soir!"* (See you tonight!)

All over Paris, the postal agents seem to be jollier. "Some are really nice!" says Julie Winn. "Be nice back!"

In rural France they have always been friendly and helpful. Just last week an agent in the Dordogne looked at a letter for the U.S. I'd stamped myself and said, "You put too much postage on it!" Whereupon, slowly, taking care not to tear it, she scratched one of the stamps off the envelope and gave it to me. "You can glue it onto the next envelope," she said, "but don't use Scotch tape."

In the Dordogne, they hold our mail if we're away, and when we're back, they drive by especially to deliver it. An agent in Nevers looked up my phone number from the address on a package and said that the addressee had just died. Should she send it to his daughter? And one in Tours called and said that I had miss-sent books to a bookstore which was not in Tours, but in Toulouse. Should she send it there?

As for the Paris post offices themselves, innovations have been tumbling on top of each other. They now have electronic letter-weighers, photocopy machines, ATMs (*distributeur* or *Point Argent*) and coin changers, as well as telephones and a Minitel, that French precursor to the Internet.

Last year they injected a quirky note of chumminess by stringing up colored banners that change with the seasons: witches and pumpkins for

Hallowe'en (though the French had never heard of Hallowe'en until a few years ago), Santa Clauses for Christmas, hearts and flowers for Valentine's Day, bunnies and colored eggs for Easter. Matching 3-franc stamps go with the banners.

Savoir-Flair Tip No. 95:
You can rent a computer at your neighborhood post office

As if this wasn't enough to blow me away, when I was passing through a small provincial town in southwest France called Condom (yes, really), I went into a post office to mail a letter and gaped: a shiny new blue iMac computer, was sitting on a desk on the customer side of the counter. The government is shelling out 100 million francs to have 1000 of these iMacs in post offices all over France. Well, it isn't free, any more than the phones nearby are free, but for a rental, it's competitive with the cyber-cafés. Like French public phones, it works with a chip-card, 50 francs for an hour's use, 30 francs an hour for a recharge.

But the most incredible, welcome and soothing change in almost all Paris post offices in the last year is the installing of one single waiting-line for all the agents, guarded by velvet ropes and signaled by signs saying *"Veuillez Respecter la File d'Attente"* (Please Respect the Queue). Gone is the misery of waiting in the wrong line, watching others shrink while someone ahead of you buys 350 stamps of different kinds and writes out 18 money orders. In some offices, take-a-number-machines have been installed instead of ropes. Whichever, we should all write to the Ministry congratulating it on the demise of multiple, excruciatingly exasperating queues.

More Post-Office Savoir-Flair Tips

Stamps (timbres)
> You can buy the 3-franc stamps, the pink ones with a picture of Marianne, for an EU letter at any Tabac. They may say they're out of them unless you order a *carnet*, a packet of 10.

Pretty new 3-franc stamps
> These are a lot more fun for your correspondents to receive than the boring pink Marianne ones. Ask for a *"timbre de collection."*

Postage to the U.S.
> FF 4.40 for a postcard or a light letter to the U.S. (20 grams or less).

Mailbox
> Just outside the Tabac or around the corner.

Prices for parcels going abroad

May vary from post office to post office. Yes. They have to be looked up in a special book. I guess it depends where the agent looks and how good his eye sight is. If you have a heavy parcel, check two or three branches. Again last week, an agent in the Lot et Garonne charged me FF 32 instead of FF 8.40 to send a book to Switzerland. Finally she looked it up in a different book and agreed with me.

Translations of useful phrases into five languages

La Poste puts out a booklet, available in all branch post offices, about its various services in English, German, Italian, Spanish and Dutch. The booklet includes translations for 44 key words you might need in a post office , including "register," "money order," "customs label," plus 21 useful phrases like "Where is the nearest telephone booth?"

Special envelopes

Ask about them. "Envelope" is exactly the same word in French, except with two p's. Padded envelopes, however, must be bought in a stationery shop.

Chronopost

This is the French version of express delivery. It has a slightly slower, less expensive rate than UPS and Fedex.

Hours

Paris post offices are open non-stop Monday to Friday from 8 am to 7 pm. Saturday they're open from 8 am until noon. They're closed all day Sunday all over France, except for two in Paris (see below). Rural France P.O.s also close at noon on Saturday but have different weekday hours, varying from village to village.

Two Paris post offices are open longer

• At 71 avenue des Champs Elysées, 75008 (Métro George V) open Saturday until 7 pm

• 52 rue du Louvre, 75001, is open 24 hours a day, every day, including Sunday.

Minitel

The Internet-like system developed by the French in 1970 for doing business in France and looking up telephone numbers all over the country, is in all the Paris and rural post offices. For giving you phone numbers, it's free, unlike the telephone information service.

Visiting the *coiffeur*

Savoir-Flair Tip No. 96:
Make an appointment and be on time

Savoir-Flair Tip No. 97:
A French hairdresser/barber can make your hair look fabulous

Hayes Dabney, a charming Detroit school teacher, prepared for his first visit to Paris with the enthusiasm of a true traveler. As he had hoped, studying the history, culture, customs and codes made up for his lack of French. What he planned on doing while in Paris, he told me during his visit, was "to try to exist like a normal person in a big city." So, soon after landing, he stopped in at a barber shop. Hayes's hair is a challenge, he says: "It's unusual, even for an African-American. I was curious what they would do." This is what he e-mailed me after he got home:

> The first thing I noticed about this French barber, a neat, simply dressed gentleman in his mid-fifties who quickly greeted me and helped me with my coat, was how carefully he studied the texture of the product he had to work with, my hair. He caught the swirls in minutes, while others whose blades I had been under didn't notice them until halfway into the haircut. He commented in French on the swirls and then made gestures to let me know what he was saying. I nodded and hoped that this wouldn't be too much of a burden for him (or me). I started having flashbacks of the numerous times I'd left a barber shop holding my head to the side, to compensate for its lop-sided design.
>
> Most of the time he switched between a pair of large scissors and a small electric razor, snipping and cutting at an easy pace. But then he did something that alarmed me: he took out a straight-edge razor. What was he going to do with a straight-edge razor? I didn't ask for a shave!
>
> Very coolly he took the straight-edge and began to work on the swirling portions of my hair, using a comb as a guide, measuring, cutting, viewing, all with an intensity that I'd never seen. It was his work that I was witnessing; his livelihood. Something he took great pride in. It seemed to define who he was. I felt as if my hair was being sculpted to fit me. By a master artist.
>
> This barber was more involved in the shaping of my hair than any place I had ever been, even in Ann Arbor, where they cut my hair, take my money and that's it. This total stranger spent a considerable amount of time actually thinking about what he was doing, how my hair worked, and what was the best way to make it look great.

131

I began to realize that one of the things people in France do is take an interest and pride in style, in their personal style and their knowledge about what it is they do, and focus more on what it is they do and the eccentricities of it, than people in America. So -- that generalization about French people being keen on style, well, I found out it's true. I discovered new effective techniques, and a professionalism and attention I'd never experienced at home.

I asked Hayes later if he liked the haircut. "I loved it!" he said. "It fit me so well, and no swirls showed!" Hayes doesn't remember the name of the barber shop, only that it was in a greyish building on the rue Pasquier going towards the Champs Elysées, before the rue de Sèze.

More Barber-Hairdresser Savoir-Flair Tips

Tipping

FF 20 for a FF 100 haircut (men) in Paris. *Coiffeurs* cost less in the provinces, as does food, generally. Same tip for shampoo and set or blow dry for women.

Cost

Extremely variable for women. I suggest Thierry Pitou, at 96 rue du Bac in the 7th arrondissement. He is talented and among the least expensive in Paris, with a pleasant boutique with television sets. FF 117 for a shampoo and set (*shampooing et mise en plis*).

Going to the movies *(le cinéma)*

French people love movies. The theatres are large, the seats luxurious, the choice of films rich: over 400 are playing at any one time. This is a painless way to improve your French. If you're feeling a little homesick, find one in English. American and English movies are either shown in the original, with subtitles in French, or are dubbed in French. If you want to see one in English, be sure that it has "v.o." after the title (for *version originale*).

A little booklet published every week on Wednesday, *Le Pariscope*, FF 3, lists what is playing where and when. It is also invaluable for everything else going on in town, including exhibitions, night clubs, theatres, guided walking tours, church services. They recently added a section in English at the back.

Savoir-Flair Tip No. 98:
Ask which line you should stand in for a certain movie

Movie lines can be long. Prudent moviegoers therefore buy tickets ahead of time, so that they'll be let in first. Tickets in hand, they stand under a sign saying *Spectateurs munis de billets*, a good place not to stand if you don't have one.

Savoir-Flair Tip No. 99:
Ticket prices vary with days of the week and hours of the day

Ticket prices are lower for children, students and *"seniors"* (over 60) on certain weekdays or certain hours of the day. Ask your concierge to fill you in.

Savoir-Flair Tip No. 100:
Ads are shown before the film you came to see

Le Pariscope notes the times of the *séances*, that is, the beginning of each show, which consists of ads plus the film you came to see. The film starts anywhere from 15 to 30 minutes later, depending on the length of the film. Some of the ads are beautiful and others are fun. Recently, the daily newspaper *Le Parisien* delighted us all with two very Parisian incidents: one showed a woman being cut in front of in a cashier's line at the supermarket, and the other showed a driver honking his horn impatiently and then having an accident.

Savoir-Flair Tip No. 101:
Don't annoy the French with talk, eating noisily or crinkling paper

French children are drilled not to be overheard or to make any noise in public. Doubtless they're louder on the street and in the Métro than they were 20 years ago. But not in the movies. Noisemakers are liable to be scolded. During the ads and quite a while before the film, Ande and I were looking for single seats in a packed house. From several rows away, Ande called to me, not very loudly, that he had found one. I was trying to enter a different row, and noticed that the young man in the first seat wasn't making any effort to let me by. I asked him if there was a problem. "Yes," he said. "You're behaving as if you're at home."

Hardly anyone buys the peanuts, popcorn and ice cream offered by the usher working the rows. If they do, they chew quietly.

Tipping the ushers when they seat you has gone out, but is still expected at the opera and big theatrical productions.

Savoir-Flair Tip No. 102:
Take a flashlight

Take a flashlight. The theatres are dark and the steps hardly ever lit.

The Pharmacy

Very often pharmacies sell homeopathic treatments as well as traditional medicine, which gives a slight alchemical flavor to these stern establishments. With their godlike aloofness and cabalistic air of secret power, the white-coated professionals behind the counter can strike fear in the sturdiest tourist heart.

Interminable waits, while other customers plow through pages of prescriptions, is part of the mythology. Anxiety builds. When at last it's your turn, you whisper an order for herpes medicine or a urine test. "OH, YOU MEAN FOR PREGNANCY?" shouts the intimidator. The other French customers don't bat an eye; they take natural things naturally. But the tourist, particularly if it's a young woman, may slink out the door without her potion.

However, those big green crosses are lit up on almost every block and you can find one in your neighborhood with welcoming and tactful professionals within, like ours on the corner of the rue du Bac and the rue de Varenne.

France supplies its residents with about the most generous free medical services in the world, but not to you. Don't faint at the cost of vitamins.

Savoir-Flair Tip No. 103:
French pharmacies are empowered to give you medical advice

The pharmacist waiting on you has had between four to six years of higher education after high school. It's a profession of prestige in France, much more so than in the U.S. Many of them have a Ph.D. and medical knowledge close to that of doctors. Very often they can solve your health problem. If you do need a doctor, they're the ones to ask.

Savoir-Flair Tip No. 104:
Your pharmacist will help you more if you make him your friend

The better the pharmacist knows you, the more he will open up his bag of knowledge. In an emergency, he will see to it that you get attention from the best doctor around. If he knows you, he'll fill your prescription even if you left it in the United States. Forget about regulations. All of France works on trust.

Marketing - at the open Markets

Open markets are the deep dark root of French gastronomy. Many of the vendors are selling produce they have grown themselves in their own *terroir*, a rich French word with undertones of soil, native land, one's own plot of ground. These are the people that bring the French to the market. They're what make it possible. The markets are lovingly cherished and frequented by French men and women alike, throughout the population. (See Chapter 15 on French food, and Chapter 21 on rural living.) French people care what they eat. They know that if you can't make a silk purse from a sow's ear, you certainly can't make a *tête de veau* (a favorite of President Chirac) from an old cow, or a thrilling soup from tired celery.

Some of these markets are permanent, all day: in Paris at the rue Mouffetard, the Place d'Aligre, the rue de Seine, the rue Cler, the Porte de Clignancourt, to mention a few. Others move from place to place in the mornings only. Every quarter of Paris will enjoy one twice a week, coming back to each spot on certain days and only in the morning, like the one on the Boulevard Raspail on Tuesdays and Thusdays, with a special "bio" natural food market on Sunday mornings. Every rural village is visited by one once a week. It takes strong arms and devotion to put up those temporary stalls, with their tents and poles, and strong arms and devotion to take them apart again. I never heard a grumble about it.

Savoir-Flair Tip No. 105:
You can learn to love those fresh-food lines

Gail Chaddock, the *Christian Science Monitor* correspondent who triumphed over the police *fonctionnaire* in Chapter 8, lived in Paris's 5th Arrondissement from 1994 to 1997. Now back in the U.S., here is what she wrote for the *Monitor* after she got home:

> Outdoor-market leeks have a certain dignity about them. They are lovingly displayed, gently handled, and only hours from the field. But you'll have to wait for them, and on a Sunday morning the lines at an outdoor market in Paris can run a dozen deep. Learning to love lines is an acquired

taste. For me, it began by waiting in line for leeks. You can buy leeks in Paris without the wait, but supermarket leeks don't taste the same. They've been lying around in a truck too long. If they have any moisture at all, it's because a clerk has just passed by with a hose and squirted them.

You can read a book in line, but it just gets in the way when it comes time to haul the vegetables home. Instead, I learned how to cook. Start by noticing how Parisians shop. They have lists, as in: two carrots, three leeks, a single stalk of celery. In Paris, buying just what you need is as important as buying what is good. For those of us whose vegetables often wind up covered with fur in some forgotten corner of the refrigerator, this insight comes as a revelation.

If a man came along to help with the shopping (often the case), there might also be discussions about the quality of a melon or which greens worked well together in a salad. Watch how Parisians select vegetables: Big is never better, and good is not necessarily beautiful.

Then, begin asking your own questions, such as "Excuse me, but what is that (hideously ugly) root and what do you do with it?" You'll walk out with a half-dozen recipes.

Standing in line also makes you part of a place. You'll begin recognizing the same people in line. So will the farmer, and he'll set aside a bag of fresh peas if he knows you love them, just in case you're running late. Sometimes, the questions will come back at you: "Excuse me, aren't you American? And can you explain to me how to cook corn?"

Alas, corn is the one vegetable Americans understand better than Parisians. Any New Hampshire farmer knows that good eating corn is white or bicolored, with names like "Silver Queen" or "Butter and Sugar." They're selling tough yellow field corn in Parisian markets. I couldn't bear to tell her. "Boiling water, 9 to 12 minutes," I said, silently adding: "Chew well."

Good lines make good neighbors. My husband and I arrived home late, tired and hungry after hiking one Saturday. Our neighborhood baker had just drawn his blinds. We'd often played with his daughter while waiting in line. Before we reached our apartment, the baker came running out a side door, with two baguettes.

"I saw you walking by and thought you might need these," he said.

When Gail and Rob left Paris for Washington, this baker gave them a going-away present of two antique cream pitchers in the shape of cows that they had been admiring in the window for three years.

Savoir-Flair Tip No. 106:
Treating the vendor as if you're in his home makes him more helpful

Food and wares belong to the vendor. Pretend you're arriving in his home: *Bonjour, monsieur* (or *madame*). He will welcome you.

Savoir-Flair Tip No. 107:
Touching fruit or wares is not acceptable

Adrian Leeds, the Web consultant we met in Chapter 9, took her newly-arrived friend, Jenny Bern, to an open market. Jenny was delighted to find a *brocante* (junk dealer) with several clocks on his sidewalk table. She picked up a small one to see it better. A French couple, who had also been admiring the clocks, began screaming at Jenny. Jenny didn't understand French. She freaked out and kept asking Adrian, "What did I do? What on earth did I *do*?"

Jenny had *picked up* a clock. The French woman no doubt would have liked to pick it up herself -- but would have been breaking the rules (Tip No. 107) of not touching produce or wares.

Savoir-Flair Tip No. 108:
Soft cheese is the touching exception; you can also taste it

In France, cheese is a living being, made from a living being, that you nurture in a cool place, not a dead thing that you wrap in plastic and put on ice. You can touch certain soft cheeses, like Brie or Camembert. But ask, first.

Also, you can ask them to let you taste (*goûter*) a sliver.

In Paris, on the Left Bank at the famous cheese store of the Barthélmy family on the rue de Grenelle in the 7th Arrondissement, and on the Right Bank at Lillo Fromages on the rue des Belles-Feuilles in the 16th, they'll give you a Brie or a Camembert which is just right for a certain hour that evening. Sometimes, before lunch or dinner on the weekend, the line (a *noble* one) at Barthélmy's goes around the corner.

More Open Markets Tips

Hours

• The twice-a-week open markets close by 12:30 or 1:00.

• French greengrocers and markets in Paris open around 7 am and close at 7 pm or later, with two or three hours out for lunch. Closed Mondays.

Department Stores

Savoir-Flair Tip No. 109:
In a department store, find a cashier without a line

If you see something you want to buy, the salesperson can't sell it to you. She gives you a bill which you then take to a cashier serving a whole bunch of counters, maybe a whole department. You wait in line, you pay, and bring the bill back to the salesperson, marked paid, to get the merchandise. These lines can be endless. Look for a cashier in a different department with a shorter line.

Savoir-Flair Tip No. 110:
Expect the fitting-room lines to be terrible, too

You're only allowed to take a certain number of things at a time to try on in the fitting room, maybe five, maybe three, as Adrian Leeds learned in Chapter 9. There's no way around them.

Marché aux Puces (Flea Market)

There are four main flea markets in Paris: at Saint Ouen, Vanves, Montreuil and Clignancourt, all near the Métros of the same name. They open around 10:00 am on Saturday, Sunday and Monday.

If you're a pro or close to it, and want to mix with the pros, the thing to do is go to Clignancourt at 6:00 am on Friday morning, or even earlier. To find them, follow signs to the Marché aux Puces, go under the overpass of the Boulevard Périphérique and look for the trucks of the merchants bringing their wares from all over the country. This is where flea market and Paris antique dealers go to replenish their stocks. Take a flashlight!

Going to Church

Catholic churches in France are often not heated. In wintertime, dress in your woolies. The American Church (interdenominational), the American Cathedral (Episcopalian) and the various UK churches, however, are fairly well heated.

In an Austrian Catholic church with Fritz Molden, my first husband, standing up, I noticed he was glaring and grimacing at me. I couldn't imagine why. Then he hissed at me, "Take your hands out of your pockets!" Catholics all over Europe are taught to keep their hands out of their pockets in church. Not to is considered *mal élevé*, insulting to God and his priests on earth.

Chapter Eleven

Enjoying Finding Something You Lost

Don't Give Up

The French don't wear tutus or stick bones in their noses, so we expect them to be like us. Wrong. They are different. In a way it's a pity they don't wear bones in their noses: we'd get the signal a bit sooner.

Don Horowitz, lawyer, San Francisco

Savoir-Flair Tip No. 111:
Always look at the bus driver's face in case you forget something

Maybe it sounds wacky, the idea of enjoying losing something, but there really is joy when something you lose is found and given back. Paris is the place for this. I've gone back to a movie theatre where I left my wallet on the floor and had it returned to me the next day, including the 500 francs inside. Salespeople have greeted me in a pharmacy with my handbag, in a department store with my checkbook, in a supermarket with some meat I'd paid for and forgotten. They kept it for me overnight in their refrigerator.

One day when it was raining hard, I asked the bus driver if he could possibly let me out at a traffic light before the bus stop, to be closer to where I'd left my bicycle. Which he did. I noticed his kind face, metal-rimmed glasses and reddish hair. On the sidewalk a moment later, I discovered I'd forgotten my gloves. My favorite gloves, black leather, a present from Ande. The bus, an 83, was stopped at another light just ahead. I ran towards it, just missed it. I cycled home as fast as I could and tapped the Minitel for the RATP phone number.

"Silly waste of time," said Ande, as I waited. "You'll never get them back."

The Minitel gave me 40 numbers for the RATP. I called France Télécom. They gave me a general bus-information number (08 36 68 77 14), which gave me the number for the 83 bus terminal (01 44 36 32 74).

An agent answered. Not a recording. A real live human being. "Call back in one hour," he said. He sounded helpful and nice. "By then we should know if the gloves have turned up."

I hung on. I figured if I lost him, my chance of retrieved gloves went from 30% down to 1%. "But perhaps if you could give me the phone number of the bus," I said, "and if I called him now, there would be more chance... the bus was just here at the Solférino stop a few minutes ago... I was sitting all the way in front on the left -- I wouldn't bother you with this, but they're wonderful gloves, and a present from my husband, I'm so upset..."

"Madame," said the agent gently, "there are buses every three minutes just now. It's impossible to know which one. In any case, it's not possible for you to call him."

"But if you could possibly call him yourself, monsieur l'agent... perhaps you know him, he has reddish hair and metal-rimmed glasses, in his early forties I'd say...."

"Oh," said the agent. There was a feeling to the "oh" like "aha, yes I do know him, hmmm." Then he said, "Perhaps. Call back in 20 minutes."

When I did, the agent said, "*Oui, madame*, we found your gloves. Also your scarf." My scarf? "If you come to the 83 terminal today, I will be happy to give them to you."

The 83 terminal is a tiny raised shack on stilts at the end of the line at the Porte d'Ivry. Inside, three men and a woman were keeping track of their buses. A tall black man got up when he saw me entering, and handed me the gloves and the scarf with a big smile. He did look really happy to be making me happy.

Savoir-Flair Tip No. 112:
Always let your taxi driver know where you're staying

Sherry Champeaux, an American from Atlanta, lives in Rennes with her French husband, an architect. On holidays they take the children across France to see their Champeaux grandparents in Besançon, a pretty town east of Dijon near Switzerland. The trip means two different TGVs, first from Rennes to Paris, the Gare Montparnasse, then from the Gare d'Austerlitz to Besançon. At Christmas 1998, Sherry and her husband took a taxi across town from Montparnasse to Austerlitz with their three children and innumerable packages and suitcases. On the train to Besançon, Sherry discovered that her handbag was missing... with cash, passport, credit cards, her address book and photos she was fond of. Sherry's parents-in-law met them at the station. Sherry didn't sleep well that night. The next day, the taxi driver telephoned that he had found the handbag in the back seat. Sherry had chatted with him in the cab about going to Besançon. He'd looked through her address book and found a name in Besançon like the one in her passport. As it was Christmas, a family holiday, he reasoned that she would be going to see family. Or, anyway, that people with the same name would be able to reach her. He'd already mailed the handbag to Besançon. He wished her a merry Christmas.

Savoir-Flair Tip No. 113:
The Police and the Hôtel de Ville will help you with almost anything

I locked my bicycle to a post in front of my hairdresser's shop and was rushing -- late, as usual -- into the shop when somehow my keys slipped out of hand and fell... not onto the sidewalk, but through the bars of a grate. I had another key to the bike lock at home, but losing the door key of our apartment house on the same ring was close to catastrophic. I'd tried to have it copied, with no success. It was a strange unique key. Without it, I would have to enter the building by a long tiresome tunnel.

However, I had only a few minutes of frenzy. The policeman on the corner said this was no problem. All I had to do was call the Hôtel de Ville and ask for the *voirie*. The *voirie* is in charge of Paris's garbage removal, with bright green trucks manned by collectors in bright green uniforms who serve us seven days a week, even holidays. The Hôtel de Ville operator asked me what the problem was. I gathered it wasn't the first time she'd heard this one. She gave me a *voirie* number (01 44 75 22 75) with an answering machine. I left my number. Five minutes later a *voirie* official called back. Talking very fast in a tone of emergency he told me that he understood my anxiety, that the rain might soon make it impossible to find the keys and that he would radio his "*gars*" (boys) right away. They were circulating in Paris on other less urgent matters. Could I meet them at the grate in 15 minutes? Which I did. The three *gars*, in smart bright blue uniforms, were already conferring with my hairdresser. There were several grates there, which one was it? I told them. They removed the bars, and one of them slipped down a long ladder, holding a flashlight. Presently he climbed up again with my keys. All three were as pleased as I was. They then said that it wasn't a *voirie* grate. It was an EDF grate, but that they were glad to help.

Savoir-Flair Tip No. 114:
Continue looking for something until you -- or someone else -- finds it

Tony Gerber, a Francophile Englishman, now lives in Paris. Before he found an apartment, Tony and Linda, his wife, hopped over to Paris from London, checked into their favorite hotel on the Right Bank, and jumped into a cab for some shopping at Linda's favorite Left Bank boutiques. After amassing a minor haul during several hours in a good many shops, they taxied back to the hotel. At the hotel Tony discovered he had lost his wallet.

"It disappeared somewhere between checking-in to the hotel and that moment," he said. "Worse yet, I couldn't be really sure when I'd last seen it. Linda had paid for all her purchases with her own credit card. Gone were all my credit cards, French francs, my California driver's license, and $2,000 in cash.

"The concierge helped us to call each shop we'd visited that afternoon. No success. We tore the hotel room apart. We went through everything we were wearing. We drove the concierge and reception staff completely nuts... and then took a cab to retrace each step of our journey. "

In three stores they searched on counters, behind counters and under counters. Finally there was no hope left but the street.

"The sight of a frenzied couple scanning gutters was pretty unusual, I guess," said Tony. "Smartly dressed Parisian ladies looked at us weirdly. We understood that no French people would behave like this in public.

"We decided to try one more store where we've been customers for years -- and were greeted by an exultant manager. Our wallet had been found. It was back at the hotel. The store manager glowed. He seemed genuinely happy for us. He didn't know any of the details, just that the hotel concierge was calling each shop to leave us the exciting news."

Back to the hotel. Tony didn't hope for much except the wallet itself, which he was fond of, and perhaps the driver's license, a nuisance to replace.

The concierge was waiting for them. He took them to the waiting taxi where the wallet had been found. Leaning against it was the driver, a

Provençal with an abundant handlebars mustache.

"I shook his hand with both of mine and urged him to tell me the whole story," said Tony. "He explained that after driving us from the Gare du Nord to the hotel, he had picked up a new fare. This passenger had found the wallet on the taxi floor and turned it over to him. The driver then returned with it to our hotel, assuming we might be guests there. On discovering from the concierge that, indeed, we had turned half of Paris upside down looking for the wallet, he had insisted on waiting for us there... at least an hour."

With a twinkle and that French look of It-happens-to-all-of-us-but-don't-push-your-luck, he then gave Tony the wallet with a flourish, and without hesitation jumped in the cab before Tony had a chance to stop him.

Tony called to him to wait. "I had quickly seen that nothing had been taken from the wallet. I took out $200 and pushed it through the slightly open window of the cab. He refused it! I persisted and eventually he accepted. He obviously hadn't thought of a reward and didn't think of accepting it.

"Tell me, do you think this would happen in New York?"

143

Chapter Twelve

Enjoying Being Young in Paris

Host Mothers, Kissing, Phoning, Eating, Arguing, Meeting Other Young People

One warm magical night, with a few friends, we bought a bottle of wine and went down on one of the quais next to the Seine. There were two Brazilian musicians playing wonderful music on their guitars. They seemed delighted when my friend Molly and I started to dance. The Bateaux Mouches were passing by on the river, lighting up the little cobblestone island under the bridge where we were. Suddenly to make the entire scene perfect, people from the bridge above started blowing bubbles that drifted down over us. I remember thinking that it was impossible that this was real, that how could it possibly be true that Paris is as romantic and magical as everyone says, but I haven't been disappointed yet!

Sarah Davis, Harvard '99, intern at *Time*, Paris

Savoir-Flair Tip No. 115:
Foreign students should be ready for tough teachers and lower marks

French teachers mark in numbers from 1 to 20, and no one has ever been known to be given a 19, let alone a 20. Students accustomed to As and A minuses in the U.S. will be given 14s and 15s. Don't be depressed, you're still the brilliant you. But make sure you prepare your college administration at home that this grading system is DIFFERENT.

Also, no pats and feel-good praise from French teachers. Not that there is a whip, or even a slap, these days, but verbal "negative reinforcement" remains their favored weapon. If you hear the teacher telling the whole class that the paper you spent weeks on is *nul* -- zero! -- and your grammar that of a two-year-old -- not to mention your intellectual gray matter being that of a flea -- you have another opportunity to demonstrate your superb *nonchalance*. Not for nothing is that word *French*.

Savoir-Flair Tip No. 116:
Young foreigners must expect French elders to "civilize" them

As far as anyone knows, the first French behavior manual was written around 850 A.D. by Dhuoda de Septimanie, a noblewoman in Provence. Values, principles and rules. Lots of rules. The French have been honing them ever since, adding new rules and nuances and degrees. The French word *éducation* -- which means manners as well as learning -- is about the transfer of knowledge... which is not only knowing what, but how. If your manners are back in the medieval stage, French people -- everyone from the café waitress to your "host mother" -- will take the trouble to enlighten you. You may wish they didn't.

What you have to keep remembering is that you're in their country, a different world, and they're telling you *for your own good*, assuming you're eager to be taught these things... in order to be, well, yes, civilized. The French mission is to civilize, a word they invented in the 17th century.

Young Americans are sometimes uncomfortable with the word "civilized," which, they've told me, is a "typical arrogant French word." But the French don't mean it to be arrogant. What does to "civilize" mean anyway? In my dictionary it says "to bring to a technically advanced and rationally ordered state of cultural development; to educate, refine, socialize; to help people to acquire the customs and amenities of a civil community, to acquire refinement of thought, manners and taste." In this case, the customs and amenities of a *French* community and the thought, manners and taste of *France*... and France is the benchmark of thought, manners and taste in the West, right?

Just the right way to make a sauce, to cut a sleeve, to shape a bullet train, to probe a molecule -- along with their creative genius, and a few other sterling qualities, *bien sûr* -- is how they got to be world leaders in everything, in the 17th and 18th centuries.

It's the same with manners.

Manners are drummed into French children from the age of 2, which is when French children begin to shake hands with grownups -- and with each other. When you break the rules, you insult people. Foreigners living in France for a long time either master the rules or risk relentless correction. In time, the rules seep into their psyche, and they're as manners-insistent as the French.

You might be staying with a French family. In this case, you're in for a total-immersion course in being civilized. French children are brought up in what seems to Americans like military rigor.* Expect your table manners to be corrected. Your phoning habits will be supervised. Your drawers might be inspected. You'll be told to talk and laugh *less loudly*, not to raid the refrigerator and to turn down your stereo. Take it as an adventure. Be cool. You'll notice little things you didn't think about before, such as that no one eats in the subway (except foreigners) and women never put on lipstick in public.

At a recent gathering of the Canterbury Group at the American Cathedral (you may want to join its weekly suppers) young foreign students compared their experiences in their "host families."

"I was in a terrible hurry, no time to eat, and I was on my way to class -- I *had* to grab a sandwich and eat it in the Métro," said Holly Scheuhinger, a lively junior from Bates College in Maine. "You should have seen how everyone stared at me! Never again!"

"My host mother gave me lessons for a week in how to hold my fork!" cried Nancy J., here with the Sweetbriar junior-year-abroad program.

"My family keeps telling me to sit up straight at the table!" said another.

"My host mother gave my host brother a terrible scolding about hunching over his food," said Holly. "I felt myself slowly straightening up, hoping she hadn't noticed *me* hunched over my food." Holly laughed and added, "My host mother not only told me how to hold my knife and fork but also how to make my bed, not to come down to breakfast after 10:00, and never, never to walk down the street holding a bottle of water or drinking a coke."

On arrival with their host families, they were all handed a printed page about rules on telephoning, on staying out late, on eating between meals, etc.

In one family, the dinner-table talk was about politics and economics. In another, art and literature. In a third, after two glasses of wine, the children -- 16- and 17-year-olds -- began saying what they thought. For the first time.

You'll be startled at the orders issued to 16- and 17-year old French children. And probably just as surprised that the fathers in these families are in constant touch with their own parents.

"My host father goes to Toulouse to see his parents twice a month,"

*For more on the French school system and the family see *French or Foe?*, Chapters 9 and 10 said Jane Gerdsen, a Sweetbriar junior from Cincinnati.

The thing is, as I keep saying, this place is different. No Reese's Peanut Butter Cups, no Mountain Dew, no Lucky Charms. They're cool in France too, but it's a *different* cool, even if you do see Coca Cola dispensers all over, even if you do see lots of McDos (McDonalds) and lots of *ados* (adolescents) in New Balance.

Savoir-Flair Tip No. 117:
You're expected to get up and shake hands (or kiss) when you greet

Watching young French people, you'll get the knack. Coming into a room where they're seeing people for the first time that day, they shake hands or kiss every single person there, unless there are more than 20 people -- no nonsense about getting away with a general "hi" to everyone at once. If they're sitting down when someone else comes in, they get up to greet and kiss their peers, and to greet older women; and yes, older men. Not all of them do -- but the ones who know, do. And you'll do wonders for your country's image if *you* do.

In the fall of 1998, a group of junior-year-abroad students in Paris from James Madison University in Virginia won a special warm place in my heart. Each one came up to greet me and shake my hand, one by one, when they entered the seminar room. It had never happened before.

Savoir-Flair Tip No. 118:
Young French people greet each other with a *bise*! right away, really

La bise (a kiss on the cheeks) is the expected greeting for young people, even if they've never laid eyes on each other before. Girls kiss girls, girls kiss boys and boys kiss girls.

(Right: boys don't kiss boys. That's in Arab countries. But if you're an Anglophone girl with a boyfriend who is half Arab, half French, don't be surprised if he holds hands with an Arab male friend. His Arab friend would be insulted if he didn't. It has nothing to do with sexual orientation.)

Back to *la bise*: the choreography is: first, right cheek to right cheek, then left cheek to left cheek. If you aim for the wrong cheek, noses clash. (This is what happens when French-custom-oriented people go to England, where they kiss in the reverse order, left cheek first.)

Just once on each cheek, please, in Paris. More than each cheek, once, is *plouc* (hick).

In the provinces it's often four kisses. There you might find yourself in the same fix as Jean H. from Scotland. "In Nantes, it's four kisses, two on each cheek," she said. "I went to a party there of 20 people. That's 80 kisses! And everyone did it, as if it was perfectly normal!"

La bise or, in southern France, *un bisou* isn't necessarily a real kiss. Often it's air to air, lips not touching anything. It's not an embrace, *definitely not* a bear hug. Your hands don't touch the other person's body, either, unless you know that person well, and want to show extra warmth.

Wet kisses are definitely out. "Very, very *plouc!*" says Julie Winn's daughter, Lucy Winn, age 17.

In case all this kissing worries you: "There's no significance to a *bisou*," said Carrie Conrad, one of the James Madison juniors.

She's right. It's just saying hello. Nicely. You'll love it, when you get used to it. In France, human beings like to touch, to look at each other, to *interact*. Tune in to the sparkles of boy meets girl, boy talks to girl. Men and women enjoy each other's company. English and American women feel they're more respected and a lot more admired by French men than they are at home.

To young Anglophone men: Pigalle and the Folies Bergères have given many of you the idea that French girls are "easy." They're not. They're not sentimental and not particularly romantic. That they're *charming* goes without saying. Court them respectfully. Preliminaries are what it's all about.

To young American women: French men have a tendency to consider assertive women, particularly assertive American women, as aggressive, which puts them off. Easy does it.

People are charming even if you fall in the apples

"Everyone is so nice!" said Whitney Melton, another James Madison junior. Whitney is a Southern belle, the kind known as willowy, from Richmond.

"You hear such nasty things about French people in the States," she said with that soft voice. "I was invited to a wedding in Normandy... and I was helping my friend with the preparations -- and I fainted. Did you ever? I never thought I'd have a chance to use an expression for fainting I'd learned just the day before -- *tomber dans les pommes*. Falling in the apples! And you can't imagine how thoughtful everyone was. When I came to, they insisted I join them, told me not to be embarrassed. It was a wonderful day!"

Pippa O'Carroll, a young South African, said the same thing. "Everyone told me the French were so rude, but everyone has been so nice to me!"

Meeting French young people

There is no word for a "date" in French. French teens rarely pair off like Americans. They move around in groups, often to each other's houses or apartments. So, to meet them, you have to find a group.

You can also meet them in a café, at a bookstore, in a library, at an exhibition, or doing what you like to do... rowing, cyber-surfing,.. or on a street corner. Why not? It's the way it's done, in Paris.

The funny thing about French people, with all those millennium-old rules, and their ease at striking up a conversation with a young woman in a public place, no one has thought up "communication rules" such as automatic introductions for the informal *verre*, a gathering with wine.

Mary J., a brunette, one of the students at the American Cathedral supper, said she went to a party with French university students and no one introduced themselves. Nor did anyone introduce her to anyone.

"I felt like an obnoxious loud American, too loud, too big, too everything," she said, "and not pretty or charming at all. I thought the male-female thing here was supposed to be so great. Was I ever disappointed."

It is. It's coded, like everything else.

Savoir-Flair Tip No. 119:
Strolling (*flâner*) à la française is a good way for finding fun

Sometimes you can have a marvelous time just strolling and enjoying what's happening. On the Pont Saint-Louis, for instance, or in the Latin Quarter.

Sarah Davis, the *Time* intern quoted at the beginning of the chapter:

"My favorite thing about Paris is wandering until I find something that is just breathtaking -- luckily it happens nearly every time I walk out my door. In early September, I was walking around the Latin Quarter near the Odéon, and the streets were packed with people. It was like a festival, but I soon found out that warm weekend evenings are always like that. There was a man sitting at a table that was covered with different-sized wine glasses, each filled with a different amount of water. He would dip his fingers in the glasses and run them around the rims of different glasses (how he knew which ones was a mystery to me), the result was a symphony that floated through the crowd on rue Saint-André-des-Arts."

Another of Sarah's favorite places is the little Pont Saint-Louis, the bridge leading over to the Ile Saint-Louis from Notre Dame. "Jugglers and street musicians, always something fascinating going on," she says.

Savoir-Flair Tip No. 120:
If you're invited to a French house, expect long, long meals.

"I was invited by a French friend to lunch," said Alistair Adams, a University of London freshman. "We had an *apéritif* at about 1:00... and then lunch... and the time went by so fast I hardly noticed that lunch had turned into dinner! And dinner went on until 2:30 am!"

Well, that's a record, but you do have to expect a dinner called for 8:00 or 8:30 pm to last until midnight. On weekends all over France, French people often sit happily at lunch on Saturday or Sunday until 6 pm. It's called conviviality. The point of their wonderful food is to get family and friends together to talk and have a good time. If you're going to have a really good time, it takes *time!*

Savoir-Flair Tip No. 121:
For a good meal, be respectful to waiters

Waiting on tables is not a summer sport for college kids in France. It's an exalted profession with a long and exacting apprenticeship. In a country where the chefs are gods, the waiters are the high priests, with the attire and dignity befitting their experience and their encyclopedic command of gastronomy and viticulture. Talking to a French waiter about the composition of a meal is like auditioning for a play. Do you know your part? Have you done the preparation? If not, why aren't you at a Mc.Do? (See Chapter 16 on enjoying French waiters.)

Savoir-Flair Tip No. 122:
You get better service ordering according to waiters' suggestions

Caroline Hutchinson, from Birmingham, UK, married a Frenchman, and feels up to just about anything that comes along in France, including speaking French. But when she was 19, visiting a French friend, the family took her out for a meal in a Parisian restaurant which still astonishes her.

"It was the kind of restaurant where you could see the chef through a window to the kitchen," she said. "I mean, not terribly classy, and you'd think it would be sort of easy going and homey. Well, I ordered salmon, and was given the choice between side dishes of green beans or pasta. My friends were helping me with the ordering, since my French wasn't that great. They told the waitress I wanted green beans.

"The waiter gave the order to the chef. I could see them conferring in the kitchen. When he came back he told us delicately that the chef thought that the pasta would be 'more of a compliment' to the salmon. My friend's father -- I'll call him Monsieur Dupont -- discussed this with the waiter, saying that perhaps the chef was right, but that his daughter's English friend preferred the green beans. They went back and forth on this. The waiter stood his ground and so did Monsieur Dupont. I don't have any idea what their various arguments were, but Monsieur Dupont was politely firm. So, finally, the waiter went back to the kitchen and announced the result to the chef. I got my green beans.

"I couldn't believe that my choosing beans or pasta was of such importance to everyone. I just found it very funny that my so-called choice wasn't really a choice at all."

Despite all that food, French girls are thin

French girls are thinner and smaller, usually, than British and American girls. They're *narrow*. I don't know if there is something in French genes that makes smaller bones, but the fact, is, when you go shopping you're bound to feel sort of, well, big.

We talked about this when Berna Huebner, godmother to visiting young Americans in Paris (and not just because her husband, Lee, is president of Northwestern University) invited the whole Medill journalism group to her apartment for supper. These young women, healthy young Americans and certainly not what anyone would call "fat," were shocked that they were unable to get into French clothes when they went shopping.

"All the dresses were too small," said Michelle Adelman, "and yet I'm only a size 8! I was getting madder and madder as I tried on one dress after another."

"All the dresses have waists! Tiny waists! There's nothing like that in the U.S.," said Jenny Rode.

"If you ask me, French girls don't eat unless you force them. I think they must all be anorexic. If I lived here and saw all these thin people all day, I'd get complexes!" said another.

"Well, one thing, you don't see athletic looking people around here," said Suzanne M.

"I think it's because they smoke," said another. "They do ALL smoke, and that's why, to stay thin."

Lucy Winn, the 17 year old quoted above, has lived in Paris since she was seven. This is what Lucy says about French girls: "True, they're thin, but they're not anorexic. They learn very early to eat only at meal-times, and to stop eating when they're not hungry. You'd think it would be obvious!"

Savoir-flair Tip No. 123:
Avoid misunderstandings by speaking French carefully

The French have perfected the veiled hint. It's called *nuancer*, a word difficult to translate which means to express a thought, sentiment, etc. with great sublety. One little word like *bien* can change the sense of the whole sentence.

Christopher Dol, a Madison junior, discovered the difference between *aimer* and *bien aimer* the hard way. While you can decide for yourself whether *aimer* standing alone in a sentence means to like or to love (the nuances are in the context), if that little word *bien* is next to it, then the word definitely does not mean love, anyway not romantic love.

"I got to know a French girl really well -- and we always spoke French," he said. "She told me, *'Je t'aime bien.'* I was a little confused and disturbed; I thought it meant she loved me! I didn't quite know how to handle the situation. Then someone told me about *bien* making all the difference. What she really said was, 'I like you a lot.' If you say *je t'aime...* well, that's what I thought she was saying."

Queue manners at ski lifts, taxi ranks, etc....

"I don't get the ski situation here," said Frank Wesley, also here on the Internships France program. "The lines are simply funnels. The skiers pour into them en masse, crowding and jostling to beat the others to the chairs -- and walking all over your skis! Skis are sacred objects to an American skier -- what gives with the French?"

France doesn't regiment people's queues on vacation -- and hardly anywhere else, for that matter. Neither does Italy. It's considered part of your liberty. Yes, I know it is very organized in Britain and the U.S. This is our culture heritage or training. For French people, ski lines are one of the few places where manners weren't engraved in a behavior manual 800 years ago. I'm afraid you'll have to stop caring about the scratches, or get some cheap skis. Better still, rent them.

No hot water unless --

"I was staying at a bed and breakfast in Paris," said Holly Stewart, of Pittsburgh, an undergraduate at Penn State. "There wasn't any hot water! When I asked the landlady about it, she wanted us to pay in advance -- for the B & B and the hot water! When I complained about paying extra for hot water, her husband said, 'Typical spoiled Americans.'"

Electricity is expensive, much more expensive than in the U.S. Any kind of energy is expensive in France, including hot water, as noted earlier. Budget hotels will ask you to pay extra for a shower.

French people are traditionally frugal and thrifty. Arletty said it all in the movie, "Terminus Nord," that she just can't help it, she's *radine* (tight-fisted).

They don't consider the pursuit of happiness a birthright. They're not even very demanding about physical comfort. It costs too much.

Savoir-Flair Tip No. 124:
Money talk being taboo, you must word your questions tactfully

"All I did was ask my host mother how much it would cost to take the train to Bordeaux," said Jyoti Schlesinger, another junior abroad. "And she blew up! She shot back with 'You Americans are always talking about money! And you haven't paid us back for all the money we spent on your Revolution!'"

Poor Jyoti. She hadn't expected to provoke a diplomatic crisis, nor to be held to account for American history. Born in Tunisia with an Indian mother, Jyoti grew up in Oakton, Virginia. Her background usually helps her to sniff out a cultural nerve a mile away. This reaction distressed her.

What suddenly went wrong? Two things.

First, talk about money is displeasing in France. Asking how much anything costs is, in principle, a taboo. French people *may* ask *you* how much something costs, or even how much you earn, because they've heard that all Anglophones do is compare prices. So, this sort of question has to be put very tactfully, roundabout. If Jyoti had said that she was on a tight budget and didn't know if she could afford the train to Bordeaux, then her host mother could have volunteered the information without having been asked directly.

Secondly, this host mother was perhaps reminded by Jyoti's question that her own beloved country was becoming greedy with consumerism, pursuing the root of all evil instead of dedicating itself to scaling cultural summits.

It is true that while, in general, French people do like Americans, many blame America and its overwhelming might and means for hyping vulgarity at the expense of depth. French columnists write thoughtful pieces about the uniformization of expression and leveling of thought to the lowest denominator. They see the American presence in their daily life and in their language -- the flower and the pride of their culture -- and many of them fear and resent it.

Savoir-Flair Tip No. 125:
Boning up on history will give you answers to hard questions

Like it or not, ready or not, you're seen as a spokesman for your country.

Jyoti, like other American juniors abroad and interns, was put in the witness box also about blockbuster American movies threatening planetary destruction by an asteroid, a monster, enemy aliens, whatever, the world to be rescued only by American genius and courage. Other countries barely exist, except to applaud the U.S. In "Godzilla," France is simply lasered off the map.

"My French friends blame 'Saving Private Ryan' for not being objective, " said Jyoti. "They complain that you wouldn't know the soldiers were in France."

"This can provoke really interesting discussions," says Sarah Davis, "but don't mistake their arguing for chastizing. The French love to go to town on differences of opinions which have nothing to do with being judgmental."

Still, the French, and Europeans in general, wonder deep down if the United States, the one remaining Superpower, hasn't turned into a Superbully. *Le Figaro* wrote in October, 1998: "America now is concerned with taking over the whole planet."

Despite family quarrels from time to time, the fact is that France is the United States's oldest and most faithful ally. But while America's other allies toe the U.S. line with scarcely a grumble, France will often play the role of court jester to America's Unique Superpower. Who would deny a king the gift of at least one dissenting opinion, perhaps a wise one? The cornerstone of French foreign policy since World War II, initiated by General de Gaulle, has been not to kow-tow to Americans. Should you resent this, it is well to keep in mind a powerful ghost ever-present to the French: their history. It is they who were calling the shots in the western world for 200 years, during the 17th and 18th centuries. Versailles was the power-culture-science center of the West. French was the only diplomatic language until 1918.

Savoir-Flair Tip No. 126:
Showing respect for French achievements will oil prickly discussions

If you aren't much on culture -- art, history, music, literature -- and not much on science or politics, then show your respect for your host country in boning up on French world dominance in certain sports, beginning with their winning the soccer World Cup in 1998. It's the solo sports where they really excel against the whole world. Maurice Herzog was the first man to climb to the top of an 8000-meter Himalaya. Their champions have won the Tour de France bicycle race, the world's most difficult, countless times. They're the world fencing champions. Their sailors, including women, are constantly sailing alone across the Atlantic and around the world. A Frenchman swam across the Atlantic in August 1998. A Frenchman rowed across the Pacific in 1992. Commandant

Cousteau explored the depths of the oceans like no one before him. A Frenchwoman walked across the South Pole alone, arriving in 2000.

Younger Teens

If you're between 14 and 19, the place you want to head for is the Champs Elysées. This is where you 'll find the shops you want and the movies you want, plus stickerphoto booths. This is also where to find the videogame arcades (Virgin, etc.), plus a McDo and a Haagendaas, and a new café popular with your age, Le Café de Paris.

For Lucy Winn, the Champs Elysées is the best place to go on the weekend. "There is always so much to do there even in bad weather. I never go to there without seeing someone I know. As for shops, SEPHORA!!!! Sephora sells everything to do with make-up and perfume. It has the advantage of letting you try on absolutely everything and not being preyed on by saleswomen working on commission.

"The nearby clubs are the Bains, the Queen, the Duplex, the Planches and others. The Queen got busted for drugs a few years ago and is a gay club. The Duplex and the Planches are for younger people. The Bains Douches is where celebrities go. It's apparently quite hard to get into. When I say club, I mean Nightclubs/Discos, with what is now known as dancing but what I prefer to refer to as bopping. Oh, I am born into the wrong era. I'd have made a great 20s chick!"

Some boys and girls between 13 and 14, friends of Elizabeth Garner, 15, got together at her mother's apartment in the 9th arrondissement to talk about France. They had lived in Paris for over a year, Elizabeth, for five years. They were Chloe Rhys, 13, from Washington,D.C., George Janin, 14, from Little Rock, Alex Brasant, 14, from Boston, Robert Gourlay, 14, from Washington, and Jocelyn Jeffery, 14 from New York. All were American except Fabrice Adriani, 14, son of the former French ambassador to the U.S. All went to the Ecole Bilingue.

And all were living with their own families, with the advantage that they could get used to the foreign country gradually, while keeping up various habits at home. They did miss Reese's Peanut Butter Cup and Mountain Dew, but, cozily living with their families at home in Paris, they thought they had the best of both worlds.

One of the things they appreciate most in Paris is their independence.

"In Arkansas you get driven around everyhere by your mom," said George. "Here you can go by bus or Métro." I remembered George gratefully from a Christmas bazaar the year before; he'd volunteered to help me carrying my books to the sales counters. "In America there's a big difference between people on the street and the people in a car," he added. "Here, everyone is in the street together. There's much greater mobility."

Elizabeth agreed. "You can go to a bar and get something to drink if you're our age," she said. "At home, you can't, so people do, and overdo it, and get drunk. Here, you never see anyone drunk, the way you do in the U.K."

"Right," agreed George. "They're not *anti* things here. They're more relaxed about drinking and pornography. There's less tension. Things are more natural."

They recognized that a lot of prudence goes with the extra freedom. All the girls and young women I've talked to, of all ages, agreed on one thing: French men feel free to talk to you, and if you're blond, you'll be stared at and perhaps approached by French men of all ages. Blond or not, second generation immigrants from North Africa may follow you and accost you.

On the street

"In the beginning I was really scared on the Champs Elysées," said Elizabeth. "Men come up and bother you. Now I'm used to it and say loudly, '*Laissez-moi tranquille.*' It's better to be straightforward, polite and distant. But I wouldn't walk alone in the 20th, around Belleville."

Lucy Winn says that over the years she has perfected a "forbidding look" for walking on Paris streets.

On the Métro

"On the Métro I'm careful to keep my hands in my lap or covering my face, and not to cross my legs," Elizabeth added. "And I keep my eyes down."

Chloe, who had been in Paris only a few months, hadn't quite got the hang of things yet: "I get totally paranoid in the Métro, when a man in the seat opposite makes a remark. I freak out and switch places."

They all said that they avoided certain Métro stations, even during the day: Barbès, Châtelet, Les Halles and Saint-Michel.

The *racaille*

For the boys, there were gangs of young teenagers from the suburbs to worry about. They're known as the *racaille*. Rabble, riff-raff. They come in groups of three or four, they're 14 or 15 -- anyway, under 19, they're all dressed alike in sweat pants and puffy short jackets," said George.

"They're on the Champs Elysées or the Trocadéro and they walk beside you and say, 'Oh, that's a pretty jacket you have on. Can I have it?' You'd better give it to them -- they'll tear it off your back anyway, and rough you up. We had a friend -- Olivier -- who wore designer jeans, designer everything to school. Then he paraded around after school. He was just asking for trouble. They got him behind a wall and made him take off everything. They gave him some cheap shorts to go home in. It's called getting *racketté.*"

"But you don't have to worry about getting shot here. And the Arabs never attack girls," said Robert, who was hit badly once by the *racaille.* "Arabs are respectful of girls."

Smile?

"Two things are really different here," said Elizabeth. "You don't smile and act friendly to people you don't know, or they think you're stupid. And they judge you on how you dress."

La bise at 14

Kissing other girls or boys on the cheek (both cheeks! once each!) on meeting them for the first time struck these young teens as very odd, or worse. They started at about 14.

"I hated it!" said Chloe.

"Well, I did too, but I got used to it," said Elizabeth. "At first when I did it, it was as a sort of joke, imitating older people. But then... well you know, it's sort of nice, more personal than just sort of saying 'hi' to everyone at once."

Culture is good!

"I play the violin," said one of the boys. "In the U.S., the other guys see you with a violin and they think, 'Oh, he must be a teacher's pet.' Here, they think it's cool! Being *inculte* -- uncultured -- is an insult here. It would never occur to anyone in the Midwest that being uncultured is bad."

George loves the elegance of Paris. "One thing I really like to go and see," he said, "is the Church of Saint-Germain-des Prés, the beauty of it, particularly at night, when the tower is lit up."

The biggest bug of all

These young people speak French. It bothers them that some of their older compatriots come here without realizing that this is a country where the language is French, not English.

"They go into a bakery and order loudly, 'Two loaves of whole wheat bread!!' and when the baker doesn't respond, they're angry," said Jocelyn. "Then they just point!"

Manners Tips for young teens and younger...

• Get up whenever an older person comes into the room, particularly a woman. Get up to meet anyone for the first time of any age over 15, either sex.

• Say *'Bonjour, madame"* or *"Bonjour, monsieur"* to older people you know. Lucy Winn: "Yes! Always! This is considered a test of class!" Curtsying for young girls has pretty much gone out, even in France, but not entirely. Elizabeth Lapierre, who grew up in Périgueux, tells of her mother's codes for a curtsy or a handshake. If a curtsy, her mother would say, *"Dis bonjour convenablement."* (Say hello properly.) If only a handshake, then she'd say, *"Dis bonjour gentiment."* (Say hello nicely.)

• Don't put your feet on the furniture, slouch in your chair, or sit on the floor.

• Don't raid the refrigerator if you're invited to a French friend's house.

• Don't speak or laugh loudly.

• As for table manners, imitate your hostess. Try to eat as she does.

Chapter Thirteen

Enjoying Being a Woman in France

French Amour, French Elegance
Enjoying Being a Man Meeting French Women

Physical love... Everything that precedes the union of the sexes and makes it more beautiful, and since François I, more romantic, from flirting to fashion -- above all, flirting -- was born in France and only has a name in French -- coquetterie. For lessons in this, the elite of other nations come every day to the capital of the universe.

Brillat-Savarin, La Physiologie du Goût, 1826

Coquetterie: désir de plaire. Coquette: Qui cherche à plaire par sa toilette, son élégance, par ses manières.

(Coquetry: the desire to please. Coquette: someone who wishes to please by her appearance, her elegance and her manners.)

Petit Larousse Illustré, 1986

La confiance de plaire est parfois le moyen le plus sûr de plaire.
(Confidence in pleasing is sometimes the surest way to please).

Duc de La Rochefoucauld, Sentences et Maximes,1670

Leafing through a French magazine you come across a beautiful blonde in a sumptuous décolleté evening dress gliding along next to a tall distinguished man, and it turns out to be the (extremely powerful) Minister of Justice, Elizabeth Guigou, and her husband. On the street, a devastating blonde roars by on a motor cycle with long hair streaming out below her cap; she's the director of a nuclear power station. In a kiosk there's a poster of another blonde so beautiful she'd make Cleopatra jealous; who is it but Odile Jacob, founder of a thriving publishing company for scientific books. And those blocks-long queues of young people lining up to see *Le Goût des Autres* and *La Bûche*, who made the movies? Women wrote and directed them, Agnès Jaoui, charm itself, and beautiful Danièle Thompson.

How do they do it, French women?

Beautiful, mysterious, competent, admired and envied by women and courted by men everywhere for their looks, their elegant, subtle sexiness and style, French women slowly, very slowly insinuated their way into key positions in all of the male bastions of this most macho-male Latin country, even, in January 2000, into major political power with the choice of Michèle Alliot-Marie as president of the RPR, the coalition of political parties on the right. Women have done this despite the dice being loaded against them, and without a feminist movement. "We want to be feminine, not feminist," they will tell you. "We want to be friends with men. We want tenderness -- and jobs." Without firing a shot, much less declaring war on men, they managed to obtain extra government allowances for each child, months and months of maternity leave, before and after a birth with job security on returning to work, excellent, almost free child care and medical services, and first rate education for their children. Not to mention, despite the traditions of a Catholic country, the right to abortion, the pill, and the day-after pill for high school girls. Equal salaries in the workplace? Not quite, not yet, but you can bet it's coming.

And they're still "friends with men."

So, how do they do it? Softly. But it takes training to get your way softly. Training and patience. About 1000 years of both.

First of all, to be a French woman you need a French mother and women role models back to the 5th century: saints and abbesses, warriors and intellectuals, royal mistresses directing affairs of state, voluptuous horizontals and splendid actresses.

Secondly, you need French men, and a climate of love.

Thirdly, you need a thousand years of male-female symbiosis. Webster's definition (1953): "The living together in intimate association or even close union of two dissimilar organisms. In a broad sense, the term includes antagonistic or antipathetic symbiosis, in which the association is disadvantageous or destructive to one of the organisms."

The French writer and Académicien Alain Decaux took 1824 pages in *Les Françaises* (1972) to give a vision of a 1000-year symbiosis disastrously disadvantageous to women yet nevertheless, a time of their ever-increasing influence on French men. After the feudal ages, women became the property of their fathers and then of their husbands, with the status of children or the mentally handicapped, and no say about their own body or dowry, no protection against the violence of their husband until the 20th century. Adulteresses like Léonie d'Aunet, a passing love of Victor Hugo, were automatically thrown in prison with thieves and prostitutes, while adulterous men, needless to say, went happily about their business.

Courtly love and the Crusades

In a sense, the elusively superb flair of French women dates to the 12th century, when feudal baronesses, countesses and duchesses held two trumps: property and professional rights of their own, and if their lords were away on the Crusades, real power over their vassals; and the new mode of romantic love, which had surfaced due to the legends of King Arthur and Tristan and Isolde, both published on the initiative of that great queen, Eleanor of Aquitaine. Marriages were arranged; love bloomed outside of marriage, particularly with the lords away in Jerusalem. Eleanor and her daughter, Marie of Champagne, played their hand brilliantly for succeeding generations by inventing *l'amour courtois*, a leap for Europe and the first step in a long process of converting coarse feudal French warriors into elegant courtiers with manners and an interest in the arts. Steeped in the troubadour love poetry of her ducal grandfather, Marie, with a chaplain called André, wrote books on the principles of love and the codes and etiquette to be followed by her vassals. The books were inspired by Ovid's *The Art of Loving* except that, as Amy Kelly points out in her *Eleanor of Aquitaine and the Four Kings*, in Ovid, man is the master, employing his arts to seduce women for his pleasure, while in Marie's work with André, "woman is the mistress and man her pupil in homage, her vassal in service." Men who refused to follow the rules were simply denied the ladies' favors. On their side, women were taught to be *séduisantes*, in the French sense of the word -- which is to please, in their dress and manner; in other words, to be *coquettes*.

Marie also inaugurated those 12th-century spectaculars, the "courts of love," in the great hall in Poitiers. Knights came to this "court" -- made up of 60 ladies -- with a "suit" or complaint about their lady's resistance despite their strict adherence to the love codes. The courts debated his case, as well as questions still alive today, such as, can romantic love be sustained in marriage?

Things would never be the same for men again. In the following centuries, powerless to save their legal rights, women threw themselves into the lessons of Eleanor and Marie: to please, and to demand male manners, softly. To please, appearance (*paraître*) was crucial. By the 14th century, French fashion was magnificent. By the 16th, fashion and perfume, the handmaidens of *coquetterie*, were the recognized domains of the French, thus, as Brillat-Savarin says in quote above, bringing the world to France to learn about *coquetterie*.

Early in the 17th century, aristocratic French women known as the Précieuses decided to extend their soft insistence to the crude language of the men around them. Men who wished to be considered distinguished now had to hark to the rules of elegant French as well as courtship. Richelieu took over this mission in 1635 by founding the Académie Française. The Précieuses also hit on a new coat of paint for gallantry. They thought up the *carte du tendre* (map of tenderness), which looks a little like a board game of Go. The suitor's route winds around preliminaries to be submitted to or overcome by the suitor (the Lake of Challenge, the Hill of Sighs) before his beloved surrenders.

The language salons of the *Précieuses* evolved into the literary and philosophical salons of the 18th century. Marriages were still arranged, wives were still a man's property, but women had widened their domain from the senses and manners to the mind, or *esprit*. They now reigned over taste. They pushed this writer or that artist to success, withheld it from another. They affected everything from letters and art to affairs of state. Madame de Pompadour, mistress of Louis XV, received ambassadors, wrote the Treaty of Paris in 1763, and gave advice and commissions to artists, architects and artisans. The style we call Louis XV is the *style Pompadour*. The paintings of Boucher and Fragonard are songs to her and to the ladies of the court. The salon of Madame Geoffrin, the first to attract Diderot, was renowned in Europe and crowded with foreign notables such as Hume, Walpole and Franklin. Gustave II of Sweden and Catherine the Great of Russia wrote her letters. When Stanislas Poniatowski was made King of Poland, he insisted that she visit him in Warsaw, where he had an apartment prepared for her furnished exactly like her salon in Paris. On the way there, the Emperor of Austria descended from his carriage to pay her homage. The Marquise du Châtelet, Voltaire's only great love, was a scientific pathfinder. She knew everything that was known of mathematics, including Newton's differential calculus, could write Latin, and had studied Leibnitz. She was also known for her high spirits. When she saw Voltaire for the first time at age 27, already married for seven years to a man she despised, instead of swooning at the sight of the great man like the other ladies of her age, she jumped in his lap.

Love, *coquetterie*, was always in play. During the Revolution, women used these skills to rescue heads from the guillotine. Thérésia Cabarrus, a beautiful and rich divorcée known as Notre Dame de Thermidor, became the mistress of one of the bloodiest assassins of the Terror, Jean-Marie Tallien, to save her own neck and intervene for hundreds of others. After the anguish of the Revolution came the Directoire and the extravagant relief and reveling of the classes which could afford it. There were 600 public balls in Paris. Thérésia, now the mistress of the powerful Directoire member Barras, led the voluptuous dance, changing wigs three times a day, wearing almost transparent dresses which stopped at the knee, and appearing barefoot at balls with painted toenails. Other women displayed their nipples erotically or dressed in trousers.

The queen of *coquetterie*

Napoleon's reign sobered things up, but all through it, as previously during the Directoire, one woman was the talk of Europe. This was partly because of her beauty, for Juliette Récamier was probably the most beautiful woman of the time, but mostly because of her skill at *coquetterie*. This goddess spent her time breaking hearts without losing her own. She led her legions of adorers, from Lucien Bonaparte and Bernadotte to Metternich and Prince Auguste of Prussia, through the frustrations of the *carte du tendre* and then stopped short before their reward. They were close to suicide but she kept them as friends. Juliette was 16 when she was married off to Récamier, who -- according to her niece -- never made use of his conjugal rights; she remained a virgin until she was 41, when she met Chateaubriand in May 1817. She fell like a ton of bricks, but kept him at arm's length until October. This love lasted until they both died in 1849.

Juliette's *coquetterie* may well have been the inspiration of Empress Eugénie. Napoleon III was determined not to marry her. The court was against it, his mother was against it, it would bring no useful alliance to France. She was seen everywhere with him in magnificent attire, but withheld her favors for two years, until the wedding. If he played wooing games under her bedroom window, she simply sang, "First, to church!"

French women today? They're as careful -- as obsessed, British and American women like to say -- with their clothes, their hair dos, with dermatology, in short with *paraître*, as ever. This is true whether it's Isabelle Autissier looking marvelous even after she's capsized during a solo sail around the world, or Juliette Binoche, after a harrowing day's shoot. Ask them what matters most and the answer is *plaire* -- to please.

Gaelle Piccard and Séverine Roscot work for Bayard, the publishing house, Gaelle, as an editor, Séverine, in public relations. Gaelle is in her thirties, a widow. Séverine, in her late twenties, is unmarried. Both are dark, slim, elegant and clearly *French*. At lunch, they launched into the subject of pleasing with gusto. In French. It is difficult to do it justice to in English.

Gaelle: "*La courtoisie française* -- French courtesy -- is to consider someone, the person you're talking to, as *séduisant* -- seductive -- to give him or her the feeling that they are *séduisant*. If that person is not *séduisant*, all the more reason to make them feel that they are... because he will be more sensitive!!! *L'injure la plus mortelle* -- the most deadly insult -- is to give someone the feeling that they're not *séduisant*."

Séverine: "And to show someone that they're seductive, you must be yourself very *soignée*... well-groomed, careful about your appearance." They learn this from their mothers, for instance, the smooth skin that results from not shaving legs and underarms, but waxing them. Painfully. They have an annual subscription to go regularly to the *épilateur*. "Then when you're 40, the hair doesn't come back any more." (Later, Etienne B., from Bordeaux told me: "I love it if women are hairless everywhere. Well, except on their head.")

Gaelle: "Yes, and all this shows in your bearing, your manners, your clothes, your way of speaking, your conversation, your wit... I want my women friends, as well as my men friends, to be *séduisantes*, charming and good looking."

Marthe de Rohan Chabot, a psychoanalyst, agrees. "*Oui. On veut plaire*," she says.

The ultimate French weapon

A foreigner who exults in *séduction à la française* is a gorgeous Japanese widow, Lady Albery. She was on her way to a cocktail party when we met at her hotel, drop-dead elegant in a black *smoking* (tuxedo), with satin lapels, and a polka dot tie with a diamond pin. She loves France.

"The game of seduction is everything here," she said. "Seducing, in the French sense of the word -- charming -- adds such spice to life. Charm is the most powerful weapon here. If you don't use it, you'll be overcharged by the taxi driver, you won't get your hotel room. The hotel concierge is the biggest test. If you can't get that cold, closed, formal face to relax and be charming to you in four days, move to another hotel."

The nuts and bolts of all this beauty, of being *coquette* and *séduisante* -- and gorgeous after 50 -- that is, what goes on at the hairdresser's, the dress shops, the boutiques for waxing, facials and body care often perplex American women. They're uneasy about pampering themselves. They're shocked at the expense (FF 180 for a complete leg waxing, FF 435 for a facial). If you grow up in the U.S. or the U.K. scolded for looking in the mirror, it's going to be difficult to get yourself to labor mightily over the perfection of your appearance.

Sophie Y., 22, a Medill student, grew up in Chicago. Her mother is French; her father, American. "I always knew I was different, because my French mother brought me up telling me that my body was wonderful, to love it and take care of it," she told me. "With American girls, it's different. They're not really pleased and proud of it, like French girls."

At a visit to one of Paris's famous hairdressing salons soon after her arrival in France, Lynn Kelley had a good look at the role of a French mother in bringing up a future French woman. Lynn, always elegant, with cover-girl blond looks, had decided on a splurge chez Alexandre to raise her spirits.

"This wasn't a salon as I knew it," she said, "but an alien world where chic women were giving each other air kisses, ordering lunch for their dogs and having their toenails painted and their eyelashes tinted. I sat there quietly for ages, ignored, too intimidated to make a fuss. Just as my 'stylist' finally waved me into a chair, a glamourous woman breezed in with her little daughter, about seven. More air kisses and excited discussions about this person or that, yesterday's party or tomorrow's. And wouldn't you know it, the stylist asked me to wait just one *petite minute*, the little mademoiselle needed her hair cut. Up she went, sitting on cushions piled up like the princess and the pea, regarding herself with satisfaction in the mirror from all angles. I was fascinated. How does a seven-year-old child get that much confidence? That much style? *La petite minute* turned into 40 minutes, time to ponder that Parisian women *are different* and that difference starts very early. Somehow they know that it's not beauty that counts, but chic, and part of chic is confidence."

To an out-of-context foreigner, every day in Paris seems like Valentine's Day. Greg Young, from Yorkshire, came to one of my seminars saying he'd figured out why Paris is known as the City of Love: "It's because everywhere you look, people are kissing." A movie-theatre ad for coffee shows an amorous young man trying to make friends with a young woman on a train. Young girls and old ladies are treated with gallantry by salesmen in stores. Every week there are prime time evening television discussions of *amour*. Books, movies, television programs show men and women enjoying each other's company. You can watch them in cafés and restaurants. They're exchanging ideas, looks, smiles, complicity... with lots of *coquetterie*.

Do foreigners understand what is going on? Not always. The

message about French *amour courtois* and *coquetterie* gets skewed over borders to the north and overseas. French mothers obliged to send their children to school in the U.S. and the U.K. tell of their daughters being taunted with 'French whore' and 'slut.' The mother of a 13-year-old in school in Cincinnati told of her daughter coming home in tears after being asked who her pimp was. English newspapers regularly allude to the French as sex-obsessed.

The French ambassador to the UN invited Sylvie Couturié to an elegant dinner in New York before she was married. "I had American men on both sides of me," she said, "and one of them ignored me completely until the dinner was almost over. Then he turned to me and said, 'Will you sleep with me tonight?' Of course I was shocked at this rudeness, and of course I said No. But I was curious why he would ask me, since we had hardly spoken and certainly had no *atomes crochus* , as we say in French -- hooked atoms. So I asked him. He said, 'Because you're French.'"

Folies Bergères to the contrary, French girls, closely guarded by their parents, are probably the most modest in Europe. Showing their shapes is not an invitation but is part of the culture of *paraître*.

"There is a true complicity between French men and women," said Emmanuella Dalyac, a young French mother and freelance jounalist living in London. "That's why they flirt. It makes it spicier. It doesn't mean they want sex as an Englishman or American would suppose. They just like being together, it feels better that way. English and American men often misinterpret the codes. French women wear lots of earrings and bracelets and rings because it's part of the fun of flirting to look feminine -- not because they're out for sex."

Emmanuella says that even her French accent brings unpleasant comments from some English men. "Last week in a taxi crossing Hyde Park, the driver recognized that I was French, and in a greasy, vulgar voice, laughing, said that the way I spoke was 'just like wearing black stockings.'"

Another skewed cross-cultural message is what Anglophones see as the "frivolous" French view of marriage. They like to quote the actor Pierre Arditi, who, when asked in an interview if he was faithful to his wife, quipped, "Often."

In *La Bûche*, the comedy written and directed by the beautiful Danièle Thompson, Sabine Azema plays a 40-year old singer who has been having a merry affair for years with a married man. He has four children, and a fifth is on the way -- no problem, except that Sabine discovers she's also pregnant. The movie opens at a cemetery during the burial of her stepfather. Her mother, discussing her late husband with his mistress over his grave, says that she buried him with his mobile phone with the messages from his mistresses -- and that she never had the heart to bother him about them.

In *Le Goût des Autres*, the other movie mentioned above written and directed by a woman, Agnès Jaoui, the main character, an industrialist *plouc*, leaves his wife for his intellectual, leftish English teacher when he sees her on stage in *Iphigénie*. Jaoui herself is moving and sad as a bar girl who warms up a romance with a former lover until he tells her he has a *petite amie* (a steady) who is away, studying in America. She shrugs and then falls in love with his colleague, who loves but leaves her.

These movies are funny and tender. They have no steamy sex scenes and no violence, but lots of talk, lots of wit, lots of fun and lots of love involving the minor as well as the major characters, as there are in all the recent popular French movies, without the coarseness of, for instance, *American Beauty*. The theme running through them is that love is good, it's there, it's tender and it matters, and so does marriage, and enjoy it all as well as you can.

So does that mean that for the French, adultery is no big deal? Some Anglophones think so, and it riles them. "French men are liars," said Elisabeth Kine, a Londoner whose company, Kilmuir, introduced cottage cheese to France. "French men cheat on their wives as easily as combing their hair."

Others find the Gallic way -- to adore women and pretend to take serious things lightly -- is preferable for the long haul.

"I used to be a hotshot stock broker in the City," said Delia Schaffer, an English dynamo married to a Frenchman, "and then I married Henri and had three children. No more stockbrokering, not much brain work. But Henri was so wonderful to me. Finally I said, 'But Henri, how is it possible that you still seem to love me? I must be such a bore!' And Henri said, quite shocked, 'But Delia! who cares about movers and shakers! You are the most magnificent marvelous *woman*!' As if being a woman was something special! And that's the way he treats me."

Frenchmen want their women seductive and happy. All the polls show them living up to their reputation of the French lover and then some; they seem to make love far more than others in Europe, which makes young unmarried Anglo-Saxon women visiting France all the more curious to know if the French reputation for being unfaithful is true or false. It's like asking if French water is pure or not. What water? Lake water, river water, well water? No doubt centuries of love outside of marriage are a cultural turn-on. No doubt the public example of the mistresses of the Kings and Presidents has an effect. In France, government scandals are about money, not sex. In Britain and the U.S., it's just the opposite. "It's not that the French are less excitable about sex," wrote Adam Gopnik in the *New Yorker*, "it's that they're a lot calmer about lies." There is no Puritan streak to the French. It's not so different in the other nearby countries, by the way, Italy, Spain and Austria. In Austria I was told that for married philanderers who want to stay married, all women are fair game except for the au pair girl, the woman next door and an American -- because she'll insist on marriage. Very often it's like father, like son. If a Frenchman grows up with faithful parents, or if he has a deep religious faith, or if he marries late and is captivated by his mate, he is likely to be faithful. Also, if they don't live in Paris.

But -- if they're unfaithful, these young Anglo-Saxon women pursue, how come French women take it -- or do they? Is it possible that they don't mind? That they're *that different* from British and American women?

The answer to the second question is clear. Indeed, French women do mind. Younger women mind violently. Their reaction is never like the one of American and British women I know: "Well, if he's like that, then I'm better off without him anyway." More likely they scheme to charm him back. Women's magazines are full of pertinent suggestions. If there are children, the equation is heavily weighted for them to weather things out. In any case, French husbands usually want to stay with their families. The divorce court is the last resort.

Tanja de Rosnay, a French author, wrote a novel called *Marié et père de famille* (*Married and a Father*) about seven young couples and how the wife found out that her husband had strayed, and her reaction. I went to see her.

"Young wives are terrified at the idea," she said. "They say things like, 'If my husband is unfaithful, I'll kill myself.' As they get older, they get more lucid. People live much longer now -- they see that for a man to be faithful for 40 years is really asking a lot. The point is that he should *always deny it*. No matter how incriminating the evidence, he should never admit it. That is just too hard on wives. And he should never have a long affair -- that hurts too much. Women today work and don't have to put up with that -- and they don't. But -- short flings in small doses, and *above all*, if he doesn't let his wife know... I mean, after all. Particularly if there are children. "

In an interview, Françoise Sagan said something similar: "If a lover is unfaithful and tells me, that's it, it's over. He just shouldn't tell me." Sylvie Couturié: "They have to be liars, if they're unfaithful. Not only not to hurt the wife, but because appearances must be kept up. But every situation is different. I have a friend whose husband's mistresses are common knowledge. Her friends have felt that it was too bad that everyone, including his wife, knew about them. She is in her 60's now, and during a game of bridge recently, one of them said, 'Really, Marie-Claire, why do you put up with Jean-Xavier's philandering?' And she very sensibly said, 'Why not? He has always been a good husband to me, a good father to our children, a good provider, we go on vacation together...' She raised her index finger and looked at it. 'Why should I bother about about a little muscle like this that he shares with someone else?' We all collapsed in laughter -- and admired her courage and her philosophy."

Savoir-Flair Tip No. 127:
Anglophone women interested in meeting French men: dress up!

In a sense, all Western women are heirs to the sensuous props to *plaire* that French women invented in the necessity of their legal deprivation. All of us can make use of French creams and perfumes, scarves, costume jewelry, facials, épilateurs and, why not, French advice. French magazines, and not just women's magazines, write tirelessly about love -- never "sex." One of their favorite themes for their feminine public is how to meet the man of your life. They tell you to, first of all, think positively about yourself. Eat healthily, exercise regularly. Circulate on the weekends; you'll never meet anyone staying at home. The "Beaubourg" (the Pompidou museum) is said to be teeming with attractive, eligible, divorced Français. Look your best every time you go out to get a baguette: the supermarket might be your lucky spot. If so, drop a handkerchief. Or, more daringly, some earrings. One magazine even suggested -- if you just can't get his attention any other way -- dropping a box of condoms.

You're in luck, if you're looking for the man of your dreams, for you're now in a Latin country where the men and women are aware of each other and strangers may decide to meet. To put it in the opposite-negative the French love, they are never together in a public place or private home without noticing each other, observing: discreetly, but surely. But *attention*: getting to know strangers of the opposite sex in a public place in Paris comes under the heading of *séduction*, and is a game that the French have been playing all their life, with a whole litany of implicit but recognized rules. France is the country of nuances and subtlety -- words no one bothered to invent in English. Blind dates don't exist here. If you are so fortunate that one of your women friends has spotted a possibility for you, remind her that French men are skittish. Nothing scares them off faster than being "paired" with someone. Get her to arrange to have you both casually included in something spontaneous and unrigged-looking, such as helping another friend move. Let him call you first.

French men look at women and what they have on. Dress richly, but not gaudily. Men as much as women have made Paris the fashion capital of the West for 600 years. Look at pictures of the clothes of kings like François I, Louis XIV and Louis XV, as well as of their mistresses. French women wouldn't care about *paraître* but for French men. If possible, go shopping with a French friend who dresses wonderfully or get the fashion advisor at Printemps to help you. Show your shapes, but not vulgarly. If you choose jeans, wear a Dior belt, designer shoes and a freshly pressed shirt. Tuck in the shirt; whether you weigh 120 or 200 pounds, you must show your waist. Don't ever wear sweats except in gym or jogging. Easy on the make-up, subtle around the eyes, little lipstick, if any. Wear big fanciful earrings and lots of bracelets and rings, several on one finger, if you feel like it. Learn how to wear one strong personal accent, a dazzling brooch, or a scarf tied in a special way. Every French woman, from the working class up, knows how to do this.

Be charming. Don't come on too strong, don't put out all your signals at once, or they'll judge you a predator. No significant looks. On the other hand, don't be coy. Keep your voice quiet. Be admiring of France but not gushing. If you don't want doors opened for you, if you don't want to play the game of being *séduisante*, I guess this isn't the country for you. If you do, and do it charmingly, the outcome of the evening is up to you. If you go to his apartment, or invite him to yours, alone, then you have clearly indicated how it will end. French men, with those 1,000 years' experience of coquettes, are tuned into the subtle codes of courting.

John Y., an American who fell in love with a Parisian, tried to describe her charms. "She's not confrontational," he said. "She's doesn't ask a lot of uncomfortable questions or talk about herself and her feelings the whole time. She is exciting to look at, every day."

Last month during a talk for a mixed group of seniors at a Paris lycée, I asked them which French woman they admired most, expecting to hear Isabelle Adjani or Marie Curie. Silence. Then one hand went up. "My mother," said a young man. Then the hands of almost all the other young people in the room went up. "My mother," they all agreed.

Savoir-Flair Tip No. 128:
Anglophone men: French women are jewels to be properly admired

Anglophone men need to remind themselves that French women, whether employees or social acquaintances, like to be treated like women, politely. Graceful compliments on their appearance are in order, and all the other gallantries you may have forgotten about in or outside UK or US offices, such as getting up when they enter the room, offering to carry their cases, opening the car door, pulling out their chair at the table. As Yapp and Syrett point out in *The Xenophobe's Guide to the French*, French women "present themselves as elegant creatures who need men in the way that a perfect jewel needs the proper setting."

If you meet socially and you're under 35, kiss her on both cheeks when you meet, even for the first time. Don't talk politics, or business. For heaven's sake, don't ask her about her family. Remember, you're in the *registre séduction* and must stay there. Look at her. Tell her that her haircut is the latest thing, and ravishing. If you decide you'd like to get to know her better, take her out for dinner, preferably to one of the restaurants in the next chapters. Keep the conversation frothy, anecdotal.

Don't hesitate to pay the bill. Don't forget to leave another 10% or 20% in addition to the *service compris*. Then suggest taking her to a discothèque.

Don't kiss her when you say goodnight at her door. It is elegant and tender to kiss her hand. Don't rush her. Court her for at least two weeks. If she invites you up, realize that she's willing. But be graceful. Don't forget the preliminaries.

Americans and Britons don't have good reputations in this domain. Marie-Jeanne N., a wonderfully coquette bachelor girl, told me this: "Jimmy had been courting me for some time, and I'd been giving him all the signals. I wasn't sure he was picking up on them. Then one evening at dinner in a romantic restaurant, when I had decided that it was tonight or never, he looked at me significantly and said, 'I've reserved a hotel room for us for tonight.' Really! I was furious. After coffee, I told him I had an appointment, called a taxi, and that was that. Too bad, you know. I really liked him. I was thinking of marrying him!"

Once you're between the sheets, be tender. There is one question which will make her leap out of bed in horror: "How do you like it?"

Chapter Fourteen

Enjoying Cafés

Cafés are for Everyone

It's odd that the French appear to be in such good shape, because the major activity in Paris, aside from trying to run over pedestrians, is sitting around in cafés for days at a time looking French... As a professional journalist, I like the idea of a society where it is considered an acceptable occupation to basically sit around and drink. In fact, I liked almost everything about Paris....

Dave Barry, the *Washington Post Magazine*

Le café est donc ce lieu où l'artiste et l'écrivain, quittant leur solitude créatrice, viennent remuer des pensées et des paroles. Car il n'est pas question ici de rentabilité ou même d'utilité, mais seulement de plaisir et de bien-être, d'intelligence et de commerce de pensées.

(The café is the place where the artist or the writer, leaving their creative solitude, come to stir up thoughts and words... For the point is not profit or usefulness, but only pleasure and well-being, intelligence and discussion.)

Patrick Kéchichian, *Le Monde*

Savoir-Flair Tip No. 129:
French cafés are like clubs, you can find one just right for you

The French love to talk. Brilliant talk is highly admired. Mastery of their language is the mark of distinction they aspire to. Talleyrand said that anyone born after the French Revolution could never understand what had been one of France's greatest achievements: the art of conversation. Maybe. But to a foreigner, their conversation, vintage 2000, sounds pretty amazing. One of the places to enjoy it is in a café, which is also the best place for a traveler who doesn't have French friends to listen to how the French do it. Or just to watch the scene.

French cafés are a gift of the French mind, the part of their soul they miss abroad, the place they rush home to, rejoicing. French cafés are like clubs without the fuss -- and they're open to everyone for the price of a *noisette* (a *demi-tasse* with a nut-size drop of milk).

In a Paris café you can sit or stand and drink alcoholic or non-alcoholic drinks, eat something simple or not eat, and make yourself at home. You can talk to the bartender if you're feeling lonely, or enjoy silence. You can set up your office there, like Sartre, or write your novels there, like Hemingway, without being disturbed. After your first order, the waiters leave you alone. That is, if it's not a place mobbed by tourists.

Cafés come in all sizes, in all types, all over town. The latest craze for the young and cool is the Café Beaubourg, almost next to the Pompidou museum.The oldest is the Café Procope, near the Odéon, founded in 1683 and favored by, among others, the new quietly exciting matinée idol, Jacques Gamblin. Writers and artists have traditionally flocked to either two on the Boulevard Montparnasse in the 14th, the Dôme and the Coupole; or to others on the Boulevard Saint-Germain in the 6th. Paris literary lights like François Nourissier, one of France's most illustrious writers and editors, and other well-known *personnalités* like Bernard Arnault, the industrial tycoon, are likely to show up at the café-brasserie Lipp on the Boulevard Saint-Germain. This is where the board of the

Académie Goncourt decide on the year's winner of their prestigious literary prize. The writers of Gallimard like to get together down the street a few blocks at the Bar du Pont Royal, in the 7th.

Upstairs at the Flore

Across the Boulevard Saint-Germain from chez Lipp are two cafés where, as at chez Lipp, the talk levels over the years have given them the status of protected monuments, the Café de Flore and Les Deux Magots. The Deux Magots was where "everyone" literary went during the Third Republic. But then came notoriety when Sartre picked it for the birth of existentialism. Tourists began flocking there in hopes of catching some of his passionate awareness. "Everyone," including Sartre, decamped to the Flore. They're still there. Not outside on the terrace, not downstairs, where it's comfortable, but upstairs, where it's uncomfortable and dreary... safe from the tourists. Meetings important to the publishing world are held there de rigueur, even *le verre* after the funeral of one of them.

Near the Observatoire, a block or two from where Hemingway wrote *The Sun Also Rises*, is my choice for the perfect Paris café, le bal bullier (the name is lower case, for some reason). The size is just right: not squeezed and yet not vast, like le Dôme. The coffee is delicious, no chicory added. The croissants are fluffy and fresh. The atmosphere is warm and friendly. The prices are as low as anywhere in Paris. You can spend the morning on le bal bullier's high leather-covered stools at the bar reading the four daily French newspapers and one American -- the *International Herald Tribune* -- on bamboo racks. Both the high stools and the newspapers are unusual. Most cafés offer you only *Le Parisien*, which is usually being read by someone else.

Le bal bullier is just opposite one of Paris's truly legendary café-brasseries, la Closerie des Lilas, beloved favorite of Paris celebrities, politicians, movie stars and authors, that is, everyone from the President of the Republic to Gérard Depardieu and Françoise Giroud. These *personnalités* and literati often stop by for a special bal bullier demi-tasse and a vigorous debate -- or just a chat -- on their way somewhere.

Like many cafés these days, le bal bullier is also a brasserie, which means they serve not only liquids but also simple hot meals. At lunchtime it's packed. Note the ballet of the waiters balancing their trays ingeniously as they race to fill orders between the crowded tables. I asked one of the waiters if it was really true that with an order of a demi-tasse you can have your table as long as you want, even when the midday diners begin squeezing you out.

"It's true, you can stay as long as you want and there's nothing we can do," he said. "But you wouldn't find it very pleasant, with everyone eating around you. We offer lingerers another table apart from the diners. They always take it."

Theme cafés

Some cafés feature weekly evenings for discussions of special subjects. If your passion is science, there is the Bar des Sciences at Les Halles. If it's earthquakes and hurricanes, not books, the place for you is the café-géo on Tuesday evenings at Café Flower's, near the Pantheon at 5 rue Soufflot.

I said passion, because when cafés were catching on in the 18th century, they were about passion. Some of them collected literary enthusiasts, some artistic, some revolutionaries. Hot political discussions of the Age of Enlightenment swept through them and swept out the Monarchy in the hottest Revolution of them all. Different political groups met in different cafés. These are the ancestors of perhaps the most passionate theme-cafés today, the Café-Philos.

Café-Philos? *Philosophy* cafés? Right. This is the country where citizens   announce their profession as "philosopher" without people cracking up. Today's most famous ones -- Revel, Comte-Sponville, Ferry, Finkelkraut, Debray, Lévy, Glucksman -- are starred on television. Newspapers devote full pages to their thoughts. Their books are *read*. The Café-Philos were born out the head of Zeus, so to speak, in 1992. A couple of philosophers began meeting on Sunday mornings to discuss their theories at the Café des Phares near the Bastille. A reporter at the next table wrote about them as if they were holding a public forum. The next week, 15 people showed up to listen to them and ask questions. The week after, 30 came, and now, between 200 and 250 people troop over to the Café des Phares every Sunday at ll am. Ten other philosophy groups meet weekly at various cafés in Paris. Each group has a philosopher-moderator. An American professor of philosophy, Gale Prawda, holds one on Wednesday evenings at the Café de Flore. Attendance is free. The public suggests subjects and the philosopher chooses. Some of the topics: Can language exclude? Are beliefs necessary? Is there such a thing as sacrifice? Is it sometimes legitimate to lie?

Why the popularity? Pascal Hardy, president of the Association of Café-Philos, thinks people are drawn partly by conviviality and partly by their feeling of being out of joint. "The old ideologies have been discredited," he said. "People are distrustful of the reign of capitalism, they feel swept along and want to connect with other people's ideas. They like the spontaneity, the anonymity, the freedom from academia, the mix of people, classes and races. The important thing is that they're free, not a business for making money for anyone."

Or, as Patrick Kéchichian put it in *Le Monde* cited above, it's not about selling, but about pleasure. Something the French specialize in.

Savoir-Flair Tip No. 130:
Greeting is expected when you enter a café

Entering a café, it might be a waiter or the bartender who greets you. It might be the owner behind the cash register. Someone will say, "*Bonjour, monsieur*" (or madame). Even if no one does (it's a busy day), still say hello in general when you come in. It will be noticed.

Savoir-Flair Tip No. 131:
You may have to signal the waiter to take your order

If you're alone, a waiter may not come right away to ask for your order. He's giving you time -- for someone to meet you, for you to gather your thoughts. You may have to signal or even call, "*Monsieur, s'il vous*

plaît!" You show much less respect if you call "*Garçon!*" For heaven's sake don't snap your fingers at him.

Savoir-Flair Tip No. 132:
A napkin isn't part of the deal if you just order coffee

The rule is that you get a napkin only if you eat something, even if it's just a croissant.

Savoir-Flair Tip No. 133:
If the café is out of croissants, it's fine to go out and buy one

Croissants must be fresh to be good, and cafés don't want to have any left over, so, often, they run out. Sometimes, a waiter will go down the street and get one for you from the closest boulangerie. If not, you can suggest very politely that you'll go and get one yourself. Do it in sign language if your French isn't up to it.

Savoir-Flair Tip No. 134:
Standing up at the counter usually costs less

In Paris, sitting at a table in a café usually doubles the bill. Stand at the counter if you're short on cash. If you're alone, it might be more fun anyway. You can join in the bartender's conversation with the *habitués*. If you go back regularly, and become a regular yourself, you'll get to know them. In rural France, the price is usually the same, whether sitting or standing.

Savoir-Flair Tip No. 135:
Don't just help yourself to a hardboiled egg or a croissant. Ask for it

Savoir-Flair Tip No. 136:
You're expected to ask for the check when you're ready to leave

One little *demi-tasse* is the rent you pay for the luxury of having your table for hours. Usually, the system is that when the waiter brings you whatever you ordered, he puts a little cashier's *fiche* under the ashtray. Each time you order something else, he serves it with another little *fiche*. When you ask for the bill, he adds up the *fiches*. It would shock a Parisian to be asked to pay the bill before he'd asked for it -- unless the waiter was going off duty, which sometimes happens. When you want to pay, getting his attention and just scribbling in the air with your finger is very French.

But what is peace and timelessness for some is unnerving for others. Tourists in Paris expect to gulp their coffee or maybe a sandwich and a beer, pay the bill almost at the same time and get back on their sightseeing track.

Chelsea Gutman, formerly a young executive at Bain and Co., had quit her job to come to Paris. When she first went to a café, she waited for the bill. Waited and waited.

"I got really anxious," she said, when I bumped into her at Shakespeare and Co. "The bill just would not come. Finally I asked for it - - and it came right away. As I got used to the system here, I began to love it." She glanced over at the Cathedral across the Seine. "It's lovely, you can spend the morning just looking at Notre Dame without being bothered. Now, if someone brought me a bill I hadn't asked for, I'd feel insulted."

Savoir-Flair Tip No. 137:
Cafés are for women alone, too. Luckily for them -- and for men

Paris is not Athens or Tunis, where a woman alone in a bar-café is *mal vu*. If you're a pretty young woman, and even if you're not, you might be addressed by the gentleman at the next table. This is perfectly correct in France. Cafés are for conviviality. If you're not feeling convivial, or anyway not with him, decline gracefully, not haughtily. He's paying you a compliment. It's a *good* place for men and women to meet each other.

More Café Savoir-Flair Tips:

• Always say please (*s'il vous plaît*) when you order. The French do.
• Always leave a tip, whether it says the service is included (*service compris*) or not. Thirty centimes, half a franc or a franc for coffee. Five francs for a sandwich and a beer. Ten francs if you have more.

Ice in your glass
If you ask for it, they may have it, or they may not.
Change
Don't come in from the street asking for change for FF 100 for the parking meter and expect the café cashier to give it to you. Change is often scarce. Even if it isn't, it used to be practically non-existent and the cashier may be still in that mind-set.

For the same reason, don't expect to pay for your coffee with a bill of FF 200 or even F 100. This is guaranteed to get you a frown or, says Sarah Davis, "sometimes worse!"

Les toilettes
>   Don't come to a café just for that. Order a cup of coffee first, then look around for *les toilettes*. If you see some stairs, it's pretty safe that that's where they are.

Un demi
>   A half pint of beer from a vat (*pression*). They usually have four kinds. If you don't specify, they'll give you whatever.

Un ballon
>   An eighth of a liter of red wine in a glass with a stem. You'll probably be asked if you want a Côtes du Rhône, a Bordeaux or a Burgundy.

Un café
>   A demi-tasse, black. Very strong, say *un café serré*. Weak, *un café allongé*.

Un noisette
>   Short for *un café noisette*: a demi-tasse with a little milk, sometimes served in a small pitcher, sometimes in the coffee.

Un café crème
>   Coffee with milk (or cream) in a big cup. Costs three times as much as *un café*.

Un petit crème
>   Coffee with milk (or cream) in a cup twice as big as a demi tasse.Costs twice as much as *un café*. The *petit* is important if you don't want a great big cup.

Water
>   Bubbly is *gazeuse*. Normal water is *plate*.

Addresses

le bal bullier: 22 av de l'Observatoire, 75014 Paris, l 01 43 21 06 06

Café de Flore: 172 bd de Saint Germain, 75006 Paris, l 10 45 48 55 26

Café Les Deux Magots, 6 Place Saint-Germain des Prés, 75006 Paris, 01 45 48 55 25

Brasserie Lipp, 151 bd Saint-Germain, 75006 Paris, 01 45 48 53 91

Café Le Pont Royal, 8 rue du Bac, 75007 Paris, 01 42 61 08 44

Le Select Montparnasse, 99 bd Montparnasse, 75006 Paris, 01 45 48 38 24

Le Dôme, 108 bd Montparnasse, 75014 Paris, 01 43 35 25 81

La Coupole, 102 bd Montparnasse, 75014 Paris, 01 43 20 14 20

Les Phares, 7 place de la Bastille, 75004 Paris, 01 42 72 04 70

La Chope, 17 rue Daguerre, 75014 Paris, 01 43 22 76 59

Au Petit Fer à Cheval, 30 rue Vieille du Temple, 75004 Paris, 01 42 72 47 47

Bar du Pont Royal, 7 rue Montalembert, 75007 Paris, 01 45 44 38 27

Café Beaubourg, 43 rue Saint Merri, 75004 Paris, 01 48 87 63 96

Chapter Fifteen

Enjoying Unique French Delicacies

Mirabelles, Cèpes, Foie gras, Truffles, Oysters, The Great Chefs

After traveling 30,000 miles throughout France, talking with hundres of farmers, shepherds, cheesemakers, fishermen, chefs:

For most of the people I talked with, their involvement with food is not a job. It is a passion, an emotion and involvement that lie somewhere between deep love and religious zeal... These people aren't doing it for money....or prestige... but unrestrained ardor for what they do and centuries of tradition.

Patricia Wells, *International Herald Tribune*

I send you great compliments and thanks for the marvelous beef stew. Would that I could succeed as well as you with what I'm going to do tonight, that my style would be as brilliant, as clear, as solid as your jelly -- that my ideas would be as savory as your carrots and as nourishing and fresh as your meat. While waiting to finish my work, I congratulate you on yours.

Marcel Proust, in a letter to Céline

Savoir-Flair Tip No. 138:
Food puts French people in a mood of happiness

If there's one annoying thing for Americans, it's the so-called French Paradox, that the French eat suicidal food and stay healthy and live longer.

A new study by a University of Pennsylvania pyschology professor, Paul Rozin, has just come out concluding that it all comes down to attitude: "There is a sense among many Americans that food is as much a poison as it is a nutrient, and that eating is almost as dangerous as not eating."

Americans look at the plate before them and cringe, he says. Eating food worries them. They know they have to eat, their body needs fuel, but they hate it; it's going to make them fat. So the body reacts to this negative attitude by doing just that.

On the other hand, the study continues, the French exult over the food before them. During holidays they revel in it. Putting on pounds doesn't occur to them. The hours they sit eating it are pure joy. So, the study concludes, the French body reacts positively to the positive French attitude.

Well, I know lots of Americans who celebrate the joys of good food, and I know some French people, women in particular, who diet constantly to get that beanpole look.

But the study is right on that French people love food. That they care about it... *French* food. This means they care about their *terroir*, that word rich in layers of nuances about the earth and its fruits. French people can shrug off floods, tempests and nuclear war, but they tremble at the thought of losing their food's specificity.

Food as Myth

Farms and farm products, also ports and fish, have mythical importance in France. Villages and châteaux in all the regions are constantly having fairs celebrating local produce. The feast of rare vegetables at the Château of Saint-Jean-de Beauregard in the Essonne lasted a week. See Chapter 21 for the fête of local plants in the Dordogne. A young fairytale-looking prince from one of France's oldest and most distinguished families, Louis-Albert de Broglie, has composed a carefully chaotic living vegetable and fruit museum near Tours for people to find out more about their vegetive heritage. He greets visitors in overalls and rubber boots and shows them around his château as well as the garden.

Until 1960, 70% of French people lived in the country. Most Parisians today have strong roots of some kind in *la France profonde*. They troop by the hundreds of thousands to the Salon d'Agriculture, the gigantic farm fair in Paris -- 600,000 went to it in 2000 -- where varieties of animals and birds from all over France are tethered cozily next to the food they yield. Look hard for farm machinery. Almost every region and every season exhibits its agricultural wonders. Farmers from the Périgord, Provence, Brittany, and the Basque countries bring their prizewinning cows and pigs and famous regional produce along with their latest creations, new ways of mixing flowers and fruits for new tastes... a *pâté de campagne* mixed with hydromel, for instance, or an eel *à la vénitienne* with sweet vinegar and little vegetables, almond paste laced with muscat, jam made with the leaves and flowers of violets... but the fundamental creed of the *paysans français* remains that what is ancient can be good, and can be even better than eternal innovation.

When they're protesting something, farmers periodically haul their animals to Paris and camp them on a layer of straw on the Champs Elysées. Television and radio programs are packed on the one hand with serious discussions of food by historians, sociologists, professors, movie stars and writers, and, on the other hand, by food professionals -- chefs and gastronomic and viticulture experts. On his Saturday morning program, "Grands Gourmands," Jean-Luc Petitrenaud, one of these epicurean television hosts, invites chefs to recount their "grandmother's cooking tricks" while they're demonstrating a special technique of one of their recipes. "My only wish," he says, "is to lead the *téléspectateurs* to the happiness which I believe to be *la table.*"

The great chefs

The status of the great French chefs like Joël Robuchon and the three Alains, Ducasse, Senderens and Passard, recognized as such from the three stars handed out with imperial fanfare by the *Guide Michelin*, is godlike. Robuchon had been elected "chef of the century" by other chefs, but Alain Ducasse soared to new heights when his second restaurant also received three stars in 1997.This made him a phenomenon, in a class by himself, the god of the gods. No one had ever achieved a sixth star before. And then, in 2000, the new Michelin came out and crowned him with yet another, a *seventh* star for his new restaurant, Spoon. In addition, Ducasse is handsome. With his high rounded forehead and tortoise shell glasses, he looks the part of what, in fact, he is -- not only a great chef, but also a professor (he has taught his secrets to many disciples) and a suave and quietly elegant ambassador of France on his wide travels.

Not only who the top chefs are but where they are is of importance to the French. When the chefs move around, it's news. Big news. The departure of Philippe Legendre from the ultraprestigious Taillevent in June 1999 to take over the kitchens of the Hotel George V, newly renovated, was described as a *coup de tonnerre dans le ciel de la gastronomie parisienne* (a thunderbolt in the Parisian gastronomical sky). Same thing when Guy Legay left the Ritz in the fall of 1999, "unable to resist," the newspapers said, the invitation to take over the cuisine of the famous restaurant Lasserre. Who could possibly replace him in that most demanding of culinary responsibilities? Who indeed? (See Chapter 16.)

These gifted chefs are also prolific writers. In newspapers and magazines as well as in gorgeously illustrated books, they're constantly reminding us of the history and gastronomical possibilities of everything from apples to oysters. Alain Ducasse's new book, *Rencontres Savoureuses* (Plon, 1999) is a poetic answer to beef with hormones and genetically modified corn, a book "describing what is real and beautiful about all the extraordinary people" involved in the diversity, the savoir-faire and the traditions of making French wine and cheese, of fishing the fish, raising the animals, growing the plants and fruits that go into the excellence of French cuisine. The book is an ode to gastronomy, of which he has no desire to be the last representative. "Taste relies on memory," he says, worrying about the French palate of the future. "People eat faster and faster, so that there is no time to develop memories of the tastes and flavors in the mouth." The government is listening: many schools now offer children classes in recognizing tastes and smells.

Songs for the commonplace

While the top chefs dote on the exceptional delicacies (see below), they go into just as many rhapsodies for the commonplace, provided that it's grown properly. For instance, potatoes. To give you an idea, Joël Rebuchon says that of the 100 varieties grown in France, *la ratte*, a small oblong pinkish potato shaped like a bumpy crescent, is the only one that makes sublime mashed potatoes. Alain Passard also likes *la ratte* but recommends as well the "BF 15" of Brittany with its flavors of seaweed when raw and its "suave perfume" of egg yellow when cooked; *la charlotte*, for its taste of beet-molasses and the *roseval* for the "grace of its bitterness."

Not only chefs, but French celebrities are lyrical about their favorite commonplace. Jean-Marie Rouart, author, member of the Académie Française, leading literary critic, was photographed in *Le Figaro* about to devour some *bonnottes*, which, he maintains, is the "aristocrat of potatoes," and which, had they known about it, would have kept Baudelaire from opium and Verlaine from absinthe. Rouart, elegant cosmopolite, reminisced about his childhood without electricity or running water on the island of Noirmoutier, brought up by fishermen, where he used to find tiny *bonnottes* in the sand and wasn't allowed to leave a single one. Paco Rabanne, the dress designer, writes in *La Force des Celtes* that fennel is linked with the Earth and the moon and purifies the digestive tract. Bestselling author Paul-Loup Sulitzer, who writes about money, sprinkles *oseille* (sorrel), which is slang for money, throughout his books. He likes sorrel in everything, soups, salad, fish, you name it. "The word evokes opulence and sensuality," he says.

Savoir-Flair Tip No. 139:
Mirabelles in August are one of a French person's joys

August is the moment for mirabelles, the golden plums the size of cherries. It's a short moment, you have just a month to find them. They're most abundant in the Lorraine. The 1999 crop was particularly splendid; the farmers said this was because of the eclipse of the moon. Mirabelles are usually picked by hand or shaken by a vibrator at their deliciously sweet peak.

At the open markets in Paris, ecstatic mirabelle shoppers wait in long lines. "Have you seen the trees full of them?" the lady behind me asked. "They seem laden with nuggets of gold."

Savoir-Flair Tip No. 140:
Find a friend to tell you where the cèpes are in autumn

The Italians and the French are rivals in cèpe mania (porcini in Italian). Some Italian restaurants offer a whole menu of this delectable wild mushroom, done in various ways. Ande starts licking his lips at the very mention. "You can't imagine how delicious they made one enormous cèpe in Rome," he said. "It was as big as a pumpkin."

The forests of the Périgord, in southwest France, abound in places to find cèpes, but you have to know where, and at 70 to 90 francs a kilo, the owners keep very quiet about them.

We have a place in the Dordogne, in the midst of this Périgord cèpe country. At the high point of the season, Emmanuella, my daughter-in-law, came back from the local market with an empty cèpes basket, reporting, "Everyone is whispering where you can get cèpes -- but they only tell their closest cronies. And they're not for sale."

Claude Lalique, whose cows graze in our field, knows where they are. He showed up for dinner with his arms full. He must have brought us five kilos. We had a feast.

A few evenings later we were invited to dinner by another neighbor, Guy de Richemont. "My gardener came by one day last week with 25 kilos of cèpes!" he told me. "*Du jamais vu*. This was a great year for them -- it rained every night, and often during the day. In fact, I *never* saw such a year for cèpes."

Indeed, in 1999, the Tarn-et-Garonne hadn't seen such a cèpe season since 1935. Already in August, much earlier than usual, a special market had to be organized in Vaïssac, just for cèpes. Barricades were put up to keep the 500 waiting gourmands from stampeding the place until all the farmers had finished their pick for the day, arrived and set up their stands. At 5:00 pm on the dot, the market opened, many farmers doing business from their trucks. On August 19 alone, between 800 kilos and 1.2 tons of cèpes changed hands. And the season lasted through November.

Savoir-Flair Tip No. 141:
Beware, some raw wild mushrooms are toxic!

French forests are full of other delectable mushrooms: the girolle, pied de mouton, lantin de chêne, trompette de la mort and morille. None of them should be eaten raw. *Morilles* are a chef's delight, but toxic when raw.

Only cultivated mushrooms, like *champignons de Paris*, can be eaten raw. Some should never be eaten, unless you're determined to poison someone. When in doubt, show them to a pharmacist.

Savoir-Flair Tip No. 142:
The exception to Tip No. 141: Truffles! (if they're mushrooms)

Truffles are different.

First of all, you can't see them. Secondly, you can't be sure they're there. Thirdly, you need a pig, a trained dog or some alertly sniffing flies or bees to lead you to them. The problem is that pigs are lazy, tire soon of truffle searches and often gobble up the truffles before you can grab them; dogs take forever to train; and flies and bees are even less obedient and more unpredictable than pigs.

If you decide to skip all that and buy them at the market, you'll probably find that at between FF 5,000 and FF 10,000 a kilo you feel just fine without them. After all, what is a truffle, anyway? They're sometimes called the *champignon d'hiver* (winter mushroom) but is it a fungus? Is it a fruit of the earth or a sap from dripping leaves? Or is it to the roots of oak trees what mistletoe is to the foliage? No one knows. Even the French tax people haven't decided if it's a vegetable or a fruit. Whatever, even a few grams render an omelette *noble* . Furthermore, the ancients back in the time of Hippocrates and Marcus Aurelius found it, according to Maguelonne Toussaint-Samat, not only nourishing but "producing a general excitement conducive to sensual pleasures."

Should you find or buy a truffle, after you've brushed it, soaked it for an hour and washed it again with drinkable water, you can eat it raw. This is how Guy Monier, proprietor of the Maison de la Truffe in Paris, likes them: raw, with a bit of salt and a few drops of olive oil on toast. But he prefers them poached for about three minutes, which, he says, enhances their perfume.

Truffle season starts in November or December and lasts until February or March -- if there are any. Well, there are always some. But for a good year, Nature has to do all the right things: rain all summer, but not too much, just rain from storms. Too much summer rain makes them rot. After the rainy summer storms, you need a cold fall. A summer drought brings Truffledom disaster. Thus truffle growers are a particularly dour group. The things they know for sure about truffles are few: that they only grow in micro-regions of France, Italy and Spain in a certain kind of soil near a tree. An oak tree is the most likely. They plant acorns and hope for truffles in, say 10 or 20 years. But nothing is certain in Truffledom, and there may never be any.

When the truffle season opens, it's front page news. Television reporters plus all restaurateurs worthy of the name rush down to Carpentras in Provence, one of the capitals of Truffledom, to interview the trufflers and sniff around their animal or insect truffle guides. They watch the careful weighing of the truffles, sometimes called the Black Diamond of the Quercy, and go into all the intricacies of truffle lore --- the type of tuber, the size, the color and the price (up to FF 4,000 a kilo wholesale, that is, roughly, $300 a pound). Same thing in the other capital of Truffledom, Sainte-Alvère in the Dordogne, where it's called the Black Pearl of the Périgord.

Later they repair to the local café and discuss what to drink with them: a Pomerol, a Pauillac, a Saint-Emilion. Or, best of all, champagne -- a *très grand champagne*, that is, an outstanding brand *millésimé* (from a certain and excellent year).

Savoir-Flair Tip No. 143:
Buy fresh foie gras or, in cans, foie gras *entier*

As for foie gras! French people eat 9,700 tons of it a year, 89% of it duck rather than goose liver. They don't make excuses for the force-feeding of the birds, pointing out that if it were as cruel and painful as the activists proclaim, the birds wouldn't waddle to their feeders so happily at meal time. Furthermore, they consider the boiling of lobsters, the castrating of horses and bull-calves and the battery-raising of chickens and pigs 100 times more cruel. Above all, French foie gras experts remind the activists that, like camels filling up their humps with water before heading for the desert, geese started the practice themselves, gorging to the limit before they migrated, unsure where their next meal would be... 5000 years ago. Egyptians happened to catch and eat some of these migrating birds before they flew off, were thrilled with the taste of their inflated liver and so began the force feeding by humans.

Around 300 B.C. the ancient Greeks caught onto the practice, and then the Romans, who stuffed them with figs. The practice found its way to France during the Renaissance.

Fresh foie gras is in a delicacy and price class up there with truffles. But you can get delicious, much less expensive foie gras vaccuum-packed or in a terrine, a jar, or a can. Be sure it is marked *entier*, or whole.

However, it doesn't compare with fresh foie gras... which costs from 600 to 850 francs a kilo. Believe me, you get your money's worth.

Savoir-Flair Tip No. 144:
Don't mix up pâté de foie gras with foie gras

Pâté de foie gras contains very little goose or duck liver, but lots and lots of pork liver. As a wag friend of mine put it, "It's a ratio of 10 to one - - one duck liver to 10 pork livers." The price of pure foie gras, even in a can or vacuum-packed, is also at least 10 to one more than pâté. Let's not even mention the price ratio to fresh foie gras.

Last year I wanted to give a special pleasure to some visiting gourmet Aussie friends of mine who had been wonderfully kind to me in Melbourne. They loved and were experts on French cuisine. I went to Fauchon's and bought a hunk of fresh foie gras. The Aussie husband commented: "Polly, what delicious pâté!"

Is it possible Australians use the word pâté as if it means pure foie gras? I hope someone will tell me.

Savoir-Flair Tip No. 145:
Scrutinize the labels on the jars to be sure it's the right duck farm

Duck foie gras is preferred by many chefs -- and many other French people -- to goose liver, as it has a stronger, more perfumed taste. It is also less expensive. You want to be sure that it is not made "industrially" from battery ducks fed mechanically on inappropriate food. Avoid the jars or cans labeled simply "foie gras," as well as the ones marked "bloc de foie gras," which is various bits of liver stuck together. Be sure the date is recent, and that the date of consommation isn't past history.

These days, foie gras might be sold in France but made in Hungary, Bulgaria or Poland, or even Israel. It might be good, but it won't have the quality of French *artisanal* foie gras. Two labels guarantee top quality French foie gras made from ducks fed *only* on corn during at least 50 meals: the "Comité Renaissance", which groups together five family enterprises of the French Southwest, and the "Comtesse du Barry."

What to drink with it? My French friends in foie gras country, the Southwest, like a Sauterne, or, better still, a Monbazillac. Monbazillac vineyards are nearby, just outside of Bergerac. So is the medieval château where the wine is bottled.

Savoir-Flair Tip No. 146:
Ortolans are delicious but forbidden, sort of

Ortolans are pretty pink-breasted buntings about six inches long with a green head, a yellow moustache and a yellow bib. They also have a plump little tummy -- and the misfortune to taste like a delectable mixture of foie gras and truffles. As you can imagine, the French are crazy about them. They've been been hunting and eating them since the Romans showed them how. Ortolans are one of the greatest delicacies of haute cuisine.

About 150,000 ortolans are trapped every fall in southwest France. They're fattened on grain for a few weeks and then marinated in Armagnac before they're ready for the oven. Just seven minutes baking, and eaten whole, bones, innards and all. The most famous ortolan feast was one of former President Mitterrand's last meals before he died, eight days later. It was on New Year's Eve in a popular restaurant. According to custom, he draped a napkin over his head in order not to lose any of the aromas and flavors. He ate two ortolans whole. The bones crunched. The other diners tried not to hear. When he was finished, from all reports, he looked ecstatic.

Ortolans aren't exactly an endangered species, as there are about 10 million breeding pairs of them in Europe. But they're songbirds, therefore legally under the protection of the European Union, which bans the hunting of songbirds. Successive French governments have been dragging their feet for years. The European Court of Justice has threatened to fine France FF 700,000 a day if the French government doesn't comply. Stay tuned. But don't hunt them.

Savoir-Flair Tip No. 147:
You can find "ortolans of the sea" in every supermarket

Joël Robuchon maintains that sardines are the *ortolan maritime*, that is, if you get the sardines canned by Nicolas Appert and take care of them properly. With patience, an alchimie is created which "ennobles each -- the sardine and the can." Treat your sardine cans like a great wine: put them in your cellar and leave them there for seven years, turning them over every six months, so that the sardines "exhale the maximum of their flavors (*saveurs*)" and that the osmosis between the olive oil and the sardines *s'accomplisse* (is completed). Taste them as they are or with a good lump of butter as they do in Poitou, and enjoy your feast.

Savoir-Flair Tip No. 148:
If you don't know the vendor, buy oysters in their original basket

The French eat 100,000 tons of oysters a year. The oysters come from Calvados, the Côtes du Nord, Brittany, the Vendée, Charente-Maritime, the Morbihan or Bouzigues, and French people know the difference. They swear by their preference.

I had an oyster-instructive day in Paris standing next to the shellfish stand of Jean-François Bohoyo, an oyster grower, on the sidewalk outside a supermarket on the rue de Sèvres. Jean-François is well known and appreciated in the neighbourhood. On Fridays and Saturdays, the only two days he's there, his customers come looking for him. Along with snails, clams and sea urchins, 10 different kinds of *fines de claires* oysters were on display, their prices varying according to size and how long they had been in their oyster park.

A friend of mine cycled up, tasted a snail, ordered two dozen, and then four dozen *spéciales fines de claires*. She asked Jean-François if he would open the oysters for her just before dinner time? Wonderful, she'd send her son to get them. A little later, her 10-year-son came skating up on his rollerblades with a tray, and said he'd come back for the opened oysters at 8:00, when Jean-François was packing up

One of the customers engaged Jean-François in a long discussion about the different kinds of *fines de claires*, and then turned to me.

"French people love oysters," he said. "A Frenchman knows his oysters the way he knows his wine, and can tell them all apart by taste." Others joined in the discussion. They talked about the fine points of the oyster flesh (*la chair*) and the different degrees of deliciousness of the best part, the nucleus (*le noyau*). Some insisted on the *fines de claires* of Marennes-Oléron (Charente-Maritime) as being the very finest, chewy and rich. Others were passionate about the flat-topped *belons* from Cancale, near St. Malo in Brittany, where, washed over by the Bay of Mont Saint-Michel, they have a specially strong taste of salt and iodine. A woman from Quimper swore by the *belons* from Belon, near Pont Aven, also in Brittany. The *belons*, I learned, are the most expensive because they need much more water -- a square meter per oyster, so that they can take in 100 liters of water a day.

Jean-François didn't have any *belons* that day. He sold dozens and dozens of various kinds of *fines de claire*, as well as *praires* (a kind of clam), mussels and snails. Then he asked me how I liked sea urchins. I had to admit I'd never dared eat one. Whereupon he took a knife, carefully cut through all the spiky bristles and poured out the gooey pink-orange seafruit into my hand. "Now eat it," he smiled. I did. It was delicious.

Oysters have 200 times the amount of iodine found in eggs, milk or meat. They're also rich in trace elements and vitamins A,B,C and D. Not only that but... here is another delicacy with special boudoir properties. Casanova called the oyster "the shell of seduction." Again, the Ancients were onto it. The Greeks liked them with honey and voted with the shell. The Roman Emperor Nero was an expert on their provenance. Louis XIV made sure that they were available to French people, as well as to himself: he ordered that there be 2,000 *écaillers* (oyster vendors) in his capital. French aristocrats had them for breakfast. Mirabeau, to fortify himself for one of his discourses at the Revolutionary Constituent Assembly, ate 300 per meal. These days, no one wants to compete with Mirabeau, but Jean Piat, the actor and writer, at 75, credits oysters with keeping him healthy and slim. He used to eat six dozen at a meal; two dozen now is about right for him.

At the market, try to find a shell pro who can advise you. The main thing is to be sure the oysters are fresh. If you buy them in the box they were transported in, you can see which fishing port they came from, and above all, the date when they were taken out of the water. You should be looking at them not more than 24 hours later. And all of them should be closed.

If you eat them at home, don't drink the water in them right after you open them. They produce another water in about 15 minutes, much better. And *chew* them -- your stomach will be happier.

As for the wine with oysters, you can't go wrong with a small Riesling, a Sancerre, a white Graves, a Pouilly-fumé or a Sauvignon of the Touraine.

Savoir-Flair Tip No. 149:
Walnuts and purslane (a weed) will do wonders for your health

French research suggests that the enviable silhouette and longevity of the French might be due not to attitude, and perhaps not to foie gras and red wine, but to the abundance in southwest France of walnuts and of a particular weed used in salads called purslane. Walnuts and purslane are both rich in alphalinolenic acid, one of the fatty acids needed by a healthy body, and a major part of the diet of Cretans, who, with the Japanese on the island of Kohama, have the world's lowest rate of heart disease. These Japanese get their alphalinolenic acid from consuming huge quantities of soya bean oil.

Whatever. Foie gras, smoked salmon and caviar are the three aces of French feasts, with oysters a close fourth, all of them best washed down by -- of course -- champagne. French people wallow in these delectables, not noticeably accompanied by walnuts or purslane, at Christmas and New Year's and Easter.

On the eve of 2000, joined by a great deal of the rest of the world in holiday gorging and festive uncorking of the famous bottles amid a blazing Eiffel Tower, the good ship France limped into the third millenium, devastated by Christmas night hurricanes, but nevertheless afloat on a vast ocean of bubbly and foie gras, everyone getting thinner and healthier. Maybe eating walnuts and purslane on the sly?

Chapter Sixteen

Enjoying French Restaurants

Love those Waiters!
Dinner at The Tower of Happiness

"Nothing is more serious than pleasure."

Claude Terrail, proprietor of the Tour d'Argent

"Humor is the best ice-breaker with waiters. It's very effective, even if in broken French. If the attempt is made, it pays off. It is fundamental to be polite and engaging here. People notice it. The waiters in France are not at all snooty. They're used to American struggles to communicate and they recognize that the meal, which is so important to them, is, to us over there, something to run through. They're very happy when they see us trying to learn about food, and taking time to enjoy it and the conversation around it."

Nelson Lees, Vice President, Chiquita International

Savoir-Flair Tip No. 150:
If you go before 8:30, you'll be almost the only diners

Restaurants in Paris are poetry. They're there to enhance your life. They're part of the reason you came to Paris. But like poetry, they take some effort on your part, if you're going to savor the best they have to offer. Restaurants are not like a theatre, where it's the actors who do the work while you sit there watching, except that, as in the theatre, everything is staged, with its own choreography. Nothing is left to chance.

You need to know that restaurants in Paris aren't just places where food is cooked and served, but both the stuff of myth and legend and part of a Parisian's everyday life. Parisians visit their favorite restaurants, like their cafés, regularly. Even if a Parisian has never been to the 3-star glories of gastronomy, Alain Ducasse, Lucas Carton, Guy Savoy, Jamin or l'Arpège, he cares that they are there, beacons of exquisite creation and energy, taste and ambiance (another French word we can't do without); bench-markers for the lesser chefs. Save up to dine in at least one of these gastronomy temples.

Some Paris restaurants, not necessarily those that are wildly expensive or sparkling with Michelin stars, are icons. If one of the icons closes or changes owners, this is a scandal for the front pages. Politicians practically went into mourning when Paul Benmussa said he was selling his famous chez Edgard on the rue Marbeuf. Both the leaders of the right and the left, including former Presidents Mitterrand and Giscard d'Estaing, President Jacques Chirac and EU Commission President Jacques Delors were in the habit of having their tête-à-têtes in private rooms upstairs. When Fouquet's on the Champs Elysées threatened to shut down, the resulting furor found an angel to keep it open.

After the sale of the Balzar, a brasserie-restaurant on the rue des Ecoles, to Flo, a chain known for cutting costs, Les Amis du Balzar (Friends of the Balzar) got together and went on the warpath. They summoned the new owner to a meeting. Describing themselves as fighting for the soul of the Balzar, they gave him an ultimatum: no frozen foods, no change in the menu, no change in the waiters. Cervelas, that Austrian sausage, where was it? It must be put back on the menu.

Adam Gopnik, the erudite Paris correspondant for the *New Yorker*, devoted a whole article to it. This was his lead: "The Balzar... happens to be the best restaurant in the world. It is the best restaurant in the world not because it has the best food -- though the food is (or used to be) excellent -- and not because it is 'hot' or even particularly fashionable, but because of a hundred small things that make it a uniquely soulful and happy place." Columnist Mary Blume explained the aura of the Balzar in the *International Herald Tribune*: "The French are concerned with the Balzar not as a mere eatery, but as a precious cultural heritage. It is what is called a *lieu de mémoire*, like the Pantheon or the Lascaux caves."

Paris newspaper columnists visited the new Flo-owned Balzar and argued about its quality. Patrick Besson lunched there several times and maintained in *Le Figaro* that everything was exactly the same, including the pleasant wait for a table on the veranda with a glass of white wine. But Dominique Jamet in the weekly *Marianne* complained indignantly that the chef *"perdait le nord"* (had lost his way), making the waiters nervous.The

Christian Science Monitor's Gail Chaddock agreed. "The life has been sucked out of it," she said. "The great thing was that their special service was not available except on their terms. It used to be that if you charmed the waiter, he would cut off all the meat for you from the *pied de cochon*, but that for a tourist, he'd just plunk the pig's foot down on the plate."

French chefs, the kitchen personnel and the waiters are conscious of their mission in tending these precious temples, from the humblest to the noblest. They do it with grace and dedication. The ones you will be dealing with, the waiters, are not college students. They are professionals with many years of training. French people respect them, and show it.

For dinner, if you absolutely can't hold out until 8:30, go at 8:00. But NOT before. The personnel will be uncomfortable. You will be all alone. Probably the room won't begin really filling up until 9:00.

"Why can't the French be a little flexible?" an American traveler asked me. "If we show up at 6:00, why can't they serve us?"

Because the waiters and kitchen personnel are eating their dinner then -- at the dining room tables, in most restaurants. Because they're not dressed. Because the kitchen isn't ready.

"But we're hungry!" she moaned. "The hotel dining room doesn't open until 7:00 pm. "Where can we go?"

To a McDo or to a brasserie. They serve non-stop all day.

Savoir-Flair Tip No. 151:
In Europe, a gentleman enters a restaurant before his lady

Restaurants in Paris are interactive: you are interacting with the waiters. The action is coded. The codes kick in the moment you enter.

A European man enters first, the idea being to protect the lady from the unknown inside the restaurant, and also, to take care of arrangements with the head waiter. He greets him warmly, shakes hands with him if he has been there before. They exchange a few pleasantries about the dining crowds or lack of them, about the weather, asks (if he's a regular customer) if the food is as terrible as ever. The maître d' laughs. The European then waves his lady ahead, and they follow the maitre d' to their table.

In the 3-star restaurants, the person who seats you is the director of the restaurant. Then one of the head maîtres d' gives you the menu and asks if you'd like an *apéritif*. If not, after a suitable pause, he comes for your order. In less celestial establishments, the same maître d' seats you and takes your order. You can tell who's who by their dress (see below).

Savoir-Flair Tip No. 152:
Making good contact with the waiter is the promise of a good meal

Your waiter is someone you want to win over. He's more than ready to give you the evening of your life... provided you do your part. Americans from the USA are in a hurry. Bringing something of themselves to the experience of the sacrament, which is what dinner is to the French, isn't part of their mental software. There are times when all of us agree with Mark Meigs, a Berkeley Ph.D. now a professor of American history at the University of Paris 13, who has been living in Paris for years: "Yes, French restaurants are wonderful. Yes, the waiters are wonderful. But sometimes I wish we didn't have to work quite so hard at it."

Ordering is a ballet. The more expensive the restaurant, the more time the maître d' expects to give you to discuss the wonders of the various possibilities. He knows all about them and is only too happy if you show an interest. Quite likely, he can cope with English. The main thing is showing that you appreciate his professional position and his deep knowledge of food and food combinations. He knows more than you ever dreamt there is to know.

Savoir-Flair Tip No. 153:
Waiters won't humiliate you without a reason

It's true, but awfully rare, that you can happen on a waiter who is impatient with your lack of gastronomical expertise. Out comes the Worm Treatment. However, it is easy to avoid.

I learned this early in my Paris life after I nonchalantly ordered a first course of fish and a second course of fish, without thinking. It was a middle-budget restaurant. The waiter gave me a long look of disgust. "*Madame, vous mangez mal*" (Madame, you eat badly), he said. Just three words for informing me that I ate incoherently, didn't have the first idea of the fine art of blending tastes and how courses should be connected and savored, resulting in the true joy of the palate, which is what all the fuss is about.

Now I rely on the maître d's advice for ordering sublimely blended flavors. If I want something else, I know how to soothe his discomfort. Before I give the order, I excuse myself charmingly, I tell him I'm afraid that he will think that I eat badly (*vous mangez mal* still rings in my ears) but nevertheless... he then protests that he would never think such a thing, and takes the order graciously.

If you absolutely must have coffee with your meal, for instance, this is the technique. (Please try not to, while in France.)

Savoir-Flair Tip No. 154:
Don't act either superior or inferior to the maître d'

Teasing is what they like, that is, within limits, and respectfully.

Nelson Lees, the Vice President of Chiquita International quoted at the beginning of the chapter, is a tall and handsome American from Cincinnati, who spent two years in Paris as an ex-pat.

From travels for Chiquita all over South America and parts of Africa, he had already become alert to cultural codes. In France, he studied them carefully.

"I knew I was hanging myself if I ordered Coca Cola in this country of splendid vineyards," he said on a recent visit, "but I noticed French people talking to waiters and they always seemed to laugh and have a great time. So I made a joke out of my Coca Cola habit. After a while, when waiters I knew saw me, they joked about it too. And if I was lunching with French executives, they'd say, 'Here comes Nelson, bring out the coke!'"

Savoir-Flair Tip No. 155:
Waiters size you up at a glance, perhaps your clothes count

One Sunday Ande and I went hiking in the country, dressed like *ploucs* (hayseeds) in jeans and windbreakers. On the way home we stopped for supper at a restaurant in Versailles we'd heard about. Not an expensive or terribly elegant one, but proper, with a maître d' in tails and the waiters in smart black dinner jackets. (In 3-star restaurants, the dress codes are reversed.) He showed us to a table with a bored look. He was cold and unresponsive to Ande's attempts at jocularity.

When he came to take our order, Ande began talking food. That leg of lamb we passed by on the way to our table, Ande said, pointing. That looked exactly perfect. Could he have the *souris*? The *souris* is the small mouse-shaped muscle of the gigot at the joint. It is succulent. It is the most delicious part of the *gigot*. The maître d' saw that he was dealing with a customer who, whatever else, knew his gastronomy. His whole body language changed. He loosened up, entered with zest into Ande's sort of jollity, and brought him the *souris* with a flourish. Later he produced a real delicacy for us, a gooey white cheese I'd never heard of called Saint Marcellin.

Savoir-Flair Tip No. 156:
Choose your French words carefully if phoning ahead

Allison Y., an artist visiting France from Vermont, went with her husband and children to look at the graveyards of American World War I soldiers near the Marne. Later they drove to the medieval town of Provins. They decided to stay for dinner and consulted the local tourist office about a nice rural restaurant.

Allison is a vegetarian (*végétarienne*). She'd heard that French restaurants weren't very pleased with vegetarians, so she telephoned ahead to take the vegetarian temperature, hoping that her French was up to it.

She asked to speak to the *patron* (owner) or to the chef, and was told that she was speaking to the patron, who was also the chef.

Then she asked, "*Comment est votre cuisine?*"

Cuisine is a tricky word. Used in a certain sense, and the way Allison meant it, it usually means, simply, food. *Cuisiner* means to cook, *elle cuisine bien* means she is a good cook. But the first and main meaning for *cuisine* is kitchen. For it to mean food, the construction of the sentence has to make it obvious. An adjective helps: the hotel has "*une bonne cuisine*" means that the hotel is known for its excellent cooking, *haute cuisine* means high class cooking. *Faire la cuisine* means to do the cooking.

To the owner of this restaurant, the word *cuisine*, as Allison used it, could mean either "Is your cooking any good?" or "How is your kitchen?" which he could understand as, "Is your kitchen clean?"

Neither question would be likely to please him. Allison, of course, didn't know which he reacted to. What she did know is that he told her she had a nerve asking him such a question, and hung up. It upset her all the way back to Paris.

Rural Frenchmen are particulary touchy (*soupe au lait*). If they're chefs, attention!

What Allison did wrong;

• she didn't greet him politely by first telling him who she was (an American tourist), which probably would have made him patient and forgiving.

• she didn't start out by asking him to excuse her imperfect French

• she didn't prepare him psychologically that she had an unusual question

• she didn't inform him, before her question, that she was a vegetarian.

A Frenchman in the same situation would go there and look at the menu posted outside, or if he phoned, he would first say the Magic Words, followed by, "What is your *plat du jour* ?" (speciality of the day). And then would feel free to ask if vegetarians were welcome.

The Magic Words would have helped Allison too: "*Excusez-moi de vous déranger, monsieur....*"

Julie Winn has had a lot of experience with vegetarian visitors. This is her solution:

"Instead of saying you're a vegetarian, explain to the waiter that everything looks delicious, but you just don't like meat! Then ask if the chef could possibly make you up a plate of delicious vegetables? They ALWAYS come through beautifully."

I can hear you groaning that this seems endless trouble for a simple question. Yes. Everything in France takes longer. That's just the point, time to ripen, whether, fruit, friendships or love... carpe diem.

Savoir-Flair Tip No. 157:
How good manners pay off

Julianne Guthrie is a consultant-analyst at Notre Dame University in Indiana, not far from where she grew up. She first came to France with her parents in 1984, then made several more trips with her widowed mother.

"We always end up having at least one evening in Paris at Au Petit Riche," she said. "Mother and I are quite fond of martinis -- American martinis -- but rarely order them. I don't have the strength of will to discuss a good martini in either English or my broken French and anyway, I'm kind of a 'when in Rome' type.

"However, my father used to say that Au Petit Riche could make a good American martini. So on our last trip, we took a chance and ordered martinis. The waiter brought us a glass of nothing but sweet vermouth -- called Martini, of course. Normally I would have simply winced and downed it to be polite, but my mother was at the end of her tether. So I first asked the waiter if he had any olives. He said No. I said fine, and then explained our disappointed hopes. He left us apologetically.

"We didn't see him for a long time (longer than usual for a French waiter). When he came back he brought us two real American martinis... with olives. He had gone down the street to get them. The martinis were a bit lopsided on the vermouth side but by that time I would've drunk mud to show him how much I appreciated the olives!"

Savoir-Flair Tip No. 158:
Order *à la française*, i.e. in the order expected by the waiter

Order the *entrée* (appetizer) and the main dish first. When finished with the main dish, order dessert. *Then* order coffee.

Mia Cunningham, of Washington, the *croissant aux amandes* addict whom we met in Chapter 5, now has an expert grasp of what to expect in France, and what to do about the unexpected. She sent me this e-mail:

> In France, coffee is served after the dessert, not before or with. Period. No exceptions. It was because my husband and I already knew the rules of French dining that we so enjoyed this incident in a small but well-known Left Bank Paris bistro. Our waiter was removing our dinner plates when, over the hubbub of the happy diners around us, I asked him for two orders of *profiteroles* (pâte à choux with vanilla ice cream and chocolate sauce) and, for Jim, my husband, one coffee.
>
> The coffee came right away - with no sign of the *profiteroles*. Feeling much at fault and determined to let the waiter know I understood and respected the rules of French dining, I attracted his attention and told him sweetly and apologetically, in French, that I feared he had not heard my dessert order.
>
> He pulled a face of mock horror and spinning on his heel, expertly whisked Jim's coffee off the table murmuring, *"Plus tard"* (later) and made a dash for the kitchen.

Savoir-Flair Tip No. 159:
If you're a pretty young woman, there may be extras

I met three pretty young Australian women on the RER train from Versailles : Emma O'Connor, 23, an opera singer, her sister Sara, 25, and Carolyn O' Reilly, 25, all from Sydney. They looked happy. They were. They talked about their picnic in the château garden and about how much they loved Paris, even in their little hotel room in the Marais without a bathroom. They had to pay the concierge an extra 25 francs for a shower.

"Paris is beautiful," said Sara. "London is loud, noisy, fast, rude, rushing. Here, people are more relaxed, people talk to us. I love the ambiance."

Their last night they went to a mid-level restaurant. They were given three complementary *kirs*. Then the waiter brought out three pink roses, one for each of them. He said that Sara's was from his wife, Emma's from his girlfriend and Carolyn's from his daughter.

Savoir-Flair Tip No. 160:
Ordering soft drinks has to be done with panache

Unless you're a regular customer and confident of your game plan like Nelson Lees above, order wine or water. Mineral water costs about as much as a *vin ordinaire*. It's perfectly acceptable to order water from the tap, and legally required to be served if you order something to eat. You can ask for a glass (*un verre d'eau*) or a pitcher (*une carafe d'eau*) whether or not you're also having wine.

Chris Cripps, development director at ESSEC business school in Grenoble, still shudders at the horror of his French friends -- and the waiter -- when an American with them ordered Pepsi Cola with foie gras.

Savoir-Flair Tip No. 161:
If you know how, everything is possible in France

Kevin Stevenson, a tall Texan, came to see me in with what seemed like a tall Texan tale about his 25th birthday in Paris on a gorgeous warm sunny day, the 20th of June. He had just graduated from Harvard Law School. He had planned for a long time to celebrate his quarter-century on Earth in the most exciting restaurant he could think of, the Tour d'Argent, with the most beautiful view of the world's most beautiful city, the city of love, with his own beautiful love, Diana. He had been saving up for it for a year.

But Kevin wanted to do something unthinkable: he wanted to bring his own bottle of Château Margaux *grand cru* 1987 to the restaurant with the most famous cellar in Paris -- 400,000 top quality bottles.

Kevin knew he had to have a strategy. He did. It worked. Here it is:

I. Planning
Step one: Reserving ahead. And making sure he had a beautiful woman on his arm.

He signed up Diana and reserved a table for two by phone from Cambridge two months before. He knew that getting a reservation at the Tour had been a serious matter right from the beginning in 1582. In those days, when it was an auberge at the gates of Paris, a cavalier who had forgotten to make one would challenge one of the seated diners to a duel, kill him, and take his place.

Meanwhile, Kevin boned up on his French.

Step two: Reconfirming the reservation that morning and gathering useful information.

He inquired about the current menu.

Step three: Convincing Diana.

"They'll be furious. They'll be insulted. They'll ask us to leave," she said. "The evening will be a fiasco. Plus, for the rest of their lives they'll talk about those American cowboys who tried to bring *their own* bottle of wine!"

"This is France, not Germany," Kevin smiled.

II. Preliminaries to the action

Step four: Being punctual and nicely dressed.

Tour d'Argent means Tower of Silver: it's six floors up overlooking the Seine and Notre Dame Cathedral. Kevin gave his name to the director of the restaurant in the reception salon at the street entrance. Going up in the elevator, he carried the Château Margaux in its Hédiard bag like the up-front kind of guy he was. Diana made faces at him, rolling her eyes.

Step five: Proper entrance.

Kevin preceded Diana out of the elevator into the restaurant, making sure that this European *politesse* was noticed by the maître d'hôtel waiting to greet him in the vestibule. He took in Madame de Pompadour's sedan chair near the elevator, then glimpsed the staggering view of Paris and the

Cathedral through the restaurant's curving wall of windows. The blue sky was just beginning to blur into shades of soft pink and orange reflected in the Seine below. The restaurant itself, on two levels with one level two steps down, was like an 18th-century drawing room bathed in a golden light: gilded bronze wall sconces against Regency wooden paneling, ornate bronze clocks, oil paintings, Aubusson tapestries.

Step six: Savvily greeting the maître d'hôtel.

Kevin spoke in French and commented that the view was as splendid as he remembered it from his last visit (although this was his first). He admired the bright gilding on Madame de Pompadour's sedan chair.

Pleased response from the maître d'. "Ah, monsieur has been here before?" he said. "If you will come this way..."

Step seven: Showing knowledge of the restaurant's menu and specialities.

When the maître d' returned for their order, Kevin ordered the de rigueur duck for Diana. For himself, he said he had heard so much about the Tour's *pigeon farci en cocotte, purée truffée*, would the maître d' recommend that? Starting with an *entrée* of *feuilleté d'asperges et homard* for them both?

Home run with the maître d'.

III. Action

Step eight: Being conversational, but not chummy, with the wine steward (the sommelier).

Kevin chatted with the *sommelier* about the Tour. It had been here since long before the Revolution, n'est-ce pas? Wasn't that when restaurants first appeared in Paris... when the chefs of the great guillotined nobles found themselves out of a job... and went into business for themselves?

Delighted response from the *sommelier*. It was a long time since an American tourist had talked to him about something other than wine. Or talked to him, period. Which revolution, monsieur? he said, adding, "We have had so many. Unlike your country, which has made do with one." Then, smoothly bringing the conversation back on track: "Indeed in the realm of efficiency we have much to learn from you. But perhaps not about wine, though your California wine is sometimes very good. About the wine tonight, monsieur? With your pigeon and madame's duck, might I suggest...."

Step nine: Moving in for the kill. Kicking in PPO (Persistent Personal Operating).

Kevin interrupted him. "Exactly, the wine... It's a big day for me -- it's my birthday...."

"*Ah, toutes mes félicitations, monsieur.* I shall tell the chef. You must have a cake with pretty candles, to honor madame's beauty," he said, with a long look at Diana. "But the wine, monsieur?"

Kevin reached under the table for the bottle of Château Margaux.

The sommelier smiled thinly. "Surely monsieur doesn't expect..."

"When I was here the last time I promised myself that I would celebrate my birthday some day at the Tour d'Argent. And here I am! And... this bottle is a birthday present from my parents."

He paused as the waiter looked more and more uncomfortable. "Napoleon said that *impossible* is not French. I mean, who will ever forget the French soccer victory over the whole world... le Mondial? Wasn't that supposed to be impossible?"

"I must consult Monsieur le directeur."

Step ten: Continued PPO.

Presently a dignified gentleman in a dinner jacket approached their table. He greeted Kevin and presented his *hommages* to Diana. "Permit me to extend my congratulations to you on your birthday, Monsieur," he said. "I am sure you understand that this request is unusual for a French restaurant... particularly one which has the most famous cellar in Paris."

Kevin cranked up his story another couple of notches. His father was very sick, and his great hope was that the Tour d'Argent would allow Kevin to drink it there on his birthday...

"Ah, monsieur, you are very persuasive, very moving," said the director. "I will have to see with Monsieur Terrail."

Claude Terrail, proprietor of the Tour d'Argent since 1952, is one of the great restaurateurs of France. He is also a celebrity, a polo player and was known in his youth as one of the playboy pals of Aly Khan. Kevin recognized him from his photos as he now approached their table with the director.

Greeting them in perfect English he said, "We are very *sensible* to the honor that you have chosen the Tour d'Argent for your celebration." He paused. "However..."

Step eleven: The kill.

Kevin, looking contrite, turned to Diana and put his arm around her. He smiled up at Terrail. "You see, we just got engaged to be married."

Claude Terrail lifted his hands to the ceiling in Gallic helplessness. "Ah, monsieur, if this is about love, what can I do?"

Interview with Claude Terrail

I went to see Claude Terrail to check out Kevin's story. In his study on the 5th floor of the Tour, I found a young and agile 82-year-old, tall and slim, as excited today by the glory of French gastronomy as when he took over "la Tour" over 40 years ago.

Did he remember Kevin and his historic concession?

"This has happened from time to time over the years," he said, "that someone has a special bottle of wine and wants to drink it here for a special occasion. I have to charge them a symbolic price -- 300 francs -- or it would be too much of a loss for the personnel. I call it the *droit de bouchon.*

"It is very moving for me that the Tour is considered a *maison du bonheur* (a house of happiness) for many people. It is the consecration of a dream for them, an exceptional moment to come here for their birthday or some other special occasion, often on their honeymoon. Since the beginning of the year we have had 20 celebrations of proposals of marriage. And the birthdays... about 35 a week. I always give a present... of jam, or chocolate or biscuits. Often people come here from generation to generation. They arrive saying their parents were there 10 years ago, or their grandparents...."

You get the feeling talking to Terrail that you're in the presence of an ageless high priest who is proudly and courageously holding the flame. He is vehement in criticizing those who say that the days of great restaurants de luxe are finished.

"Gastronomy is one of the Beaux Arts," he said. "It is true that it is more difficult today, as the produce we look for is more difficult to find. For instance, the big white peaches of Valence, in the Drôme, that went into one of the Tour's great classics, Pêches Flambées de la Vallée de l'Eyrieux, have disappeared. But great cuisine has many rich days ahead."

Terrail speaks of France with reverence -- "this exceptional country that I call France" -- and famous chefs with devotion and respect. He has known them all. The Tour as it is now was started by his grandfather as a successor to the Café de Paris, the dining favorite of the great of the nineteenth century. The most famous event there was the "Feast of the Three Emperors," when Napoleon III entertained Kaiser William I of Prussia and Tsar Alexander II of Russia. Terrail was a pilot during World War II and served in the celebrated Deuxième Blindée division of the French army, General Leclerc's division which landed at Anzio. Leclerc?

"I adored him. We all did," he said.

After the war, Terrail often paid to have Notre Dame lit up in the evening. Now City Hall does it from time to time. Whether the cathedral is lit or not, la Tour is the place to see Paris at night.

Savoir-Flair Tip No. 162:
What the great food temples serve, and how

At the end of a meal in a famous restaurant, my English host, a gourmet, turned to me and said solemnly, "This was very good. But, Polly, tell me, was it celestial?"

I had to say honestly that no, it was not celestial. However, Paris is one city in the world where you may actually find a Paradise of cuisine. That is, glorious food presented on the plate as a work of art, served with perfection in a setting of charm. When you find it, it seems like a pretty good investment. I mean, after all, how many times do you get to visit Paradise in a lifetime?

With this as my criterion, and with the good luck to be invited again, I recently (1999) investigated several candidates for Paradise.

At Lasserre, the service was charming and impeccable and the setting was elegant, but the food, though very good and decoratively presented, was also short of celestial.

And there was one big problem. Lasserre's particularity is a roof that opens and closes dramatically during dinner, just over some of the diners' heads. It does this automatically every 20 minutes or so. It's lovely to see the stars as you dine, provided there are stars.

My hostess, Kathryn Davis, a philanthropist of 91, plays tennis and took the train across Siberia last summer; that is, she is a feisty senior-plus if there ever was one. We were directly under the roof. Kathryn was probably the least disturbed of all of us when, as we were happily tucking into dessert, the roof opened and we were drenched in a sudden shower of rain.

Celestial but not quite Paradise

My cousin Basil Cox, an ex-radio producer now running a Pittsburgh restaurant, took his wife, Jayne, to Lucas Carton to celebrate their 20th wedding anniversary. Basil is one of my favorite cousins. I was away and missed what proved to be a truly celestial feast, signed by the celebrated 3-star chef, Alain Senderens. Was it Paradise?

Here is the report of a professional, in Basil's own words:

The food was truly sublime. Coquilles St. Jacques (scallops) with the texture of a cloud; laid in a lovely light something sauce with no resemblance to the heavy white sauce one ordinarily encounters.

Then Cèpes (wild mushrooms) Trois Fois, meaning prepared three different ways. First raw in a marinade; secondly, very lightly cooked; thirdly, more complex. Each were little chamber music pieces, very subtle yet intense.

Next, Canard Apicius allegedly derived from some ancient Roman recipe by a man of the same name. This is their most famous dish -- a whole duck from which the breast meat is carved first, then it goes back in the oven to cook the legs a little more. They are served with greens as sort of a salad course. The skin is thickly coated with a highly aromatic and very honeyed concoction that must have at least 20 different ingredients, mostly unfamiliar.

Whereas the first course was the essence of delicacy and nuance, the duck was very bold. So bold the recommended wine was apparently very much like a Port (we didn't go for it). Exploded in the mouth with a bang, instead of a puff. Amazing.

Last, we did cheese. Flawless.

What I remember most about the food was how absolutely perfectly prepared it was. Somehow, another dimension of taste gets teased out of the ingredients. Each mouthful is memorable.

At Lucas Carton they make a deal out of suggesting a specific wine with each dish, by the glass or the bottle. We took all of their suggestions except the duck wine. The interplay between wine and food was wonderful.

They have two prix-fixe menus, neither of which we took. Ordering à la carte, no dessert, one bottle of wine and several glasses, the bill was a pleasant surprise - just about exactly $500. Seems like a lot, but once every 20 years I can handle it!

The service surprisingly did not seem to me to be flawless. Not bad but just not perfect, which it really should be -- just like the food. The *sommelier* either didn't know as much as he should have about the wine or was unwilling to share his knowledge with me. Some of the servers lacked polish. My plate was removed before Jayne was finished. The gentleman who greeted us at the door was never seen again. Things like that. Language was not an issue.

Total Paradise at the Ritz

Some time after Basil's celestial but not-quite-Paradise feast, I was invited to take part in a feast myself that was, truly, Paradise. No Hollywood producer aiming at a royal dinner of utmost voluptuous refined elegance in all the details could have attained, much less surpassed, that evening at the Ritz. Already just arriving at the Place Vendôme in the evening, all the lanterns lit, the gilt glowing on the black iron gates, prepares you for the extraordinary.

The Ritz has changed owners several times in my 31 years of living in Paris, and l'Espadon, its restaurant, has changed areas in it, but the grand sweep of the entrance hall setting the tone of discreet, sumptuous luxury is exactly the same, giving you the feeling of being king for a day yourself. L'Espadon is a grand *salon* of crystal chandeliers and 25-foot-high mirrors with three tall French windows draped in delicate folds of beige silk trimmed in light blue, looking out on a courtyard subtly furnished with greenery and potted, blooming plants. Each table had a little vase in the center with a red rose and an orchid of pale yellow flecked with red. The tables were comfortably set apart from each other so that while the room was full, noise was not noticeable.

The food was one amazing smooth delectable taste after another. Talk about nuances. The flavors came to you slowly, like the notes of an aria. Even the French of the menu was poetry :

Fine crème champenoise aux aiguillettes de foie gras sautées et feuilles de cresson (thin slices of foie gras in a fine watercress sauce)

Bouchon de saumon mi-fumé au tartare de Saint Jacques et aux huîtres, beignets d'olives aux épices (a "cork" made of a thin slice of smoked salmon coiled around a raw scallop that had been marinated in olive oil, dill and basil)

Filet de Saint Pierre en écrin de champignons, corne d'abondance aux petits légumes du potager à la coriandre (a filet of John Dory roasted with a film of mushrooms and a cornucopia with little garden vegetables with coriander)

Médaillon de veau et raviole de homard au vin jaune, gratin d'épinards et topinambour au macis (medaillon of veal and lobster ravioli, spinach with cheese topping, Jerusalem artichokes)

Le plateau de fromages affinés. Triangle marbré au chocolat blanc et croustillant praliné, crème glacée au jus de griotte (triangle of chocolate and almond with ice cream and Morello cherries sauce)

This nectar of the gods was served by a team of waiters with a grace and efficiency that was its ultimate blessing, and as essential to the effect as the beauty of the arrangement on the plate. It was an exquisite ballet of sustained elegance and rhythm. Every wish of the diners was sensed without being expressed. The waiters were solicitous, attentive, warmly, quietly charming without being in any way obsequious or obtrusive.

Remembering my cousin Basil's disappointment with the service at Lucas Carton, I decided to go and talk to the man responsible for it at l'Espadon.

This turned out to be a lively, witty Frenchman full of charm called Jean-Marie Marcadier. His title, which he has held since 1996, is Director of Food and Beverages for the whole hotel. Which means he has one of the most arduous and exacting, and according to *Le Figaro*, most difficult food jobs in France: the supervision of the restaurant, l'Espadon (two Michelin stars), le Club, the bar Vendôme, the banquets, the Ritz cooking school, the 24-hour room service. In addition to breakfasts (187 rooms), the Ritz serves an average of 550 meals every day.

A Bordelais, Jean-Marie Marcadier started his career in Bordeaux at age 14 as a busboy.

"Here, in France, to be a waiter -- *a maître d'hôtel* -- is a respected profession," he said as we sat one afternoon over a glass of Perrier at a table in l'Espadon. "You have to spend two years being a busboy. It takes years and years and much experience before you can be what we call a premier maitre d'hôtel. There are many levels before you get there. In France there is insistence on all the details of perfect service. When I started out, we waiters had to show our fingernails to the director of the restaurant, to be quite sure they were clean. My mother washed my white jacket every day and put so much starch in it that it was hard to get my arms in the sleeves."

Marcadier laughed and pushed the air with his hand as if trying to put it in a sleeve. "Some days I just couldn't!"

He climbed up the intricate levels of waiter proficiency, first in the south of France and then around the world, in Australia and New York, learning also to be a *sommelier* as he went along.

"Our *sommeliers* at the Ritz can tell the vintage of a Burgundy or a Bordeaux by the color," he said. "Being a *sommelier* is like being a doctor -- you have to read up on all the wines all over France, keep abreast of developments. But if you don't have a sense of taste and smell, and a sensitive palate, forget it."

At l'Espadon there are 30 waiters, including busboys, for a full capacity of 55 diners. In the kitchen 60 chefs, sub-chefs and sub-sub-chefs are preparing the food for these 55 diners, and for whichever hotel guest would like dinner in their room. A table of eight will have three or four waiters serving in one capacity or another, according to a strict hierarchy, which is military-rigid, and clearly labeled by the language of dress.

He made this chart of the various ranks for me:

1.The Director of the Restaurant.
Dress: in the daytime, gray and black striped trousers,
black jacket, gray vest and gray tie.
In the evening, a dinner jacket with a black bow tie.
Function: overall supervisor
Shows the customers to their seats
2. Maîtres d'hôtel
Dress: tails, black bow tie
a) Premier maître d'hôtel
Function: Assistant to the director, supervises
takes the orders, explains the dishes to the customers
carves the meat, *flambés* a dessert
b) Deuxième maître d'hôtel
Function: similar to premier maître d'hôtel, slightly less prestigious
c) Troisième maître d'hôtel
Function: captain of the waiters
takes orders, explains, carves
3. Chef de rang
Dress: tails, white bow tie
Function: serves the dishes, takes them away, carves
4. Demi (1/2) Chef de rang
Dress: tails, white bow tie
Function: same as Chef de rang, but fewer tables
5. Commis de rang
Dress: black spencer, black bow tie
Function: brings the food from the kitchen,
takes dirty dishes back to the kitchen

It takes at least two years experience for a *commis de rang* to reach the lowest level of maître d'hôtel, or *demi-chef de rang*. The sommeliers also have ranks: first sommelier, second sommelier, commis sommelier, apprentice sommelier. At the Ritz, they wear wine-red jackets and black aprons.

"There is more respect for this profession in France than anywhere else in the world," said Marcadier. "It makes the aspirants ambitious to improve, to know everything about food and about their profession. Any maître d'hôtel in France knows ten times more than a maître d'hôtel in the United States. He can tell you when the morels come out -- those special French mushrooms we call *morilles* -- when and where the truffles are best and if the Vacherin is good that month. He knows most of the wines of France and which food they best accompany, so he can tell you which wine would go best with the food you order.

"Before the Revolution, waiters were servants and obliged to show humbleness and discretion. We've tried to keep these qualities, and to bring pleasure to the people we serve... with a smile and an attitude of 'what can I do for you?' I've also tried to import some of the good things about the American system, though not the obtrusive attitude of letting it all hang out and 'Hi, my name is Joe, I'm your waiter tonight' -- our customers don't come here to make friends with the maîtres d'. We think they prefer a respectful attitude.

"Another important thing is for a maître d'hôtel to be a bit of a psychologist, and from the customer's *mine*, his general appearance -- his dress, his expression, his behavior -- to guess at what he wants."

Marcadier laughed. "Of course, here at the Ritz, we want perfection. We investigate meticulously any complaint. We have standards we want to keep up at all costs, but we don't believe in being totally rigid. We can also make exceptions, for instance, if a customer absolutely wants to bring his dog, or if he is passionately attached to a special bottle of wine he has brought with him. In that case, there is a corking fee of 200 francs. "

L'Espadon, unlike most restaurants, does insist on a minimum of correct dress. If a monsieur appears without a tie, the Ritz has one to loan him. If he doesn't have a jacket, the Ritz offers him a choice of a single or double-breasted dark blue blazer by Hugo Boss -- in his size. It arrives fresh from the cleaners in a handsome dress bag, as does a pure wool shawl in peach or blue if a lady is shivering.

"We do want to do the impossible," Marcadier said. "You want to have dinner with friends at 2 am in your room? You can have it. You can have a party at the Ritz Club downstairs at 3 am if you like. Once, a guest ordered a special kind of vodka that you could only get in London. We had it flown in from London in two hours. A little expensive, of course -- but he had his vodka."

Marcadier gets really poetic when he starts describing the attention given to preparing the vegetables, the meat (a quarter of an ox), poultry, all chosen fresh at Rungis, near Orly, every morning at 6:00 am. Between 7:00 and 7:30 am the fish arrives fresh from fish farms and the Atlantic, including the shellfish and oysters. *Belon* oysters are the best, he says. Everything is inspected and sniffed by the director of the restaurant.

As we talked, it was now 7:00 pm and all the waiters, the sommeliers and the top chef of the kitchen formed a circle on the other side of the dining room. "They're having their daily pre-dinner conference. The chef explains the specialties of the evening, and the director tells them which VIP's are expected and where they will sit. Would you like to see the kitchens?"

Chapter Seventeen

Enjoying Business (and Pleasure) Meals

Inviting French Business Contacts:
Where, When and How?

"While I ate a succulent stew, I noticed four gentlemen who not once touched their meat to their fingers. They carried forks to their mouth and bowed deeply over their plates. Having no experience, I didn't dare do so, and merely ate with my knife."

A chronicler, about 1600, Paris

Savoir-Flair Tip No. 163:
Reserve -- perhaps a month -- ahead of time

Anne-Elisabeth Moutet, a French journalist and editor, covered the French political, literary and business scene for 10 years as head of the Paris bureau for *The European*. We put our heads together and came up with some restaurant suggestions for meals with your business associates as well as for the pleasure of being with family or friends. As I've noticed a few foreign business executives handling their cutlery not so differently from the chronicler above, I've taken the liberty to add a few contemporary pointers.

Always reserve ahead of time. It's a good idea to have a look at the restaurant the day before to be sure you reserve a good spot. If he smokes, reserve in the smoking section. If he doesn't, see where the non-smoking section is. It's often next to *les toilettes*, and if so, you're better off in the smoking section. Most smokers are polite, and will try not to bother you.

If you find out you can't go after having reserved, call and cancel. The whole restaurant system depends on this basic politeness.

Where you invite a business associate depends on what your business is. Many of your kudos will come from taking him to the right place, where he'll feel well, eat well and even perhaps run into other business associates. Places for having a fine time with family and friends are not only all of these places, but also the much simpler bistrots listed at the end of this chapter.

When -- at what hour -- you invite him depends on what his business is. It will be most likely be for breakfast or lunch. The French usually reserve their evenings for family and friends, concerts or theatre... although, like many other things in Paris, this is changing.

How you host your business contact will also have a lot to do those kudos... and putting through the deal. The way you welcome him, seat him, order food and wine; your conversation and, yes, your table manners will have an effect on him.

Savoir-Flair Tip No.164:
Breakfast is your best bet for busy Frenchmen

Breakfast is the likeliest free moment for a French contact. His lunches will be booked three weeks in advance.

Savoir-Flair Tip No. 165:
Where you take him depends on what he does

For breakfast, the grander hotels (Crillon, Bristol, Ritz, Royal Monceau) are favorites of the mergers & acquisitions crowd and older conservative politicians. They might also enjoy the sense of savoring something new on the market at two just recently luxuriously renovated hotels, the George V and nearby on the rue de Berri, the Warwick, both starring excellent chefs.

Younger politicians and the literary lions prefer the Café de Flore, Jean-Paul Sartre's favorite haunt in Saint-Germain-des-Prés after he fled the tourists at Les Deux Magots, as mentioned in Chapter 14. Measure your guest's true influence in the Paris power structure by the number of people he greets here. The media & movie crowd like the Hôtel Raphaël on the Avenue Kléber and Le Fouquet's on the Champs-Elysées.

Savoir-Flair Tip No. 166:
What time you meet also depends on what he does

It takes an Anglo-Saxon (according to the French) to have a business breakfast at 7:30 am.

8:00 am is still considered early, that is, industrial and investment banker hours. 8:30 is civilized. 9:00 and 9:30 is for public relations and media types. Never invite journalists for a press breakfast before 9:00 am - - it's still a full hour before they usually start their working day. (But they're often still at their desks at 9:00 pm.)

Savoir-Flair Tip No. 167:
It's worth trying for a table in one of the great restaurants for lunch

If you want to host your French contact grandly and memorably at a splendid meal, then try one of the great 3-star restaurants. It's easier, and (relatively) cheaper to get a table at one of them for lunch than for dinner. An invitation to Taillevent, Alain Ducasse, Lucas-Carton or Arpège (where the waiting list for dinner is more than two months) will be treasured by the most blasé of French grandees (but still set you back at least $150 a head if you take wine).

Only slightly less grand and slightly less gastronomically sublime but a lot less expensive, full of charm and very popular with French ministers, is La Ferme Saint-Simon in the tony 7th arrondissement around the corner from the Prime Minister's office-residence, the Education Ministry, the Agriculture Ministry and the Parlement. Any French or foreign executive is happy to be taken there.

Nearby, with a charming, quiet terrace far from traffic for spring and summer, is Le Basilic, just behind the Church of Sainte Clotilde.

Also nearby, less expensive and popular with French high civil servants and executives is the lively and delicious Du Coté 7ième, where there's a menu-fixe of FF195 including wine, with several choices for each course and an excellent chef. Their *foie gras de canard* (duck foie gras) is delicious.

Two other Left Bank restaurants popular with cinema, journalism and industry alike are La Closerie des Lilas in Montparnasse, near the Observatoire, and the Balzar on the rue des Ecoles, both mentioned already in Chapter 14. More sophisticated and surprisingly affordable, is the newcomer Le Six Bosquet, with inventive cuisine and "second wines" from the best Bordeaux, a real find your Parisian business contacts and friends will be delighted to discover.

Try Pharamond on the Right Bank for a discreet meeting in quiet, provincial surroundings, a century-old establishment in Les Halles specializing in Norman cooking. It used to be a favorite of the late President Mitterrand.

If you're in the fashion business you probably already know about lunch and tea at the super cool, Jacques-Grange-decorated Hôtel Costes, the former France et Choiseul. Sit in a series of knick-knack bedecked, mock-library rooms, watch supermodels air-kissing *Vogue* editors, and enjoy better food than this sort of place usually serves.

A meeting place centrally located on the Right Bank, favored by French business people, with excellent food at more or less moderate prices, is Le Petit Yvan near the Champs Elysées.

If you have time and want to get away from the bustle of Paris without hardly going anywhere, try Le Petit Poucet on the Ile de la Jatte in Neuilly. In the summer, you can sit on the terraces overlooking the Seine and have a wonderful lunch for FF 300.

Savoir-Flair Tip No. 168:
The time for lunch also depends also on what he/she does

Industry lunches at 12:00 noon. Services (banking, lawyers, etc.) lunch at 1:00 pm.

12:30 pm is usually acceptable to all, except, again, for media types, who are watching/listening to the crucial midday news at that time.

The famous French two-hour lunches are usually, but not always, shorter these days, but if you're lunching at one of the 3-star restaurants, expect it to take two hours. Be careful not to make an important appointment afterwards before 4:00. Remember, lunch is where the important decisions are made. You might find yourself negotiating for a half hour on the sidewalk after lunch.

Savoir-Flair Tip No. 169:
Try out a restaurant before you take a guest there

Unless it's one of the restaurants mentioned above, arrange to have at least one meal at the proposed restaurant before you invite your business contact. Make friends with the maître d', test the food, check out the service and decide on the best table for your negotiations.

Turn off your mobile phone before you arrive, and be sure to get there well ahead of your guest. Seat him on your right, with the best view of the restaurant. If there are to be several guests, figure out the seating ahead of time. French people never sit down before their seat is indicated. The most important guest goes on your right, the next most important on your left, the third most important opposite you.

Savoir-Flair Tip No. 170:
See to it that the waiter pours the wine. As for the water...

Keep track of the wine, watch the glass of your guest (or guests) so that it isn't empty for long. Even if you're not a wine drinker, drink a little. Please, please don't order Coca Cola or beer for yourself. Nelson Lees (Chapter 16) can get away with it, but only just. Order another bottle without waiting interminably. For the cheese course, the wine must flow.

Don't pour the wine yourself, just see to it that the waiter does.

If you're the one who is invited, whether at a restaurant or at a French friend's house, be careful *never* to pour wine for yourself, unless your host specifically asks you to "take care of the wine" at your end of the table. How often I've seen the long arm of one of my American guests reach out to pour himself, or, more likely, herself, some more wine. This is one big no-no in conservative circles, but less shocking now than before to business people.

Remember that everyone will be waiting for you, the host, to take the first sip, whether of the *apéritif* or of the wine with lunch. I found out about this when I noticed that a French business associate I'd invited to lunch hadn't touched the Porto I'd served him at least 15 minutes before. "But I'm waiting for you to drink yours," he said. So, take one sip even if you don't want any.

As for water, if you're the host, ask the guest if he'd like it plain or bubbly (*plate ou gazeuse*) and see to it that the waiter pours it. The funny thing about water is that when you're the guest, and water is on the table, no one serves it. You have to ask for it, unlike wine, which is automatically poured, unless you have your hand over the glass --- the thing to do if you don't want more.

Savoir-Flair Tip No. 171:
Order the apéritif first, then the first two courses

If your guest passes up the *apéritif*, then you should order, but only the first two courses. At distinguished restaurants you'll be served a tiny dish of some special delicacy while waiting for the first course. This is called an *amuse-gueule*, or, more elegantly, an *amuse-bouche*.

The cheese or the dessert, or both, are ordered when you've finished the main course. Coffee is ordered *after* or during the dessert course.

Insisting on ice in your water glass, or ketchup with your food will not make a hit with your French guest.

Savoir-Flair Tip No. 172:
You'll be judged on your manners!

In France, culture is everything. French business people don't rise far without it. Technique at the table is part of culture. Your French business contact will notice yours. He has learned his own through determined application or at his mother's knee. The knees of most American managers' mothers these days are at work and not supervising whether little Johnny eats with his hands or his feet. Since major decisions in the U.S. are not usually taken at lunch, as in France, American managers haven't been lectured about the manners involved and often haven't any more of a clue about them than they do about the difference between *fines de claires* and *belons* oysters.

One of the things you probably have heard is that Continentals always keep their hands on the table when they're not actually eating. Well, it's true, and it's nice if you can remember, but not crucial. The important thing is how you wield your knife and fork, and how you position them on the plate when you've finished.

The main points

- Your arms and hands are horizontal to the table, elbows close to your side. Never wave a knife or fork at someone while you're talking.
- Also don't point your finger at someone when you're talking.
- When you cut your meat, your right hand should have the fingers and thumb around the knife, the forefinger along the blunt edge; the tines of the fork are turned over with the convex side up.
- You can eat holding your cutlery in this position throughout this course, placing the meat and some vegetable on the back of the fork, and bringing the back side of the fork to your mouth.
- Or you can switch hands, parking the knife on the side of the plate, and taking the fork in your right hand, handling it as you normally would. Fine, providing you park the knife entirely on the plate, not half on the table.
- What you can NOT do, while keeping the knife in your right hand, is to turn around the fork in the left hand so that the concave side of the tines is up, then load it and bring it to your mouth. No Frenchman would fail to notice this with horror.
- When you're finished, the knife and fork should be placed neatly

side by side on the plate, diagonally. That is to say, at 4:00, if the plate were the face of a clock.

•They should NEVER be left sprawling all over the plate, half on it and half off it, the knife on one side, the fork on the other.

•But don't park them at 4:00 if you're not finished. The waiter will think that you are, and take your plate away. If you're not finished, but for the moment not eating, the knife and fork should rest diago nally towards each other on the plate, the handles at 4:00 and 8:00 (or at 5:00 and 7:00), the tips of the tines and top of the blade of the knife touching at noon.

• Don't put bread on your plate or cut it with a knife. Leave it on the table. Break it with your fingers. Crumbs on the table are cool. The waiter will handle them.

• Butter and butter plates are provided only in more expensive restaurants. Don't butter the entire piece of bread or half a roll before eating it. Butter just enough for the first bite.

• Your napkin belongs in your lap. Use two hands to wipe your mouth with it. Napkins are not for blowing your nose. (Yes, I have seen even preppy managers doing this.)

Savoir-Flair Tip No. 173:
First talk culture and politics, then business

France has speeded up like everywhere else. Business people are wired to the Internet. Websites are proliferating exponentially. So the tradition of never, never mentioning business until *"entre la poire et le fromage"* (between the pear and the cheese), or until the last course is giving way. But proceed carefully. Let your French contact open the business talk.

Incidentally, the *poire* (pear), meaning the fruit course, never comes before the cheese. Why the saying? Who knows?

For pleasure without business

Any of the above, plus the bistrots below.

Bistrot food is closest to what the French eat at home or in family reunions. It is wonderful and robust. In a bistrot, your guests can relax, wind down, open up. (Most bistrots don't mind your coming in to dine alone.) For the best *Tarte Tatin* (caramelized apple pie) in town, go to Le Vieux Bistrot, just across the street from Notre Dame, if you didn't already during our walk in Chapter 4. Don't miss their beef *entrecôte en papillotte à la moëlle* (a steak cooked with bone marrow) and their *Gratin Dauphinois* (baked slivers of potatoes in cheese and cream.)

The more bourgeois Chez Pauline has venison in season and a great Burgundy wine list (rarer than a Bordeaux list).

For charm and a stupendous view (but don't expect too much of the food) try Le Totem, inside the Palais de Chaillot. The Champ de Mars, the Eiffel Tower and a vast view of Paris stretch out before you.

The quiet streets of the 16th arrondissement (Paris's Upper East Side) hide Chez Géraud, a bistrot specializing in the cuisine of the Southwest. The dishes are inventive and the foie gras is superlative.

Marcel Baudis is the chef at L'Oulette in the 12th arrondissement, not far from Lafayette's burial place at the Picpus Cemetery. This accomplished chef also offers southwest specialities from his hometown in Montauban. Try his *cabèche de calamars* and his *millefeuille de sardines*.

For budget watchers

Chartier on the rue du Faubourg Montmartre is a happening in itself. It has been delighting its habitués since 1870 with its Belle Epoque decor, lots of big brass lamps, dark-wood tables and chairs, and faïence on the walls. Its speedy waiters race about with their delicious dishes at the best prices in town. It's absolutely authentic from the time, nothing has changed.

Near the Bastille is a small, cozy restaurant that Ande fell in love with, Le Temps des Cerises, with a menu-*formule* of three courses for FF 71. It looks like a traditional French bistrot of the 50's. It was crammed when he was there, no place left to sit down at all, with people of all ages and, according to the proprietor, all walks of life. If you're alone, and since it is always crammed, even if you're not, they put you at someone else's table. Only open for lunch.

If you want a delightful, really inexpensive, really Parisian evening which is also delicious, try Le Petit Saint-Benoit on rue Saint-Benoit near Saint-Germain-des-Prés. The cuisine is traditional. So is the clientele. One elderly Frenchman keeps his napkin there in a little pigeon hole, and retrieves it every day at lunch. As at Le Temps des Cerises above, it feels like one big family, partly because you're seated at long tables with other people, unless it's the summer and you're on the sidewalk.

Gail and Rob Chaddock love Polidor, between the Odéon and the Luxembourg garden on the rue Monsieur le Prince, where you'll also probably share the table with others. They rave about the *crème de lentilles soupe* and the *foie gras*, "unbelievably good," they say.

L'Annexe, chez Maurice et Alice, near the lively open market on the rue Mouffetard, is in the same category. You won't have to wait and the tables are separate. Maurice and Alice have been cooking in this small charming restaurant on the rue du Pot-de-Fer (Street of the Iron Pot) for 45 years and serve a remarkably good three-course lunch for FF 65.

In the Marais, A 2 Pas du Dos, at 101 rue Vieille du Temple, offers a three course menu, two choices for each course, at FF 78, including wine. I had a really delicious lunch there in February 2000.

Farther afield in the 20th arrondissement, just down the street from the Père Lachaise Cemetery, is Mère Lachaise, a brasserie-turned-restaurant frequented and waited on by a young, hip crowd of ethnic and artsy residents, all of whom you might run into in one of the newly hip cafés on the rue Ménilmontant nearby. The menu is simple, reasonable and appealing. Each day there is a different *plat du jour*. Friday's was *perche aux champignons* (sea perch with mushrooms).

If you're down and out, try to find a family-run bistrot and pour out your heart and bad luck. I know an American who was fed for a whole month for free.

Dine -- at what time?

The earliest you can invite a French person to dinner, or go by yourself is 8:00 pm -- and you'll start your meal in a three-quarters empty restaurant that will only fill up gradually as you eat. (See Chapter 16.)

8:30 pm is acceptable; 9:00 pm not uncommon. Most good restaurants will accept orders until 10:00 pm, but always check in advance.

More Restaurant Savoir-Flair Tips

A *kir* is appropriate only as an *apéritif.*

When the students of Chris Cripps's ESSEC group of graduate students in business wanted to continue with *kir* throughout the meal, Chris simply told them:"Impossible. We're red wine now." "But we like it," they said.

Chris reports that his only answer is:*"Tant pis."* (Tough.)

Sharing the bill

This is full of nuances and depends on many things: how the decision was reached to eat together, how clear the invitation was or if there was no invitation. It's one of those context questions that you can answer in your own culture but is very subtle in someone else's.

In general, the French, if there was no clear invitation at the beginning, like most southern Europeans, don't usually share the bill. They pay for the whole thing, or you pay for the whole thing. Be alert.

Keep the decibels down, above all, your mobile telephone.

Addresses

(Note that the French, all the way to the Michelin Guide, are unfairly supercilious about hotel restaurants. L'Espadon at the Ritz, Les Ambassadeurs at the Crillon, and the Bristol restaurant all could have earned three stars had they been stand-alone establishments. Yet there is almost no waiting list there for lunch or dinner. Consider them for a memorable meal at short notice.)

Very expensive

Hôtel Ritz, 15 place Vendôme, 75001 Paris, 01 43 16 30 30

Hôtel de Crillon, 10 place de la Concorde, 75008 Paris, 01 44 71 15 00

Hôtel Bristol, 112 rue du Faubourg Saint-Honoré, 75008 Paris, 01 53 43 43 00

Hôtel Royal-Monceau, 37 avenue Hoche, 75008 Paris, 01 42 99 88 00

Hôtel Raphaël, 17 avenue Kléber, 75116 Paris, 01 44 28 00 28

Hôtel George, 31 avenue George V, 75008 Paris, 01 47 23 54 00

Hôtel Le Warwick, 5 rue de Berri, 75008 Paris, 01 45 63 14 11

The great 3 star restaurants

Alain Ducasse, 59 avenue Raymond Poincaré, 75116 Paris, 01 47 27 12 27

Arpège, 84 rue de Varenne, 75007 Paris, 01 47 05 09 06

Lucas Carton, 9 place de la Madeleine, 75008 Paris, 01 42 65 22 90

Taillevent, 15 rue Lamennais, 75008 Paris, 01 44 95 15 01

Guy Savoy, 18 rue Troyon, 75017 Paris, 01 43 80 40 61

La Tour d'Argent, 15 quai de la Tournelle, 75005 Paris, 01 43 54 23 31

Medium priced or more

Le Fouquet's, 99 Champs-Elysées, 75008 Paris, 01 47 23 70 60

Au Petit Riche, 25 rue Le Peletier, 75009 Paris, 01 47 70 68 68

Le Balzar Brasserie, 49 rue des Ecoles, 75005 Paris, 01 43 54 13 67

Brasserie Flo, 7 Cour des Petites Ecuries, 75010 Paris, 01 47 70 13 59

Brasserie Lipp, 151 bd Saint-Germain, 75006 Paris, 01 45 48 53 91

Café de Flore, 172 bd Saint-Germain, 75006 Paris, 01 45 48 55 26

Chez Pauline, 5 rue Villedo, 75002 Paris, 01 42 96 20 70

Chez Géraud, 31 rue Vital, 75016 Paris, 01 45 20 33 00

Hôtel Costes, 239 rue Saint-Honoré, 75001 Paris, 01 42 44 50 25

Le Gave de Pau, 147 rue de Charenton, 75012 Paris, 01 43 44 74 11

La Ferme Saint-Simon, 6 rue Saint-Simon, 75007 Paris, 01 45 48 35 74

Le Basilic, 2 rue Casimir Perrier, 75007 Paris, 01 44 18 94 64

Pharamond, 24 rue de la Grande-Truanderie, 75001 Paris, 01 42 33 06 72

L'Oulette, 15 Place Lachambeaudie, 75012 Paris, 01 40 02 04 77

Le Six Bosquet, 6 avenue Bosquet, 75007 Paris, 01 45 56 97 26

Le Vieux Bistrot, 14 rue du Cloître Notre-Dame, 75004 Paris, 01 43 54 18 95

Le Totem (in the Palais de Chaillot), 17 Place du Trocadéro, 75016 Paris, 01 47 27 28 29

Le Petit Yvan, 1 bis rue Jean Mermoz, 75008 Paris, 01 42 89 49 65

Willie's Wine Bar, 13 rue des Petits Champs, 75001 Paris, 01 42 61 05 09

Inexpensive

Chartier, 7 rue du Faubourg Montmartre, 75009 Paris, 01 47 70 86 29

l'Annexe, chez Maurice et Alice, 16 rue du Pot-de-Fer, 75005 Paris, 01 45 35 57 07

La Mère Lachaise, 78 bd Ménilmontant, 75020 Paris, 01 47 97 61 60

Le Petit Saint-Benoît, 4 rue Saint-Benoît, 75006 Paris, 01 42 60 27 92

Restaurant des Ministères, 30 rue du Bac, 75007 Paris, 01 42 61 22 37

Polidor, 41 rue Monsieur-le-Prince, 75006 Paris, 01 43 26 95 34

A 2 Pas du Dos, 101 rue Vieille-du-Temple, 75003 Paris, 01 42 77 10 52

Chapter Eighteen

Enjoying the Fabled SNCF

Catching the Right Train
Travelers' Tales

J'ai recherché avec une sensibilité exquise la vue des beaux paysages; c'est pour cela uniquement que j'ai voyagé. Les paysages étaient comme un archet qui jouait sur mon âme.
(With an exquisite delight I have sought the view of beautiful landscapes; this is the only reason I have traveled. The landscapes were like a bow of a violin playing upon my soul.)

Stendhal, *Vie de Henry Brulard*

Savoir-Flair Tip No. 174:
Ask someone for help in deciphering your ticket

France would be worth a visit if only for the trains.

The SNCF, the French railway, is one of the prides of France. The trains, both fast and less fast, are possibly the world's most agreeable -- rapid, comfortable, clean, punctual and safe. The TGV (bullet trains, or, literally, High Speed Trains) go boiling along at 300 kms an hour with never a serious accident; not a single person has ever been killed since their appearance in 1981.

And the conductors. They're dreams of compassionate humanity. They have to be, to hold the hands of the foreign passengers, because the TGV is very high context. That is, you're expected to know everything vital you need to know in order to board the right train, without anyone telling you.

The French themselves, very high context, of course know everything, such as that three different stations (*gares*) serve the south: the Gare de Lyon, the Gare d'Austerlitz and the Gare Montparnasse. It's easy for foreigners to go to the wrong station and even if they go to the right one, to get on the wrong train, even if, like Ande and me, you've lived here for 20 years or more. What I mean is, it takes a certain amount of concentration.

Your TGV ticket gives you all the pertinent information; the problem is that it's in a kind of coded shorthand.

Six SNCF Tales
First Tale: Three American girls, my grandsons and me on the TGV

A good day not to travel in France is the Friday before Bastille Day, July 14, France's most joyous, frantic holiday when it seems as if the whole country is on the move. Motorists are advised not to go near the expressways. Trains and planes are reserved weeks if not months in advance. Canny Frenchmen stay home or else leave a week earlier.

Thanks to a last-minute change of plans, this was the very day I was taking my little grandsons, Stanislas, 10 and Alexandre, 8, on the TGV No. 8417 to Libourne at 10:45. Without a seat reservation. Our tickets specified car No. 9: no seat numbers, but maybe *strapontins* (flip-down seats at the end of the car).

Savoir-Flair Tip No. 175:
Have a 10-franc coin ready for the luggage cart (*caddie*)

At the Gare Montparnasse we rushed with our mountain of heavy duffle bags to an escalator and rode up to the upper level. The boys ran off to get two carts (*caddies*) with their 10-franc coins, loaded them and raced them over to me.

The electronic departures monitor is vast and if you look up, you can't miss it -- unless you're looking for a tiny airport screen. Stanislas spotted the track number first: "Track Number 5!" I remembered Ande's near disaster with this train (the Second SNCF Tale) and checked the board myself that track No. 5 was lit up next to train No. 8417 for Bordeaux, stopping at Libourne.

Savoir-Flair Tip No. 176:
Don't forget to validate (*composter*) your ticket

You validate the ticket (*composter le billet*) yourself by inserting it in a sort of post that can look like an orange fire hydrant about waist high, or like an orange postbox hung on a wall. There are two good reasons for this:

1. You can be fined 150 francs by the conductor if you don't.

2. Should there be an accident on the train and you are hurt, the SNCF is relieved of paying damages if your ticket isn't punched.

If the machine doesn't punch right away, and you're late, catch the train and explain to the conductor right away -- he won't fine you.

The boys and I validated our tickets and dashed to the platform. We fought our way through a crowd bottlenecked by two railroad officials checking tickets. Our tickets finally okayed, we ran along the track on the left. At the end of each car next to the boarding steps, we looked for its backlit number in a little window at the beginning of each car. At car No. 9, we scrambled up the steps with our luggage, found three flap seats (*strapontins*) and flopped into them.

Just as the train was leaving, three American girls -- early 20s, pony tails and backpacks, pretty in a scrubbed, wholesome way -- came scurrying through our car, screaming in English: "Where are we? Where are we going? What car is this? Where is car No. 17? Doesn't anyone speak English?"

I explained that they were too late to get to car no. 17. The train was in two sections of 10 cars each, with two engines linked nose to nose between them. Thus no traffic was possible between the two. Their car was in the other section. So, since the train was very crowded, they'd have to stand until the first stop.

"We've only been here 3 days," said one, tearfully, "and you can't imagine all the things that have happened to us! Why doesn't anyone explain anything?" They rushed on to the next car.

"They're from out West somewhere," said an American near me. "We don't have trains out there -- we're just not used to this."

We were pulling out of the station. The loudspeaker announced that we were on a non-stop express to Bordeaux. I looked at the American. "That's crazy, what about Poitiers, Libourne..."

"No no, that was the other train... on the same platform."

The boys and I looked at each other. Stanislas burst out laughing. Alexandre burst out laughing. I just hoped they'd laugh all the way to Bordeaux and back to Libourne.

Second Tale: Ande and the lost Serb

Ande was to meet a Serbian friend, Stevo Ognjenovic, in Libourne when he made the same mistake I did, boarding the non-stop express to Bordeaux instead of the other Bordeaux train on the same platform stopping at Libourne. At Libourne they were to change to a local Corail train. Stevo was a 60-year old refugee from the 1990 war in Croatia. He spoke only Serbo-Croatian. Ande, himself a Serbian refugee years ago, had no trouble imagining this former high civil servant, now a destitute emigré, stranded on a train platform somewhere in a foreign country without a word of the language.

Ande told his tale to the conductor (*contrôleur*). The conductor nodded his head gravely several times. Then he said, "I will see what can be done." He disappeared into the next car. Presently he returned.

"We will make a special stop at Poitiers," he said.

Ande was startled. "A special stop?"

"You will get off at Poitiers," the conductor went on, "and explain the situation to the station chief (*chef de gare*). He will put you in phone contact with the station chief at Libourne. You will give him the message for your friend. Then you can take a local from Poitiers to Libourne to join him."

The express train to Bordeaux from Paris actually did make a special stop for Ande at Poitiers. The station chief, stunned by the unprecedented unscheduled stop of a TGV express, promptly contacted the station chief at

Libourne. Ande then dictated the message for Stevo in Serbo-Croatian, letter by letter. The Libourne station chief took down the message. He made a sign with Stevo's name in large letters. When the train pulled into Libourne, he himself walked the platform holding the sign.

Stevo, getting off the train and not seeing Ande anywhere, had only a few sinking moments before he noticed his Serbian name being paraded around the station. Seeing Stevo's face telling us this story later was a story in itself. Refugees need stories like this.

Third Tale: Tom McTigue's Scare on the Corail

Even Tom McTigue, the culture detective and veteran of France we've met in previous chapters, wasn't immune to an SNCF alarm.

Corail trains are normal express trains, with few stops, that don't go as fast as the TGV. Tom and Carol, his wife, and Matt, their 13 year old son, boarded a Corail at Toulon on the Mediterranean, making sure that the car they sat in was headed all the way to Chamonix in the French Alps.

"I'm always careful to check the destination sign on the side of the car as I enter," Tom said, "because some cars fork off to go somewhere else."

At Avignon, Matt asked his father if he could go back to the bar car to get a pizza. Tom gave him about the right amount of money for a pizza and ham sandwiches for Carol and himself. A few moments later the loudspeaker started squawking in fast French that the train was about to separate into two sections. As Tom dashed back towards the bar car to get Matt, his part of the train jerked and pulled out of the station, leaving Matt and the bar car behind in Avignon.

Matt had no train tickets, no passport and only pizza-sandwich money. He spoke no French. Tom tried to explain to the conductor, but couldn't understand what he answered. Carol was getting upset.

"By this time the French people near us realized what was happening and began all talking at once," Tom said. "Finally one of them turned to me and explained in English that Matt's train would follow ours to Valence. Both trains would be in the Valence station at the same time for '3 *minutes précises*'!! Our train would get there first. The plan was for me to get off, cross to another track and wait for his train to arrive. And then try to find him in 3 *minutes précises*."

It takes 45 minutes to go from Avignon to Valence, "very loooong minutes," Tom said later. "In Valence, I dashed off the train and ran over to the track where Matt's train was to arrive, and waited. Finally it pulled into the station. I waved my arms frantically as each car passed by."

Then the train stopped. The first person off the train was Matt, grinning.

"Here's your ham sandwich, Dad," he said.

"We ran back to our Chamonix train just before it pulled out of the station," Tom said. "Everyone in our car was looking out the window for us. When they saw us, they stood up and clapped."

Savoir-Flair Tip No. 177:
Have a contingency plan for an emergency

Tom's epilogue: "The moral of this story is that travellers should have a contingency plan in case they get separated. We decided that ours would be to call our next-door neighbor in the States and tell them where we were, and let them call us back telling us where our lost brethren were."

Matt e-mailed me about being 13 and lost in France:

> I was just about to go back through the electric doors with the sandwiches to my parents' car when all of a sudden, it was no longer part of the same train. My first reaction was WOW. I am now all alone in France (thank God I finally got rid of those parents -- just kidding) with a pizza, two sandwiches, no passport, and no money. Not to mention no French.
>
> I was sitting next to the electric doors when the conductor came by to ask for my ticket and passport. I tried to explain. It gave me comfort to see the English flag on his conductor's hat, which meant that he spoke English. He said that the trains would meet in about 45 minutes, and he'd make sure that I was on the other one. He made me feel comfortable in a weird situation.
>
> That is my story about being lost in Avignon, but I'm not so sure if I was supposed to be found. I do not think my parents took into account that I might meet a very understanding conductor who spoke English. They must have overlooked that when they made their plans. Ha Ha!!"

Fourth Tale: Kathie Kremer woke up in Brittany by mistake

Kathie Kremer, from Wichita, Kansas, is a passionate traveler who runs a bookstore, the Travel Den, with her husband in suburban Saint Louis. It outfits people going anywhere with all the information they need. Adventures that sound funny when they happen to other people won't happen to Travel Den customers, if Kathie can help it.

When I visited her at the Travel Den, she told me about one she'd had herself during a college vacation. "I was with a friend and we wanted to go on a bike trip, starting in Bordeaux," she said over a cup of coffee. "We took an overnight Corail train to Bordeaux from the Gare Montparnasse, planning to sit up all night to save money. On the platform, we checked on the outside of the first car that there was that little sign that said 'Bordeaux.' However, there were no seats in that car, and the train was so crowded that we went through eight or nine cars until we finally found them in the very last car, and promptly went to sleep -- without, of course, having been able to check on the outside of the car where it was going, or thinking of asking someone.

"I woke up at about 5:00 am in a station with a name that didn't look right. I got out my map and realized we were heading west instead of south. Our car had been uncoupled and hooked onto another train going to Brittany."

Kathie and her friend got off at the next station at 5:30. The station house was locked, but the sun was coming up and they had sleeping mats in their backpacks. "We found a pleasant field close to the station, so that we could see when a train was coming," she said. "We caught one going back at 9:30, and eventually got to Bordeaux. Actually, it was beautiful lying there in a Brittany field. But I don't recommend it for people with children and luggage."

Fifth Tale: Sara Terrell's Serendipity

Like Kathie Kremer on a college summer vacation, Sara Terrell and a friend bought tickets in Florence for the shorter of two train routes to Nice. However, they boarded a train taking the longer route. The conductor demanded more money for the extra mileage. They didn't have it, so they had to get off, go all the way back to Florence and start over.

"But the next ride from Florence to Nice was a revelation," Sara wrote in a fax. "We shared a compartment with a French mother and daughter. They didn't speak much English, and we didn't speak much French, but we had a delightful time talking with them in a roundabout way. We shared a good many of those coveted smiles, and even a bit of laughter when the conductor told us we had to move down a couple of cars, because the one we were in was staying at the station. When we said we were going to Nice, they told us about St. Paul de Vence. So we visited St. Paul de Vence and spent an unforgettable day in a walled town exploring windy streets, discovering artisans and quaint shops."

In a couple of sentences Sara then summed up the poetry of travel:

"That train ride, for all the frustration that led up to it, remains my fondest memory of France. The feeling of actually having a meaningful, enjoyable conversation with people of a different culture is one that cannot be duplicated. It is something I wish for everyone to experience at least once."

Sixth Tale: The Perrys miss their stop

David Perry, in charge of Microsoft sales in Europe, and his wife, Laurie, whom we met in Chapter 6, one of the few "trailing spouses" to be employed in Paris by her husband's company, are from Seattle, where there aren't many trains for travelers to practice on. Laurie's father was visiting them. To show him the châteaux of the Loire, they were going to take the TGV for an hour to Saint-Pierre-des-Corps and then rent a car for the day.

The Perrys went to the right station in Paris, and boarded the right train. Twenty minutes after they were scheduled to arrive at Saint-Pierre-des-Corps, David glanced at his watch and realized that it must have been the last stop, and that they were now boiling along at 300 km per hour away from it.

Savoir-Flair Tip No. 178:
Check your watch for arriving at your station.
Stations have very few identifying signs.

"We'd heard the loudspeaker saying something but couldn't understand it," said Laurie. "When the train stopped, we hadn't been able to see any station signs from our window. I guess we thought someone would tell us."

The conductor reassured them. At Poitiers, they could call the rental agency to hold the car in Saint-Pierre-des-Corps until they got back by the next train. And then, because Laurie's French was good (and I'm sure also because she is so pretty and polite) he wrote some scribbles on the back of the ticket which meant that their ride back to Saint-Pierre-des-Corps would be free.

"He was just so nice," said Laurie. "No governessy remarks that we should have paid attention, no reproaches, just niceness. It made all the difference."

The *grandeur* of the French State

The SNCF or, in all its *grandeur*, the Société Nationale des Chemins de Fer, is not just about transportation. To think that would be to imagine that trains are just to get people from one place to another, or that Paris is simply a place to live and do business. Like Paris, the SNCF is a state of mind.

When I said *grandeur*, I meant that trains in France have glamor, splendor and nobility. Roads of Iron are strong, fast, reliable and mythical. They are owned by State, which is a word -- *Etat* -- which resonates with the power and glory lying deep in the national memories of great Kings like Louis XIV and Emperors like Napoleon.

The TGV was conceived in the 1960's on reflections by General de Gaulle. The Germans had efficiently confiscated all French locomotives and destroyed the tracks during World War II; de Gaulle was determined to replace them with the best trains in the world. The engineers (*les Polytechniciens* from the Ecole Polytechnique), who very likely are the best in the world, went to work. The TGV's speed of up to 300 km per hour means that you can get from Paris to Lyon in two hours (instead of the normal five hours) and from Paris to Bordeaux in three hours (instead of overnight). Local trains connect with them seamlessly. You can even walk out of the airport into a TGV in Paris (Charles de Gaulle Airport) and in Lyon.

Their sleek appearance, punctuality, and seats designed for ease are as felicitous as their speed. Maybe a little squeezed in second class, but the first class is a dream of sumptuous comfort. Even the second class is luxury stuff on the Paris-Lyon line, with double decker cars and legroom to please a Gulliver. The trains are warm in the winter and air-conditioned in the summer.

Savoir-Flair Tip No. 179:
Don't clog the aisles with enormous suitcases or backpacks

TGV trains are popular and crowded. There is plenty of space for baggage à la française, that is, if everyone travels light. Recently I took the same one as 40 American college students. The young men all seemed to be seven feet tall with backpacks the size of toboggans. The baggage area soon overflowed. Duffles blocked the aisles. If you needed to stumble over them to *les toilettes*, good luck.

Dogs are different. There is always plenty of room for a French Saint Bernard. French people pat them and coo to them as they climb over them.

A smart option is to bring your lunch and eat it in your seat. In the bar car, you can get salads, hot and cold sandwiches and a variety of drinks, but you'll probably wish you'd brought your own.

Unfortunately, the TGV design engineers didn't waste time

worrying about the pre-boarding concerns of their customers. As the French are expected to know everything, no thought was given to signs, even in French, for people from other parts of the country, let alone the world. Water fountains and numerous, nearby *toilettes* in stations, forget it: the French don't drink much water and their bladders are endlessly elastic. These design engineers were young and healthy so they didn't insist on escalators that always work.

The station at Libourne is pretty typical. Arriving at the other end of platform 3 and obliged to get to platform 2 for your *correspondance* (connecting train), you're lucky if you find a *caddie*. There are no escalators. So you not only have to drag your luggage along an endless platform, but also down a long flight of stairs and up another. Luckily there are always kind people ready to help.

Savoir-Flair Tip No. 180:
You can buy your ticket in special salons without queues

And the ticket queues. There are several ways around them, but mostly only French people know this.

1. *Electronic ticket dispensing machines* inside the stations save waiting if you don't need a reservation. You'll need a genius level of competence in both French and computers to use them happily.

2. *The special ticket salons:* In the major train stations, even in some RER stations, there are comfortable, enclosed, heated, pleasantly furnished areas like living rooms, with several ticket agents seated behind low counters, no glass barriers. You pick your number in line from a number machine, and wait in upholstered armchairs to be called. At the Musée d'Orsay RER-Métro station, newspapers on bamboo racks are provided for you on a low table.

3. *Reserving by phone or Minitel* with your credit card number, you can pick up your ticket just before the train's departure. Without it, you have to get it 48 hours before the train leaves. But at least you have your reservation. Or you hope you have it. The trouble is, sometimes the agent on the other end of the phone makes a mistake in the date, the class (first or second), the window or aisle, smoking or non-smoking.

Savoir-Flair Tip No. 181:
Check your ticket's date, etc., right away

Rob Chaddock, the husband of Gail, is a computer whiz. He gave up his job to "trail" Gail to Paris. When they moved back to Washington last year, he was genuinely sad to leave. But arriving in France was a different story. Rob didn't speak a word of French. He was used to getting things done the U.S. way -- fast. The French rhythm is different. Even if you speak French, things take longer. Lots longer. Rob was blowing up at an average of three times a day.

Rob Chaddock's story, in his words

One time weeks in advance, I reserved on the phone. I got the number of the reservation and went to the nearest station (the Gare d'Austerlitz) to get it. I had to stand in the regular ticket line to get it -- a LONG line. Everyone ahead of me had an issue to argue about. It took 45 minutes. I finally got my tickets.

I checked them when I got home -- and they were for a smoking car. An eight-hour train trip to Munich in the midst of a wall of smoke? No. Neither Gail nor I could stand it. So I had to go back to the station and stand in line again to have it changed. This time the agent told me he couldn't change it -- the train was completely booked. He told me to go early to the Gare de l'Est, where the train was leaving from.

I followed his advice. I got to the Gare de l'Est early, and again stood in line at the ticket window, this time for 15 minutes. My turn at last, the agent said he couldn't change the ticket. They would only do that at the "Information" counter.

Another line. This agent said changing tickets was not his job, I should go back to the ticket agent. So I went back there -- and this time I screamed at him.

He came out from behind the window and talked to me, then went with me to the Information counter. They had a long discussion. And decided I should talk to the conductor on the train. The conductor on the train said the train was fully booked and there was nothing he could do. So Gail and I had eight hours of breathing smoke to Munich.

Savoir-Flair Tip No. 182:
Don't expect helpful signs at the stations: ask!

The Gare de Lyon

The busiest and least traveler-friendly station in Paris is the Gare de Lyon. The bus and the Métro trains stop miles from the trains. Once you're inside it, the place is vast, with complicated corridors and levels and endless possibilities for taking the wrong turn and missing your train. This is the station French people use to get down to their favorite spots in the South, Aix en Provence, Avignon, Cannes, Nice and other French Riviera (Côte d'Azur) points, not to mention Rome and Florence. They, of course, know where they're going.

A taxi dropped me off at about 7:20 on the TGV side of the station for a 7:40 am train. The train platform was two stories higher. The escalator wasn't working. I dragged my suitcase up two high stories. At the upper level, a clock said 7:24. I panicked when I saw the electronic bulletin board posting the train as leaving at 7:30, not 7:40, and from Track B. No sign anywhere in that enormous station indicating where track B might be. Some signs about tracks with numbers, no letters. I switched myself from System SA (Self-Automated) to System TYOPM, or Throw Yourself On the Public Mercy. I turned around to the other people studying the electronic board and cried, a little hysterically: "Does anyone know where Track B is?"

I said it in French, but English would have done as well. Right away a Good Samaritan came forward. I screeched that I couldn't miss that train, I would miss my group at Roanne and the chartered bus for the tour of Romanesque churches would leave without me! He was soothing. He seemed to know the train. There was plenty of time, he said, and led me around corners, down corridors and upstairs to Track B, where the train was posted for departure at 7:40.

The Gare du Nord

After visiting Paris, a television salesman I'll call John Miller, from Grand Rapids, Michigan, led his wife and two little girls, 8 and 7, onto the RER, which his concierge told him was a quick, reliable and relatively inexpensive way of getting to Charles de Gaulle Airport. At the next station after Saint-Michel, everyone got off. Assuming it was the airport, the Miller family got off too, with their cameras and two sofa-sized suitcases on wheels, plus backpacks for the girls.

The other passengers disappeared. The Millers saw a sign near some stairs saying "Sortie" -- whatever that meant (exit). No escalator. They went by another sign they didn't understand saying "Gare du Nord."

Dolores remarked that it was funny not to have an escalator in an airport.

They dragged the suitcases up the stairs, dragging the little girls as well, and found themselves on a busy street. So they went down to the platform again, and walked to the other end. Here they saw another meaningless sign saying "SNCF Grandes Lignes." Still no signs about airplane departures. The children began to cry.

The Millers were on the edge of a seriously miserable end to their nerves and their vacation when a young man in a snappy red wind breaker and a baseball cap came up to them. Peter Lundt was a German student at the Sorbonne who had recently been hired by the SNCF to wander around the Gare du Nord and find people who looked lost and desperate. He was to explain as gently as possible that the SNCF was obliged to reroute people to the airport on a different train during the construction of the Stade de France.

He gave the Millers a big welcoming smile. "Is there some way I can help you?" he said, with a slight German accent.

John Miller smiled his salesman smile with gritted teeth. "This is a funny kind of airport," he said.

"Yes, sir. Well you see, sir, it isn't an airport. It's a train station."

More SNCF Savoir-FlairTips

Getting food

The snack bar or "bar car" is always car No. 4 and/ or car No. 14. Sometimes a sandwiches-and-drinks wagon comes rolling through the train, but not always.

Stations in Paris

Gare du Nord -- north, northwest. Brussels, Scandinavia, London

Gare de l'Est -- northeast; southern Germany, all eastern Europe, Moscow

Gare de Lyon -- south and southeast; Switzerland

Gare Saint Lazare -- suburbs and long distance. Brittany, western France

Gare Montparnasse -- suburbs and long distance. West and southwest

Gare d'Austerlitz -- south and southwest

Reductions

There are many, depending on your age. For French or foreign seniors over 60: a "Carte Senior" pass for about FF 270 gives a reduction of up to 50%, on all trains, or a Carte Vermeil Quatre Temps for FF 140, good for four one-way trips. They're valid for a year.

BIJ (Billets Internationaux de Jeunesse) are for international travel for anyone 25 and under.

BSE (Billets Scolaires et Etudiants) are for students aged 12 to 25 for traveling within France.

Eurail, Europass, Euro Domino France, France Vacances Pass, Brit-France Railpass, and many other formulas are available, depending on where and when you want to go. A good travel guide explaining them all is the Lonely Planet Guide for France.

Holidays

Study a calendar of all the French school, State and religious holidays, when everyone in the country and the countries next door seems to be riding the TGV, and take your trip some other time. These crowded times are usually: between Christmas and New Year's; two weeks in February and early March; two weeks in April around Easter; every weekend in May; the first week of November; and the whole months of July and *August.*

Reserving a seat on the TGV

• It's obligatory. You have to reserve ahead, but can cancel and get a refund up to three hours after the train is due to leave.

• In the second class, the seats at the tables -- usually only four tables to a car -- have much more leg room.The key word in trying to reserve one is *"un carré."* They're supposedly reserved for families with children, but are often available for anyone. Nos. 53 and 54 will have a table between them, also nos. 51, 55, 52, 56, 57 and 58, and a few others.

• Seat numbers in the second class: no 9's, no 0's. If the number is over 100, it's the last car of the train.

• First-class tickets are not double the price of second-class tickets -- not even near double -- but they have triple the comfort and aesthetic pleasure.

Baggage service

The SNCF will pick up your luggage and deliver it to your hotel or other destination.You have to reserve. Recommended for families going on ski vacations.

SNCF Stations in the provinces

• Many stations in rural France have big panels on the platforms showing charts of where your car will be on the platform when it arrives. The chart says *"composition des trains."* You look for the departure time of your train. If you see that your car is at a spot marked E on the platform, look on the floor of the plat form for a big letter E, probably yellow. These letters are usually quite far apart and painted on the floor of the platform itself.

• Trains can come from the right or the left. (Métro trains always come from the left.)

• Trains in the countryside don't necessarily arrive on the track posted. Try to confirm with three different people.

• Loudspeakers often make announcements in the station when a train is arriving, making such a racket you can't hear them.

• Loudspeakers inside the TGV trains usually announce the stations. In the local or Corail express trains, they might, or might not, it depends. Don't ask me on what.

- Loudspeakers in French on the trains are as hard to understand as on the platforms. You're better off asking another passenger to tell you when your station is next. In any language. Just say the station name, distinctly, with a questioning look and "*s'il vous plaît?*"

SNCF vocabulary

conductor	contrôleur	en retard	late
train	train	suburban	banlieue
car	voiture	local	régional
section (of TGV)	rame	connecting train	correspondance
flip seat	strapontin	ticket	billet
long distance		to punch (a ticket)	composter
trains	Grandes Lignes	à l'heure	on time
luggage cart	caddie	station	gare

Chapter Nineteen

Enjoying Motoring Around France

Priorité à Droite!
Navigating *la France Profonde*

Each of the sites (you visit) should bring to life its age as does the Pont du Gard (near Nîmes) whose hugeness and classical proportions can overawe us today with the power and the rigid rationality of mighty Rome, as it did the Celtic barbarian two thousand years ago, or the Cathedral of Conques, whose Romanesque mystical beauty can make the most agnostic of us feel the Age of Faith. In other words, the site should possess that indefinable quality which makes us classify a work of man as Art, that quality which gives one of man's creations life enough to survive through the years, a quality that made it please not only the generation of its creator but future generations as well.

Ina Caro, *The Road from the Past*

Savoir-Flair Tip No. 183:
Don't drive after lunch or after 9:00 pm

Before you set off, some soothing words about driving in France. The autoroutes, secondary roads and even small, tertiary roads are excellent. They're practically empty, compared to UK roads. Many of the straight ones were created by the Romans, who paved over the roads of Gaul.

French drivers have swift reactions. What they're likely to do takes a little getting used to, and so do the regulations, which is why this chapter is crucial if you're planning to drive in France. Read it carefully and you'll be fine.

You may be worrying about what you've heard about France's high rate of accidents. First of all, there are not nearly as many per inhabitant as in Spain or Portugal. Secondly and most important, the Ministry of Transport finally got serious a few years ago about the cause of most of the accidents: speeding. In 1998 the government tightened up the laws and enjoined the police, especially the gendarmerie, to pursue the guilty mercilessly. Drivers caught speeding at 50 kilometers (30 miles) an hour over the authorized limit can face up to six months in jail and a fine of 50,000 francs ($8,200). Random breath tests are routine. This is locking up a lot of trouble. Results are already in: the numbers of road deaths in 1998 were down to around 8,000 from 13,787 in 1976. The Ministry is determined to grind those numbers down to 4,000 dead in one year by 2008.

Thirdly, most of those fatal accidents happen with drivers under 25, who drive too fast after drinking too much wine at lunch and dinner, and parties on Saturday night. Paris taxi drivers have told me they never work Saturday nights: "People come in from the suburbs who drive badly, or drink too much, and next thing you know, your car is smashed up."

Everyone in France eats lunch, and since lunchtime begins sometime between noon and 1:00 and lasts until 2:00 or 3:00, the trick of safe motoring is to drive when they're eating and not drive for an hour or two after they've finished. The same goes for dinner, which starts usually at 8:00 pm but can start as early as 7:00 pm or 7:30. It goes until 9:00, perhaps 10:00 pm.

Timing your long-distance driving according to French mealtimes makes it not only safer but also pleasanter. You have the roads to yourself.

No road rage

Maybe you've also heard that French drivers are aggressive. Aggressive? But road rage doesn't exist. No one whips out his pistol because you passed him on the wrong side or because your rap music is playing too loudly. No one whips out his pistol, period. Not even if you bash in his rear fender. Although he might be pretty upset. French people, particularly south of the Loire, are what Ande calls *soupe au lait*, or like a soup made with milk. They overflow instantly and dramatically. But only for a minute.

Savoir-Flair Tip No. 184:
In any sort of accident, never admit you're in the wrong

You're pretty sure to experience this if a Frenchman runs into your car with his, which happened to me near Périgueux in the Dordogne. There was no sign of a turnoff I was looking for. I decided to check my map. As I slowed down and turned, perhaps a little suddenly, onto the shoulder on the right, a huge truck rammed my left rear light. The driver slammed on the brakes, jumped out of his truck and strode towards me waving his arms fiercely. Showing lots of missing teeth, he shouted -- "harangued" is really the word -- that this was "unheard of," "unbelievable," he had "never seen such a thing," that I should learn how to drive, etc.

As the thing to do in France is never to admit you're even the tiniest bit in the wrong, I protested vehemently that it was I who was shocked and furious, he had been driving much too close, totally illegally, was he so blind he couldn't see my blinker, etc.

He stomped off back to his truck. When he returned with his car papers, he was quiet as a lamb. I noticed his clean, smartly pressed, elegant shirt and that he was quite attractive when the gaps in his teeth didn't show. He was politeness itself as we filled out the damage claims together, and when he saw that I had a Lauzun address nearby, he was transported with neighborly joy. We chatted about the charms of the Dordogne, and parted friends.

Spirited driving

The word I use for French drivers is spirited. Spirited driving is as inseparable from Frenchness as love, food, style and strikes, and believe me, it's addictive, even to foreigners (except maybe the British). You get to love it.

Edouard Zarifan, professor of psychiatry at the University of Caen, maintains that French road "aggressivity" (his word) is a result of the strict behavior codes of France and that inside their automobile is the one place that French people can let go, ignore the rules and do as they please.

"If the rules of savoir-vivre inhibit or channel a person's real nature, they disappear the moment this same person gets behind the wheel," Zarifan told *Le Figaro* (April 14, 1998). "There, he is alone with himself. He can behave according to his own temperament. Someone very courteous and civilized can become aggressive and rude. His car obeys him without other people interfering."

I personally think it's because they don't have enough sports -- if any -- during their school years. All that energy is crammed into their books. So when they grow up, it bursts out.

Americans are particularly tried by the Battle for the Parking Space. Zarifan explains that French people often identify themselves with their car.

"The less people are intellectually structured," he says, "the more they feel that the car is a part of themselves... and the more aggressive they

241

will be to people who compete for the same parking space, or the more likely they are to make a *queue de poisson* in front of someone whose driving displeases them."

A *queue de poisson* (a fish tail) is when a car passes you and then cuts in front of you, too close for comfort. You'll be tempted to show him you can do it even better, and more scarily. Which will inevitably stir his sense of competition. And so forth. Sometimes in the city, but truly not often, drivers get out of their cars and award victory to the strongest fists.

Remember that in France, rage comes out in a burst of words -- and then it's over. If you stay calm, you have the advantage.

Rent or lease?

If you're staying a month, or even less, leasing a car is the way to go. Less expensive. No restrictions on other people driving it. Total insurance against any mishaps (see my Cousin Anna's accident below).

The leasing system has also the advantage of anonymity. Not so, with rental cars. The two last digits of all French license plates end in the number of the *département* where the car is registered. Rental cars are almost always registered in the Marne, *département* No. 51, where the inspection stickers are the least expensive. *Donc*, as the French say, highway robbers are interested in a licence plate ending in 51, probably driven by unsuspecting foreigners. French authorities have taken note, and the 51-labeling is said to be on the way out. Until it is, be careful.

The accident of the Mississippians

My cousin Anna Packer, from Natchez, Mississippi and her sister Muff, an author known under the name of Ellen Douglas; their brother Dick Ayres and his wife Jo-Anne, all in their seventies, leased a Peugeot and rented a house in southern France in Uzès, north of Nîmes.

The car was fine and the house was fine, but on a two-lane *départementale* they had an accident. Dick was driving. Jo-Anne, navigating in the front seat, was looking for a turn-off to a small village. When she saw it, Dick made a sudden turn and landed in a ditch lined with concrete, the car on its side.

"It was quite a shock, so the first thing we did was to see if we were all o.k.," said Anna. "We were -- everyone had been buckled up. That was one thing. Getting out of the car was another. We couldn't."

Quite soon, two Frenchmen in different cars stopped. One had a mobile telephone and called the police and a wrecker. By the time they'd helped everyone out, the police had arrived, two men and one woman.

"The next minute an enormous wrecker arrived," Anna said, "with a big man driving it. He got out and looked at the car and shook his head -- walked around and shook his head some more."

None of the French people spoke English. The Americans couldn't speak French. Muff, with a few words of school French from years ago, managed to assure the police that everyone was o.k. and that no other car was involved.

Skillful French wreckers

Anna continued: "Finally the big man in the wrecker stopped shaking his head and went to work. He attached various ropes and very gently with remarkable skill, lifted the car out of the ditch.

"The police were grand -- they stayed the whole time, stopping traffic and generally helping and soothing us. We toasted the wrecker and the police for several days. When we got to the airport three weeks later, we had dents and scratches on the undercarriage and a big scratch on one of the fenders. The Europe by Car people didn't even LOOK at it. They said, 'You're fully covered by insurance.' I thought we were, but it was very nice to find it out."

Savoir-Flair Tip No. 185:
In strange towns, keep the doors locked and the windows rolled up

This tip is especially important in tourist areas like the Mediterranean.

Ande and I rented a car a while ago in Cannes. The concierge of a friend who had loaned us his apartment met us at the train from Paris, and showed us the way. Later in the dark, after dinner in a restaurant, Ande drove slowly trying to figure out where to go. In a few minutes we heard the screech of motorcycle tires stopping suddenly and found ourselves surrounded by a gang of four teenagers, obliging Ande to stop. Before I knew what was happening, my door was opened and one of the boys had grabbed my handbag from the floor next to my seat. I had just time to hang on to one of its two handles for dear life while Ande battled the boys in front and on his side. He put the car in gear and moved forward. This scared them. The boy tugging at my handbag fell back and they all drove off. The police next day sighed and said this happened frequently, usually French-born boys from the immigrant families in the hills of Valbonne.

Savoir-Flair Tip No. 186:
Keep your luggage out of sight in the trunk

Foreign license plates, of course, interest robbers the most. Charlotte Stone, a glamourous Scot from Inverness with glamorous luggage, drove her new Fiat from London to the French Riviera to visit various friends in October, 1999. In St. Tropez she stopped for three minutes in a boutique, locking her car first. Her luggage was visible in the back seat. When she came out, it was gone.

State Department warning

The U.S. Department of State hands out this warning to Americans driving in southern France (see Appendix for more):

Thefts from cars stopped at red lights and tollbooths are commonly reported, particularly in the Nice-Antibes-Cannes area, and in Montpellier and Marseille. The thief is usually a passenger on a motorcycle. Car doors should be locked at all times during travel and windows closed or left only slightly ajar.

Purse-snatching by motorcycle riders is also common in the area.

Savoir-Flair Tip No. 187:
Give cyclists enough room

When overtaking a bicycle, the legal margin you're supposed to leave between you and the cyclist is 1.5 meters. In town it's one meter.

Savoir-Flair Tip No. 188:
If renting, insist on maps, automatic shift and air-conditioning

A rental agency in a smallish town may not equip the car with a map. Insist on two: a map of France showing all the service stations on the auto routes, and a detail map of the special area you want to visit.

Also, specify that you want a car with automatic transmission. As you can see from the above, motoring in France is more fun in a car you feel comfortable with. You should also mention air conditioning.

Driving with Grace

Grace Anderson is a beautiful Chinese-American account executive with a big firm in Los Angeles. After buying a house recently in Belvès, in the Dordogne (southwest France), she ordered a powerful Mercedes for her vacation, with air-conditioning and automatic transmission. She had never driven a stick-shift car.

"I took the train down from Paris to Périgueux," she said. "When I showed up at the Hertz office there, I was given a 5-speed stick-shift Renault Twingo the size of a Harley Davidson with a roof. I had no idea how to drive it. The Hertz agent gave me an hour's lesson and off I went."

Grace's route from Périgueux to Belvès was by way of Brive and Sarlat. She drove very slowly, keeping behind trucks so as not to have to shift. Concentrating hard, she missed some signs. The first one she saw indicated that she was on N-89... for Bordeaux. That is, going in the opposite direction.

Since she didn't know how to go into reverse, she just kept going. Presently another sign informed her that she was on the road to Spain.

"At this point I decided that I didn't know where I was or where I was going, what difference did it make whether I was going to Spain or to hell," she told me on a later visit. "Then another sign said I was going towards Toulouse. It dawned on me that Toulouse was en route to Spain and Belvès was en route to Toulouse, so I might just as well keep going. Not that I made the other motorists very happy. If looks could have killed, the Twingo and I would be long since in a Renault graveyard."

Two days later, a friend found an automatic Peugeot for her in a local Belvès garage.

"I was delighted," she said. "The mechanic, Jacques, knew me and all about my house because he'd helped move in the furniture. Well, the car stalled within a few yards. And then again. It stalled at every stop. I filled up the gas tank but it still kept stalling. The next morning I had an appointment with Jacques to have the car serviced in the garage -- but it wouldn't even start.

"Jacques made a house call. Water was in the spark plugs. He said I had filled the gas tank with unleaded fuel instead of premium leaded. I told him that unleaded fuel was what the instructions manual in the car prescribed -- and he told me, well, fine, but that manual was not the manual for that car."

Where to motor to from Paris?

Hemingway knew how to get the most out of France... by mastering the French technique of letting moments unfold as they come. You simply rent a car and take off, with only the vaguest plan of where you want to go, stopping for meals wherever you feel delighted. The theory is that you can't go wrong in France. This technique doesn't appeal to most foreigners. They usually like to complete projects according to an advance analysis, if possible by someone who has been there before, for instance, Ina Caro. Her book, cited above, is a chronological revelation of France's marvels over the centuries. It is also a beguiling tale of her adventures driving about.

Savoir-Flair Tip No. 189:
As in Paris, the road coming from the right has priority
(*In case you skipped the part in Chapter 6 about driving in Paris*)

You're on a major road, a *nationale* and a car turns into it from the right, from a small road, without stopping. It is **your fault** if anything happens. **This is a most dangerous surprise for foreigners on French roads.**

Unless there is a traffic light, a stop sign, or a sign with a yellow triangle on your road, you must yield to the right.

"This *priorité à droite* still gets me -- after 10 years," said Amy Porter, head of European marketing for Sun Microsystems. "I'm on a big road, and at a crossroad, anyone coming from the right has the right of way -- no matter if it's a cowpath. Unless there is a stop sign, which practically doesn't exist. Same thing in a village or town. But woe to you if someone comes at you from the right and you didn't stop!"

If you're driving along a major road that has the priority, you may notice French cars roaring up to your road from a side road as if they're not going to stop. They do stop, finally, but not without making your heart stop first.

Savoir-Flair Tip No. 190:
Priorité à droite, except -- usually -- at roundabouts!

Roundabouts are the exception to *priorité à droite*. The priority is not to people coming from the right, but to the people already inside. Almost always.

There is a sign at the entrance to the roundabout indicating that the priority is not for the people entering. It says either "*vous n'avez pas la priorité,*" or "*cédez le passage.*" If you don't see the sign, then you're on your own.

Road and route signs: another French Mystery

Patricia Henderson of Kent, an experienced traveler, after driving around France with her husband, Robert, one summer. "I don't know how the Germans ever got to Paris," she said. "In the UK, you get on the M1 and keep going. The route signs match the maps. Not so in France. The route signs on the map are different from the route signs on the road. You'll come to a fork and both roads will have signs to the same place, or no sign at all. You end up pointing the car in the general direction and praying. We often ended up on a cowpath."

Savoir-Flair Tip No. 191:
Memorize all the towns for 200 km in the direction you're going

My niece, Karen Dondero, a judge in Chester County, Pennsylvania, motored from Paris to southwest France, with her husband, David Dondero, driving, the two children in the back seat. Before leaving they equipped themselves with various guides and special detailed Michelin maps.

"Americans navigate by direction," she said. "All our major routes have signs with numbers and directions of the compass at important intersections. You take U.S. 1 South and simply keep on it, no problem. The signs on the road always exactly correspond to the numbers on your map.

"The problem for us in France was that since the numbers indicated on the map very often do not tally with the signs out there on the roads, I just couldn't find where we were going. I had to ask David to pull up on the side at every roundabout. None of the signs seemed right. Finally I figured out the system. It's according to place-names, not directions. The logic of where the place-signs are put is something I haven't figured out yet. They will sometimes direct you to a place and then the signs for it will disappear long before you get there. Basically, they drop you in the middle of nowhere and offer a whole other menu of destinations. So the system is, you memorize *all* towns of any size for about 200 kilometers between where you are and where you want to go, and about 200 others for the places you *don't* want to go to."

André Leroy agrees. He's French, but has lived in Detroit for 20 years, and lost some of the knack of Frenchness. "There's a Hansel-and-Gretel element to driving around France," he said. "There are masses of often meaningless route signs, but that's not the problem, it's the town signs. The town signs are everywhere -- the sign budget here must be enormous -- but they're not consistent. Almost as if they're playing a game with you -- will you really get where you're going? -- and someone is taking bets. First, it takes quite a while to get used to where they're pointing. Left or straight? Hard left or sort of left? And while I'm

accustomed to the system -- that you go by town signs, not route signs ---
the worst is that you'll be going along according to three different towns
and then they drop one of them -- the one you need -- or else there are no
signs at all. We often felt forgotten. You know, all alone in the dark woods."

For foreigners with hazy memories for French names, Tom McTigue
has the answer. Copy all the towns ahead on Post-It Notes and stick them
on the steering wheel or the dashboard. If you get confused somewhere,
you can unstick a likely Post-It and take it with you to show someone when
you ask for help. Plus, no worries about your pronunciation.

As you might expect, French people have no problem with the signs.
"If it's a sunny day, I keep an eye to the sun," says author Sylvie Couturié.
"If it's on my left in the afternoon, I'm going West." Yes, but if there's no
sun? "Oh well, I ask, someone will know."

Savoir-Flair Tip No. 192:
Heed speed limits - French radar works!

The big fuss being made about speeding includes a New Age radar
that could track a grasshopper. The speed limits are simple: 130 km an hour
(90 miles an hour) on autoroutes, 90 km on other roads, and 50 km in
villages. How much you can safely add to these speed limits depends on
the time of day, whether it's a national holiday and how near
dinner time it is.

French autoroutes are built for these legal high speeds and consequently are in better physical condition than American roads. So French drivers don't hesitate to gun their cars up to speeds that put newly-arrived American passengers into shock. Newell Wright told of his parents shrinking into the back seat when he drove them to Normandy. After Ande drove a visiting friend of mine out to the country for the weekend at 100 miles an hour, she refused to drive back with us. She took the train.

Flashing lights

If a car flashes his lights coming towards you on a *nationale* or a secondary road, slow down. Gendarmes are hiding in bushes up ahead. They're particularly strict about the speed limits in villages. At lunchtime and after 6 pm they're usually less vigilant.

Traffic lights

Traffic lights in France look different. They're positioned on posts on the side of roads and streets, not hanging from central overhead cables, as in the U.S. The colors can be quite faint. Sometimes you can't see the red. Or the green, for that matter. Gail Chaddock went through two red lights driving around the Dordogne before she figured out where and how to look for them.

What kind of gasoline/petrol?

Sally Lipscomb and her husband Jay, a geologist in air-pollution consulting in Chicago, began their first month-long trip in France with a French-English dictionary, very little French, and lots of enthusiasm.

"We were very excited," said Sally. "We hadn't been here since our honeymoon and backpack-bicycle days."

They rented a car at Charles de Gaulle Airport and headed north for Lille. It started getting dark. They worried about running low on gasoline/petrol. They still had quite a drive ahead, so they pulled into a self service station. It was closing. The man inside the office, however, nodded to them.

Jay found himself facing an array of pumps with different names and *liter* prices in green and blue. When he figured out what the francs meant in dollars, and that a *liter* -- one-fourth a gallon -- cost the same as a gallon in the U.S., he made a beeline for the cheapest. He filled up the tank, paid for it and took off.

After about two kilometers, the car started jerking and sputtering and hissing. Smoke billowed up from the motor. Jay groaned. He realized he'd put diesel -- *gasoil* -- into the tank instead of regular or super.

There were some exciting minutes as they jerked and sputtered their way back to the service station, wondering if they'd make it, and if so, if anyone would still be there. And then, how to explain without speaking French.

The station was still open. The owner came out to see what was up.

"I took out my tiny dictionary," said Sally, "and after looking up 'smoke', I said 'FUMER!' and pointed."

"FUMER!" echoed the owner. He threw up his hands and rushed excitedly to take the pan apart.

"He was so nice, " said Sally. "And he refused to let us pay!"

Savoir-Flair Tip No. 193:
Memorize on-duty hours for service stations

In rural France, service stations probably close for lunch, at 7:00 pm weekdays and all day on Sunday, holidays and perhaps Monday as well. In rural France, you might find one open at lunchtime in a town, but never in a village.

I know this, of course, but the gasoline/petrol indicator on our car doesn't work. Ande is usually the one who drives it and he has a mysterious instinct about the gas/petrol level. Last summer I was driving a friend, Frances Jones, a young Doubleday editor from New York, to a Buddhist center isolated in the Dordogne countryside. The center is not far from our place, but not that near either. I knew the gas/petrol was low, and planned to get some in Duras, a town on the way. However, before that, there was a meandering detour through empty countryside on a road hardly even marked on my local detail map. The car stalled at a crossroad in the middle of a forest. It started up, but only just.

At the next crossroad it stalled again. Panic. What if the car didn't start this time? No mobile phone, a 5-kilometer walk to the next village, and Frances missing her lecture. The car did start, but only just. We decided to try to borrow some gasoline/petrol and hailed an approaching tractor. The attractive young farmer inside politely regretted that he had no extra fuel. Behind the tractor was a beaten-up old red Peugeot with an elderly bearded driver. I hailed him too. He told me solemnly, no smiles, that he thought he had some petrol at home, but that was in the other direction. Right now he was going to get his son. Then he would turn around and go home and have a look. Where was his son? How far away? He didn't say. No other cars were likely to come by: it was lunchtime.

We settled in for a long wait, but it was just a few minutes later when the beaten-up old red Peugeot came back, heading in the other direction, with the young farmer of the tractor sitting next to the driver. (So the tractor driver was his son.) The bearded driver nodded to us as he drove by.

"Do you think he'll come back, even if he doesn't find any gas, and tell us?" asked Frances.

"He'll come back with some, somehow," I said. "Matter of honor. Two foreign women stranded in *la France profonde*? Of course he'll rescue us."

Not 15 minutes later the old red Peugeot reappeared, with father and son inside. They got out of the car perfectly equipped with jerry can and siphon. The son held the siphon while his father poured the petrol into my car, with a certain amount of ceremony. He then explained that he hadn't found any petrol at home after all, but had gone to borrow some from a neighbor.

I fished around for some coins for the neighbor, and then we all shook hands, or tried to. The son was shy. He shook my hand, but Frances was young and beautiful and he couldn't look at her.

Savoir-Flair Tip No. 194:
Always have plenty of cash for emergencies

Tom McTigue, driving through Burgundy, had forgotten about Sundays in the French countryside. With a petrol tank nearly empty, he passed one closed (*fermé*) service station after another. Finally he found one that was open, sort of. Of the six pumps, one was functioning, but only on credit cards, Visa and Master Card. Tom was ready for it with a Visa card, but the pump spat it back. Tom was ready for that too, with a second Visa card, a backup he'd used successfully at stores the day before. However, the Sunday pump didn't like that one either.

Now, what? Kick the pump and break your toe? Wait for Monday? Not Tom. He went to talk to the man in the car behind him. He carefully introduced himself with the Magic Words and proposed borrowing his Visa card in exchange for francs. The Frenchman handed over his Visa card. The pump accepted it. Tom filled up his tank and returned the card to the Frenchman with the right amount of francs, and drove off, tickled at having triumphed over another French challenge.

More Savoir-Flair Tips for driving:

Gasoline/petrol at bargain prices

At all *grandes surfaces* (super and hyper-markets): Leclerc, Intermarché, Carrefour, etc

Buying gasoline/petrol

Gasoil is diesel

In green letters: super *sans plomb* is unleaded (*plomb* is lead)

In blue letters: *super* (leaded unless marked *sans plomb*)

Service stations hours

- Closed at lunch time in rural France, except at the big super-and hypermarchés like Intermarché and Leclerc, where, like the village gas stations, they close at 7:00. Only big towns will have one open at night, and probably not all night.
- Closed all day Sundays except in big towns.
- But on autoroutes: open at lunchtime, all night and Sundays.

Car rentals

Renting is less expensive if arranged outside France. All international car rental firms, e.g., Hertz, Avis, Budget etc. will do international bookings from your country of origin on their central toll-free numbers.

- Be sure you arrange in the U.S. for the second driver and check with the French office where you pick up the car, or you may be charged more.
- Ask for air-conditioning and automatic transmission or you probably will not get either.
- Be sure you know the name of your rental company and where to find it at the airport. Julianne Guthrie couldn't find hers at Charles de Gaulle Airport; they subcontracted to another agency at the airport, with a different name, but didn't tell her.

Car insurance

- Based on your age, the number of years you have been driving and how many accidents you had. This doesn't show on an American driver's license, so have this information available just in case.
- The French government discourages foreign imports in various ways. One of them concerns specific regulations for size of headlights, etc. Your car, if you bring it over, must be changed to suit these French regulations. Lynn Kelley went through this and doesn't recommend it.

U.K. Driver's licenses

Britons assume that as members of the European Union, their driver's license is valid. Technically this is so, but local police may not accept it if you're caught speeding or not wearing your seatbelt, etc. French licenses now have points, and you might have to deal with this.

U.S Driver's licences

U.S. citizens need a French license after living in France for more than one year. Then, even if you've been driving for 30 years, getting one means going to a French driving school for an expensive series of lessons -- yes, really -- and then taking a police exam. It's made hard to pass on purpose, since you pay more each time. I know lots of Americans who have failed it more than once, even three times, after having driven in the U.S. for 20 years. American rage at this system has had an effect in a few states, which now have a reciprocal agreement with the French government accepting each others' driving licenses: Connecticut, Florida, Illinois, Kansas, Kentucky, Michigan, New Hampshire, Pennsylvania, and South Carolina. Residents of these states just exchange their licenses for French ones, avoiding the lessons and the exam. The American Embassy in Paris and the French Embassy in Washington are trying to persuade the other states to go along.

• The Fehrenbach driving school in Suresnes gives lessons in English and arranges for students to take the written exam with a translator. Tel. 01 45 06 31 17

On the autoroutes

French autoroutes are supplied with frequent pleasant wooded areas for relaxing during a long drive (as well as service stations). These rest-stops may have changing tables and disposable diapers for babies, courtesy of Nestlé, as well as play grounds. Many of them have restaurants or snack bars.

Chapter Twenty

Enjoying Rural Cycling

The Tour de France with Paul Salacain
A Television Producer's Adventure in Cannes

Rien n'est excessif, tout y est modéré, le climat, les saisons, les formes. Tout y semble obéir au souci d'un être invisible de proportionner les rapports entre les collines et les plaines, les labours et les pâturages, les rivières et les bois... tout y ramène l'esprit à des équilibres stables, aussi éloignés d'un lyrisme sans contre-poids que d'un réalisme sans échappées.

(Nothing is excessive, everything is tempered, the climate, the seasons, the forms. Everything seems to obey an invisible being ordering the harmony of hills and plains, fields and pastures, rivers and woods... so that the spirit itself is in harmonious balance, as far from the extremes of lyricism as from realism without vision.)

Elie Faure, *Découverte de l'archipel*

Savoir-Flair Tip No. 195:
Knowing what motorists are likely to do might save your life

France created the Tour de France, the most televised and tele-watched spectacle in the world. Year after year since 1903 it has been the home of "The Tour," a solid month of excruciating fast cycling, not just up hill and down dale, but up mountains, *steep* mountains with 11% inclines, and then -- even more strenuous -- down again, faster, always faster around hairpin turns, sometimes slippery in the rain. Winning it is one of the ambitions of healthy young Frenchmen. Also of Americans. Lance Armstrong won it in 1999, the first American in an all-American team to do so.

Twenty million French people own bicycles, one-third of the population. French children grow up on them. Later, many commute to work on them. They take their families on biking trips. There are special biking maps for routes all over the country, with suggestions where to stay, no matter what your purse. There are biking associations and biking tour groups. There are many excellent tertiary roads -- marked D on your map -- with very little traffic except tractors. The Ile de Ré, a small island off the coast of La Rochelle popular for summer vacations, numbers 40 bike rental shops, one of them with 900 rental bikes.

Right now, a handsome young French fireman called Alain Soulat is touring the world by bike with his wife Sylvie and their four-year-old son, whose name is pretty tour-promising: Aymeric-Ulysse. They set out from Angoulême, in western France. At 50 kilometers per day, they reached Seoul, South Korea, in the summer of 1998, where Aymeric-Ulysse was caught by an Agence France Presse photographer. Behind his mother and father, on a tandem bike, the little boy is sitting up proudly between duffel bags in a bike-trailer, holding his pet bear. They hope to make it through five continents by 2001.

See Chapter 6 on cycling and motoring in Paris and Chapter 19 on motoring in the provinces. It's important to know what French drivers are going to do, and what the regulations are.

Savoir-Flair Tip No. 196:
You need front and rear reflectors for dark or foggy rural roads

Country roads are dark and may be foggy. Early morning mist can be dense, as well as beautiful. It often rains. There are no streetlights in the countryside; you and your bike are much harder to see than in the city. The mandatory headlight and front and rear reflectors are really important for your survival, even in the daytime.

Otherwise, the regulations and warnings for country biking are the same as for the city. But it's a lot more fun. The air is lovely, the landscapes are charming, and you feel popular. The French love cross-country bikers.

American bicycle associations are overbooked for tours to France. Lyn and Bob Petricca, from Lenox, Mass., took a popular Canadian tour, Butterfield and Robinson, from Toronto, around Provence and loved every minute. They were in good shape after cycling the Berkshires.

"We found out all kinds of things we didn't know," said Lyn. "For instance, how they grow that delicious white asparagus. The moment the shoots show above the ground, they pile earth on them. They keep piling on the earth as the shoots grow, until they decide they're high enough."

Roberta and Lou Nucci, from Williamsburg, Virginia, signed up for a tour around Burgundy, also with Butterfield and Robinson. There were 22 people in five groups of various ages, including two retired businessmen and a judge in his 70's. Where they were going was sometimes a little confusing, sort of on the order of: Go to the oak tree and turn left; but that was part of the fun.

In Roberta's own words:

> Butterfield and Robinson's motto is "slow down and see the world." They think they're the world's premier biking company and they may be. They're expensive, but you definitely get what you pay for. We have loved our trips. It's sort of "shack elegance"! You're casual and comfy all day (bike clothes and helmet!) and you can look forward to a wonderful evening of French wine and "bonne cuisine." And you can "eat the whole thing" because you EARNED it!
>
> The guides are young, vivacious, knowledgeable, well-trained, and ready to do anything to make your trip everything you want. The accommodations vary -- all are 4-star; some are 4+. Each place offers average to extravagant rooms and they try to rotate people, so that we all have one of the best and one of the not so best! The Château de Bagnols is a 15th-century château and is one of the most unique and lovely places any-one could have the pleasure of visiting. Last year we had a "Hollywood" room at Château de la Treyne. Both of our trips have included one or two hotels in the Relais and Châteaux category.
>
> I think the French love bikers! We were always well received... even when we stopped for lunch at a quaint, colorful country inn, where normally I would never have stopped, if I weren't "properly dressed." I mean... knowing the French!! One little village we were entering, I remember a gentleman standing at his front door, raising his fist and shouting, "Bravo Bravo!" as the 14 of us pedaled by! I loved that.
>
> One of my memories of this past trip in Burgundy is looking ahead at the bikers (I was usually LAST) in their colorful attire -- they looked like a snake, circumventing the beautiful, immaculate, rolling hills and vineyards. Absolutely breathtaking vistas!

I asked Roberta to sum it up and she said right away, "I can't wait to do another one next year. The highlights? Beautiful food preparation. Marvelous ambiance. The beauty of the French countryside, stone fences, quaint houses, cattle, sheep, rolling hills, pristine vineyards... very little litter. The charm of the French villages. I loved using my French; I think I'm getting better!"

Paul Salacain, the engineer from Maine with the Heidelberg Web Press mentioned earlier, joined a different tour. Paul is a runner. The kind who runs every day for miles and miles and competes in 5-mile races. But Heidelberg Web sent him to France, and Carol, his wife, whom we met in Chapter 6, dreamt of living in central Paris. The running he'd been doing in Maine was clearly out for a while. He bought a bicycle. He hadn't been on a bike since he was 18. He loved it.

He began thinking about the Tour de France. After all, *he was in France*. Well, maybe he wasn't really in shape to join it. At 46, a little beyond the age, not much experience. He thought about it a lot, on his daily bike rides in Paris. He longed to at least really see it, up front, like a racer.

When he heard that Breaking Away Bicycle Tours from California brought groups over from the U.S. to *follow* the Tour de France, Paul signed up.

"It was great," he said. "Our leader was known as the 'Tour Nazi.' Tough, that is. He had to be. There were 40 of us, with 40 bikes we kept in our hotel rooms. The system was that we loaded the bikes in vans at 6:30, breakfasted until 7:15, checked out of the hotel and left in the vans to wherever our day's biking start was. We would do a long ride, 50 kilometers or so, biking over different terrain than the Tour, each of us with a map, and then bike over to the Tour route, getting there about two hours ahead of the Tour. The routes would be closed to the general public, but as we were on bikes, we got through.

"When the tour began arriving, it was really something. First the publicity caravans came through with the sponsors, they'd throw out all kinds of things to the crowds, key chains and hats -- one even threw out video cassettes. Around 200 of these vehicles. Then about an hour later, the Tour riders came along. A real rolling event. The television cameramen were on motorcycles -- two men to a motorcycle. The still photo people were also on motorcycles, about 100 of them. A helicopter hovered above.

"In a few days we were in the Pyrénées. We had to go over a lot of mountains with an 8-11% grade. I'd never biked on mountains before. At first, I put up too much effort, pushed too hard and my heart was going much too fast. I had to learn to go more slowly, as slowly as possible. Getting to the top of the Col d'Aubisque was really something for me -- that's a peak of 1,710 meters and a grade of 11 %."

At first, when they got to the top of the Col d'Aubisque, it was so foggy they couldn't see the racers coming. It started raining.

"Suddenly we saw them," said Paul, "just before the top, and then going down -- like bats out of hell. The route was very twisty, the rain made it slippery -- so it was very dangerous and they were falling all over the place.

"Then it was time for us to go down. That was the hardest. The Tour Nazi warned us several times. The rain had made it terribly slippery. Really something. Our group were of all different levels, everything from a triathlete to women in their fifties to a guy who just quit smoking. Well, we all made it. It was exhausting, it was taxing, but I loved every minute. It was almost as good as being part of the Tour itself."

France is equipped with bikes. You can rent them in most towns, big or small, and most big SNCF stations. If you own one, you can take it with you on certain trains if you have a bike case, or you can ship it separately south or west or wherever you want to be, via the SNCF. (You can also ship your car on the SNCF.) However, it's not as simple as it sounds.

Savoir-Flair Tip No. 197:
Check different SNCF bike-carrying rules for different trains

Ship your bike separately only if you feel absolutely certain where it is going and how you'll find it again.

Robert Lovenheim and his Road Warrior

Robert Lovenheim, a television producer, goes regularly to the Cannes Film Festival. He discovered years ago that renting a bike and snaking around the cars was the best way to finesse the annual gridlock traffic jams on the way to the screenings.

Until the 1998 festival he never took his own. It's a special Holland bike that he loves, cherishes, and guards. He keeps it *inside* his apartment in Paris, where he lives when he's not in Los Angeles.

"Holland bikes are Road Warriors in Europe," he said. "You sit up high and look out at the traffic while the solid frame and the big tires give you the security of believing you can take on anything."

Robert missed his Road Warrior in Cannes. When a friend gave him an SNCF brochure called *Guide du Train et de la Bicyclette* proclaiming that bicycles were "welcome on trains" and "easy and inexpensive" to ship anywhere in France and pick up the next day, Robert jumped at it.

The day before his train left for Cannes, he took his bike to the Gare de Lyon. At the Information desk, he was waved off towards what he assumed was the location of the SNCF bike shipping office.

"I couldn't see any sign of it," he said. "In halting French I asked another SNCF employee where I might *expédier mon velo*. He said something that sounded like 'surname' and pointed to the area back behind the station. Why would he want to know my last name, I wondered, and why wasn't the office in the station?"

Finally, blocks away, Robert found a dirty brick warehouse with a large "Sernam" sign.

"I took another look at the brochure," he said. "Yes, it did say the bike service was provided at Sernam centers. However, that vital information was missing from the section in English."

Several employees were standing around the warehouse. As soon as they saw his bike, one of them produced a gigantic cardboard carton. Two men lifted the Road Warrior inside it. Robert filled out a form for expediting the bike to Cannes, signed it, and paid 100 francs. In 10 minutes he was on his way with a receipt tucked in his knapsack. At Cannes the next day, he walked into the baggage room and confidently handed over his receipt.

"They stared at the receipt, they stared at me," he said. "No bike was there, they said. I insisted it must be there. They invited me to look around for myself. No bike. I asked when it would arrive. That night? The next day?

"Never," they told him. "Cannes doesn't have a Sernam freight warehouse."

Robert pointed out that Cannes was clearly marked on the receipt. At this, one of them, the boss, blew up. He kept hitting the paper with his hand as he complained loudly to his companion. Finally he picked up the phone, dialed somebody, and went on raging at whomever was at the other end. After 20 minutes and several more phone calls, he handed the receipt back to Robert with a triumphant look. He had found the bike. It was in St. Roch.

Where was St. Roch? Near Nice, they said, and added that it could not be brought to Cannes. *Impossible.* There was no Sernam warehouse closer to Cannes. But he could "easily" go to St. Roch, which was "just beyond" Nice, by taking the train to Riquier, and then walking the mile to St. Roch.

Fine. Luckily Robert had a friend in Cannes who drove him to St. Roch. The Road Warrior was safely waiting. They loaded it and drove back to Cannes.

"For the next 10 days," Robert said, "I was the envy of movie stars and megamillionaires caught in hour-long traffic jams along the Croisette as I glided by on my trusty Holland. Their drivers raged over parking spaces. I locked my bike to sidewalk grills, and never walked more than 10 paces."

Then the Festival was over, and glory with it. The Road Warrior had to be sent back. Robert's friend with the car had gone home. Still, Robert was confident. By now he was an SNCF-Sernam expert.

He picked up an SNCF timetable and plotted his itinerary by train to Nice and Riquier, so as to arrive at St. Roch before Sernam closed for lunch. And then back to Cannes.

But three minutes after he boarded the train for Nice with his bike, he was ordered off by three SNCF conductors. It was forbidden to take bikes on trains, they said. Their advice? Take a bus. With a bicycle? Yes. Paris buses never take bikes, but long distance buses take bicycles, if they have space in the luggage area. He caught a bus to Nice in time to bicycle to the

Sernam office at St. Roch. He filled out the paper work, left the bike, and hiked the half-hour back to Riquier where he boarded the commuter train back to Cannes.

Just for fun, in Cannes he went to the SNCF information kiosk and asked if it was possible to take a bike on any of the regional trains. "Certainly, sir, you can take bicycles on all regional trains," he was told.

More Rural Biking Savoir-Flair Tips

Taking bikes with you on trains

This is very complicated, as you can see from Robert's adventure.

• There are different rules, times, etc. for short-distance regional trains (*trains régionaux*), long-distance trains (*trains grandes lignes*), TGV and express trains (*Corail*). Try to find someone at the SNCF who knows. If you have a bike bag, you have some chance of being able to take it with you.

• Sometimes the conductors don't know themselves whether bicycles are allowed on their train. Then they say "no" automatically. If you are sure of your position (because you have something written, for instance), they will probably let you. It was actually a *grande ligne* train coming from the north that refused Robert and his bike. But the train timetable makes no distinction between regional and national trains, so there was no way he could have known, even if he'd known that the rules were different. The three conductors who ejected him and suggested he take a bus never mentioned that the commuter trains took bikes, and that one would be coming about 20 minutes later. See Chapter 8, Enjoying Getting Information.

Tour operators around France

All of the tour operators below are luxuriously upmarket. However, La Bicyclette Gourmande will custom design budget trips. All arrange for your luggage to follow you to your hotel room. La Bicyclette Gourmande - Alsace offers 2-, 3- and 4 -star trips to Alsace, Provence, Normandy, Switzerland and Italy. You can custom-design your trip, with or without a guide.

• Breaking Away Bicycle Tours Inc,
1147 Manhattan Avenue, Suite 253, Manhattan Beach, Calif. 90266
tel. 310-545 5118, fax 310-545 6625, e-mail: breakinga@aol.com

• Butterfield and Robinson, Toronto

• Backwoods Tours, San Francisco

• La Bicyclette Verte
tel. (33) 5 49 35 42 56, fax. (33) 5 4935 42 55,
web site: http://www.bicyclette-verte.com

Cycling clubs
- Fédération Française de Cyclotourisme: liaison for France's 2800 cycling clubs. Write to them in advance and they'll send you everything you need in English.
8 rue Jean-Marie Jégo, 75013Paris
tel. (33) 1 44 16 88 88, fax. (33) 1 44 16 88 99

Biking vocabulary

vélo	bicycle (much more used than bicyclette)
casque	helmet
roue	wheel
pneu	tire
chambre à air	inner tube
selle	seat
frein	brake
antivol	bike lock
pompe	pump
changements de vitesse:	gears
cataphote	reflector
guidon	handlebars
huile	oil
faire du vélo	go bicycling

Chapter Twenty One

Enjoying the French Countryside

La France Profonde: The Dordogne
The New English Colony

This year... there will be short trips and, I hope, plenty of them, but I am trying to spend the entire year within the boundaries of France. I shall still be able to visit different countries -- the Loire, the Camargue, the Auvergne, Gascony -- and should I feel a particular urge for Alps, beaches, forests, museums, cathedrals or Roman remains, the geography and history of France can provide them all in glorious abundance. And then, of course, there's the food.

Peter Mayle,The International Herald Tribune

We others, good Americans, are too inclined to identify France with Paris... France is perhaps Paris, but Paris is not France.

Henry James, A Little Tour in France

Savoir-Flair Tip No. 198:
Pick a village and linger

Paris is Paris, and there is only one Paris, and Paris is many things to many people, but Paris wouldn't be Paris without the immense diversity of rural rhythms and harmonies surrounding it. Now that you've mastered the complexities of the capital, and of circulating by car and TGV, you deserve the crowning treat..*la France profonde*. The only problem is *l'embarras du choix* -- the rich choice Peter Mayle mentioned above.

An Alp or a Pyrenee? Or the tall pines and Germanic order of the Savoie, l'Alsace and la Lorraine? Perhaps the wheat plains and wide skies of the Beauce, or the ocean waves, oysters and stern architecture of

Brittany... the exuberant grandeur of the châteaux on the Loire or the rugged, wooded emptiness and craters of the Auvergne, the vineyards of Burgundy, the hedgerows, grazing horses and whitewashed fences of Normandy, the olive trees, cypresses and Roman ruins of Provence, the sands of the Mediterranean, the perfumes of Grasse, the medieval fortresses and the prehistoric caves of the Dordogne. All this to choose from and much more, not overlooking the mysteries of the soaring medieval rock churches at Mont Saint-Michel and at Rocamadour, the inspired piety of the Cathedrals of Chartres and Conques, and the pilgrim churches on the road to Saint Jacques de Compostelle.

All of these places were settled up to 2,000 or more years ago by the ancestors of the people living there now. Whether Basque, Languedoccian, Alsatian, Burgundian, Norman, Provençal or Gascon, they evolved their own traditions, their own way of speaking, their own way of building churches, fortresses, castles, villages and houses, depending on the material at hand, the taste of the ruler, the period and the state of the art of the weapons of war; and their own cuisine from the kinds of food, depending on what grew best.

To Julian Green, an American member of the Académie Française whose first language was French, you have to *waste* time in a place to know it well, to see into its life and soul. How to start? Camping or renting, the important thing is that you base yourself in one place, where you get to know its sounds and smells... and the local people.

Where?

If you speak only English and prefer not renting from a French person, why not rent from an "Anglo -Saxon?" A good place to find a rental is in American university alumni magazines or in *The Lady* (London).

Jack Wallace, a cardiologist of Galveston, and his wife Sally, my old friend from Wellesley, were undecided about exactly where to go in France. They found an ad in the Yale alumni magazine for a château with a swimming pool in the Gers, in southwestern France close to the Pyrenees. It sounded just right for housing their children, their children's spouses and in-laws, their grandchildren -- and friends. They rented it sight unseen from Americans in July 1999. The fax and telephone lines kept getting mixed up and the washing machines weren't always perfect, but the salons, kitchen, bathrooms and, above all, the location were. They had only an hour's drive to watch their fellow Texan Lance Armstrong boiling down the mountain on his bike, on his way to being the first American leading an all-American team to win the Tour de France.

Renting in an area popular with English people has the advantage of English-speaking facilities abounding. The English have had about 1,000 years of experience with various parts of France, which almost became English several times. Their national sport may be complaining about these historical rivals -- and ridiculing them whenever possible -- the "Froggies," whom they call their "hereditary enemies," but France is where they go, some on vacation, some to retire, many for good. They go to Normandy, they go to Provence, they go to Burgundy. And an awful lot of them go to the Dordogne, a *département* deep in southwest France near Bordeaux, in the *région* of Aquitaine.

They discovered the Dordogne about 800 years ago. In fact, in their imperial English sublimity, they will tell you that, really, old boy, the Dordogne -- and all of Aquitaine -- is English, not French at all, except, well, legally, you know... It's been their own property ever since Eleanor of Aquitaine, who inherited it from her father the Duke, took it back from her former husband, the King of France, and handed it over to the future Henry II of England when she married him in 1152. Later the French wanted Aquitaine back, so the English and the French fought over it on and off for 100 years, during what is known as the The Hundred Years War. The French finally won this war in various decisive battles; the one in the Southwest was at Castillon-La-Bataille, near Bergerac. Now the whole village dresses up 10 times every summer for a son et lumière resurrection of this victorious last battle against the English in 1453. Don't miss it if you're in the neighborhood.

After 1453 the English pretty much forgot about Aquitaine until the 1980's, when a popular French movie called *Les Visiteurs* (*The Visitors*), filmed at the Château de Beynac, a medieval fortress on the Dordogne river, reminded them of it. They began trooping back to Aquitaine. In due course, I landed there myself with my family, in a centuries-old farmhouse. So, because I know it the best, this chapter indicates ways to approach the heart of a village in the Dordogne, but you could replace it with any *département* in France.

Our village, Eymet, is a bastide, or fortified village built during the The Hundred Years War. It's in the midst of farming country, rolling green hills, tilled fields and vineyards. The weekly market sells local fresh fruit and vegetables that taste the way they're supposed to, foie gras that was made four fields down the road, animals raised nearby, forests with truffles and those delectable mushrooms called *cèpes*. No tourist buses, and, in fact, few cars. The only traffic jams on the roads around Eymet are when two tractors are trying to pass a corn picker.

265

Uneven white stone arcades with varying arches, some peaked, some rounded, some wide, some narrow enclose three sides of Eymet's central square. Above them are low one-story 13th-century houses with soft brown or light blue shutters. The fourth side of the square doesn't have stone arches, but rickety-looking stilts holding up crossbeams trying to be arches, some of the stilts seriously buckling as if they might not make it much farther than the millennium. One of the timbered one-story houses above them has a crossbeam that is supposed to be horizontal, but which heads slightly downhill as well as across, as if the mason went out for a beer and forgot about it.

When you look at them for a while, the houses seem to be winking at you with wacky medieval jokes -- unmatching windows, lopsided or cut in half, the way a six-year-old might draw them or make a cutout of them, next to windows with ornately sculpted ogival frames. A small tower juts suddenly out of a corner wall, a wooden balcony sags like a hammock. One of the houses has a steeply pointed roof, others are flatter, one is topped with something that looks like an upturned hull. Chimneys stick up from almost anywhere. The whole uneven jumble has an aesthetic unity that reminds me of top-class modern fashion designers. It's as if the builder of each house said, I'm doing my own thing and it's not going to be anything like yours -- much crazier and much more splendid -- but it will have the same theme and the same tone, a sort of sister feeling of all of us holding hands around the central fountain.

Savoir-Flair Tip No. 199:
Check that the amenities are what you want

The area around Eymet offers medieval châteaux, caves painted 20,000 years ago, and sports galore: cycling, rowing, canoeing, swimming, tennis, cricket, rugby, horseback riding. In nearby Bergerac you can ride down the Dordogne in a barge. Three golf clubs are in the area, at Castelnaud, Tombe Boeuf and Le Vigier.

The main clubhouse of Le Vigier, a 16th-century château built by the Duke of Toulouse, is a hotel for club guests. On the grounds are small houses and apartments built by foreign club members digging in for a few weeks a year. The greens are surrounded by vineyards supervised by a prize-winning oenologist. A swimming pool, massage parlors, tennis courts and a restaurant are grouped around the renovated 16th century farm buildings. Its founder and director is a Swede who went to the Harvard Business School. Tired of traffic jams whenever he wanted to play golf on the Riviera (the *Midi*, to the French), he told me he'd searched all over southern France for a non-touristy place with good weather. He picked this area because it was practically unknown, only one degree less warm than Marseille with just as many sunny days, and only two hours from a big city with an international airport, Bordeaux.

"I told my classmates at the Harvard Business School about it and sixty signed up to invest," he said in his office at Le Vigier.

The Castelnaud golf is similar to Le Vigier. Many of our French neighbors find them both too chic, too international and too expensive. They play at the more informal, more rustic golf course in Tombe Boeuf.

The Eymet cricket club was started by Richard Crow, a smooth-looking and beetle-browed Englishman with a ready grin somewhat resembling Tony Blair's. Crow bought a farmhouse and restored it with his own hands, as well as assorted other buildings on the property which he rents out to tourists.

Gareth Mulloy, formerly a British civil servant in Hong Kong, retired in 1997 to nearby Duras and organized and heads the DOG, the Dordogne Organization of Gentlemen, a men's weekly luncheon club with guest speakers that meets in Bergerac. Mulloy also supplies another welcome asset, a lending library of books in English.

Savoir-Flair Tip No. 200:
Knowing what's going on locally makes you a part of a place

Another Englishman, Clin Bond, about as charming as the other Bond called James, founded an English-language monthly newspaper, *The News*, in Eymet. English, a former hotel manager from Dorset, he has reduced his *News* contribution to a spicy column, but *The News* itself continues to report on what the French government is doing in Paris, what the regional Aquitaine and departmental Dordogne officials are doing locally, what's on at the Bordeaux opera, which towns are holding which fairs, advice on gardening; and perhaps most important, letters to the editor describing the problems of other English-speaking residents and how they've solved them.

Savoir-Flair Tip No. 201:
Get someone local to fill you in on the officials and tradespeople

In every French village there is one person who knows everything about everyone, who can move mountains just by his/her intimate knowledge and connections. In Eymet, this oracle is Madame Lopez, the greengrocer. She is the only source of fresh fruit and vegetables grown locally, except for market day, and everybody goes to her. Standing in line in her store, talking with the locals, hearing them talking to each other and to her, is itself a way to the soul of Eymet. Madame Lopez is a once beautiful woman who is still beautiful, always immaculate and always elegant. She knows who your friends are, and will tell you who's around as she chooses your pears and artichokes, picking them out with gloves on. She sells eggs from her next door neighbor's hens, egg by egg, and hands them to you in a brown paper bag. Madame Lopez never takes a vacation. She works every day of the year except Christmas Day, from 7:00 am until 7:00 pm. Her husband cooks dinner. Her mother and father were Italian. They met on a pilgrimage to Lourdes.

This year Madame Lopez became a grandmother for the first time, and made the radical decision to take off also Easter Day. She went down to the Gers to meet her grandchild.

Savoir-Flair Tip No. 202:
Introduce yourself to the people you might need in an emergency

Stop in and see the mayor, the gendarmes, the doctor, the firemen, before you need them. If possible, be introduced by a local French person -- your landlord, for instance. Madame Clavier, our closest neighbor and the widow of the farmer we bought our place from, took Ande around. When a 10-year-old visiting friend of our grandson Stanislas was stung by a wasp, the firemen came instantly to clear out the wasps' nests. One of them, who lives just beyond one of our fields, stopped by the next day and found three more wasps' nests.

Madame Clavier lives in an ancient farmhouse the color of the Eymet earth, like all the houses around there. Its walls are light beige, the color of the soil when it has been baked by the sun. The roof is the darker color of the earth just turned, or after it has been raining. When we moved in, Madame Clavier told us which of the three Eymet bakers had the freshest baguettes and most interesting *pain complet*, and which of the three butchers had the best meat. She was too discreet to mention the penetrating stare with which this butcher fixes beautiful young women. Sashie, my daughter, objects vigorously to this stare and refuses to buy his meat, even if it is the best. That you have to be careful with butchers I found out from Peter Mayle's *Encore Provence*.

Madame Clavier did warn us against the grumpiness of one of the pharmacists, but warmly recommended both generalist doctors in Eymet. For dentistry she advised going to another nearby village. As for missing roof tiles after a strong wind, she found us Monsieur Robert. Strong winds being as they are down there, we often have had occasion to bless the talent and reliability of Monsieur Robert, handlebar mustaches and all. She told us about the cleaning establishment of Madame Hervon, who will put your slipcovers through the machine six times if necessary to get them clean, without charging extra, and about the sewing skills of Madame Frey, almost 90, who does wonders with hems and reversing shirt collars. Madame Clavier described Monsieur Mesquita, the Portuguese owner of Eymet's television shop, as a wizard with anything that plugged into a wall. When our dishwasher broke down in the middle of a dinner party on a recent Saturday night, Monsieur Mesquita arrived at 10:30 pm to fix it. You are getting to the soul of the place when that happens.

The reliable and responsible services of Monsieur Bottin, an all-round master of everything, we also owe to Madame Clavier. He repairs masonry, fixes the plumbing and mows the grass. He is competent, strong, agreeable and full of initiative. We were in Paris for the tempest that hit the Southwest just after Christmas 1999. We knew that the electricity was out for the whole area, trees uprooted, roof tiles flying about. We worried. We were particularly upset for our walnut tree. It gives us shade on our terrace in the summer and bears abundant, delicious walnuts. It's the preferred playground and supermarket for three of our squirrel friends. Monsieur Bottin went to look at our place without being asked, and telephoned that the damage could have been worse. The iron lid had flown off the well, window panes were broken, trees were uprooted, roof tiles were missing, but the walnut tree was fine. While we were still in Paris, Monsieur Botttin climbed up on the roof and replaced the missing roof tiles.

Madame Clavier grows delicious tomatoes and zucchini, which she shares bountifully with us, as well as the delectable jam she makes from plums and apricots. She invites us to breakfast after an absence to fill us in on the local happenings in the meantime. Talking with Madame Clavier is part of what Julian Green meant about taking time. Also, getting to know her family:

Madame Clavier's, daughter, Geneviève Le Lannic, is the mayor of a nearby village, Monteton. Her son-in-law, Claude Le Lannic, Geneviève's husband, grows crops on two of our fields, often working them on his tractor at night with strong headlights. Claude is an enterprising farmer with 50 cows. Thanks to their milk, two years ago he built a swimming pool and last year he added a tower to his house. Twenty of his cows give us the pleasure of watching them grazing in our meadows, as well as the displeasure, when they break through the electric barbed wire fences, of eating the tops of our pecan trees. The cows are nudged about the meadows by the horse of Daniel, the owner of the Eymet pizzeria, who is our next closest neighbor. One of my visiting friends, admiring the pastoral scene of the horse and the cows from our terrace, asked me if we rented them.

Savoir-Flair Tip No. 203:
Treat your service people like friends, almost

When your Monsieur Bottin, Monsieur Mesquita or Monsieur Robert, or any other people like the firemen come to fix something or mow the lawn, don't tip them -- this would "wound their pride," Ande says. But when they're finished, sit down with them and have a coffee or a pastis -- Ricard, by preference. Ande always does. They may refuse, but they'll remember the offer.

The firemen are a service of the state, therefore free. But if they do something special like cleaning out wasps' nests, it's appreciated if, in addition to the *pastis*, you slip them FF 100, saying, for the sake of their pride, that it's "for the Red Cross."

If they do something really extraordinary, then give them more. Ande was polishing an *objet d'art* of his collection when it fell into the well, which is 15 meters deep. Five firemen showed up in a truck with a winch for letting one of them down into the well. He descended in full diving gear with harness, an oxygen bomb and an underwater light attached to his head. The object was quite small. It took him an hour and a half to find it. Then they all sat down on the terrace with some *pastis*, under the shade of the walnut tree, to discuss the unusual affair in detail.

Savoir-Flair Tip No. 204:
Everyone in the village is addressed as Monsieur or Madame

All the French people mentioned above, except for Claude and Geneviève, who have become friends, are addressed as Monsieur or Madame. This is true for your gardener, carpenter, cleaning lady and everyone else you come in contact with, unless they're under 20. There is no point at which you cross over to first names with them. Our all-round-lifesaver, Monsieur Bottin, is still Monsieur after 10 years. He calls himself Monsieur Bottin when he phones us. Sometimes he adds his first name, after his last name. *"Bonjour, madame,"* he says. *"C'est Monsieur Bottin Jean-Louis."*

Needless to say, this is also true for the professional people you have dealings with, doctors, insurance or real estate agents, notary publics and so forth. The only French people you might find yourself calling by their first names are people you meet socially. But wait until they do. And don't ever call them *tu*, just because you're on first names with them.

Savoir-Flair Tip No. 205:
Be wary of calling someone *tu* ; it could insult them

Tu, the intimate form of French, is for dogs and children, people you are closely related to, friends you went to school with and... big loves. Black Africans tell me that they are invariably addressed condescendingly by the police as *tu*. They resent it. I hope that gives you an idea.

Yes, many -- perhaps most? -- young people call each other *tu* nowadays almost automatically. Yes, they kiss cheeks right away, too. But if you're over 40... well, like everything in France, it depends. But as a foreigner, you would do well to forget all about *tu*. Except in certain workplaces, where they insist.

Savoir-Flair Tip No. 206:
Be sure you like barnyard noises and farming country smells

One of the games in Eymet in the spring is identifying the different manure smells on the fields. If you walk by, they can be overpowering. It's better to bicycle, but even so, last spring a neighboring field layered with cow manure was so choking as I cycled by that I almost turned back. But that was perfume compared to the overwhelming stink of a thick layer of pig manure in another field sometime later. At breakfast, I asked Madame Clavier, about it. She nodded and told me that when Geneviève hung up her wash near a field where the pig manure had been sprayed that morning, the laundry smelled so dreadfully that she had to wash it all over again.

Savoir-Flair Tip No. 207:
As in Paris when marketing, don't touch products or produce

Madame Lopez would be shocked if you touched her pears or grapes yourself. You tell her how much or how many of something you want, and then watch quietly while she puts it in a paper bag and weighs it. Only in supermarkets can you serve yourself.

Savoir-Flair Tip No. 208:
Don't miss the neighborhood events

Every village has fairs, festivals concerts, spectacles all year long in addition to market day, including gardening days, *vendanges* (grape harvest) parades, livestock competitions, jousting tournaments featuring medieval knights. Everyone in the community around takes part. During the Bergerac *vendanges* festival in 1998, medieval barges came down the Dordogne with huge barrels of wine. Elderly couples in folk costume danced folk dances, accompanied by guitars and ancient musical instruments. Around the dance floor were stands selling different kinds of wine from the nearby vineyards. Artisans had their own stands where they were carving table legs and stools, painting ceramics and making baskets.

A favorite event in Eymet's *vendanges* season is organized by its beloved and talented first lady, Catherine de La Source, mistress of the Château de Pouthet. The 15th-century-towers of Pouthet are just barely visible through the woods on a promontory high above the village. Madame de La Source, a skillful and seemingly tireless gardener, flower arranger, hostess and *chef de cuisine* -- she gives lessons annually to legions of friends in preparing foie gras and *confit de foie gras* -- opens Pouthet to the community on her Plant Day, when everyone is invited to bring a special plant and go home with a different one. They're also invited to stay for lunch if they bring a dish for 10 people they've cooked themselves, its recipe in 50 copies, and 30 francs.

Savoir-Flair Tip No. 209:
Getting to know the neighbors will give you insight to the village

You'll enjoy renting more if you meet some of the people around. Renting from French people is obviously a more direct route to the soul of a French place. In the Eymet area, Ségolène and Mark Dauger have given a Tuscan twist to the Dordogne. Speaking impeccable English, they offer various possibilities of charm -- rooms in their vast château as well as recently-renovated farmhouses on the property, each with its own pool.

Renie and Bob O'Callaghan, from Laguna Beach, California, loved their rented house in the Dordogne. They found it by searching the Internet and when they arrived, did exactly what Julian Green advised; they took time.

"We didn't just like the Dordogne, we loved it!" Renie said. "There were so many glorious sights -- each turn in the road would reveal another spectacular scene. Sometimes we would just keep following roads with no real destination in mind because it was all so beautiful."

They gradually met their French neighbors -- "they were delightful" -- but caution against coming on too strong with French people.

This is what Renie e-mailed me about getting to know one of her neighbors:

> Our house was on a tiny little road, off of the main road. Just down from us was a "walnut mill." A little elderly lady owned it and it was open to the public. Her home was right next door. She would wander up and down our road with a constant scowl. Each time I saw her I greeted her with *"Bonjour, madame"* and a smile. No response.
>
> After reading your chapter (in *French or Foe?*) on how the French are suspicious of smiles, I tried the "non-smiling greeting," having to say to myself the whole time, "Don't smile, don't smile, don't smile!" It was difficult, but from then on she was quite friendly and began to converse with me, babbling on in rapid French from which I could only make out a few words. I nodded and smiled or h-m-m-med or whatever I thought was appropriate, watching her face for any sign that my response was inappropriate.
>
> My darling son-in-law went for a tour of her mill and bought Walnut Oil and Walnut Liqueur. We really enjoyed the oil but none of us could take a second sip of the liqueur.

If you rent from English people and you don't speak French, you'll meet other foreigners at the weekly market. Many of them linger in a café later. Another way to meet your neighbors is to throw a little dinner or cocktail party and ask your landlord to supply the guest list. It's a help to know something about the guests before they arrive. Your landlord can fill you in, and the local Madame Lopez can add details the next time you go for your fresh fruit.

The artist

In the Eymet area, Norman Douglas Hutchinson and his wife, Gloria, are one of the foreign couples it's fun to meet. Hutchinson was born and grew up like an orphan in India. He never knew his Indian mother or his Scottish father, a lord of the Queensberry clan, who had been -- briefly -- in India en poste. At 15 Norman left boarding school in northern India to work, painted in his spare time, and met and married Gloria, who is half Indian and half Russian, in an Anglican church. They turned up in London

30 years ago, more or less on a bet of Lady Mountbatten's that he would hit the jackpot there as an artist. He did. Norman is now a famous artist often commissioned to paint the Queen and Prince Philip.

In 1971, with his fortune piling up, he decided to build a house somewhere in the country. But where? Italy was his choice but too far for a London commute, so he brought Italy to the Dordogne. He transformed the houses and barns of a small village -- using French workers -- into an Italianate villa complete with cypress trees, marble statues of scantily draped nudes, cascading terraced gardens and a topiary requiring the services of four gardeners. Deftly placed outside spots light it up at night so that approaching it from the north, it looks like a Hollywood set of a Tuscan hill town.

Norman doesn't play The Artist. He is unpretentious and likes to tease. He is enthusiastic about French people. Gloria also loves France and French people. "I came home, when I came here," she said.

The house on the hill

Charming English hosts overlooking the valley of Eymet's river, the Dropf, two other Eymet residents, Christopher and Sally Anne Brough (pronounced as in "rough"), farm and raise sheep and, as Ande puts it, "tourists," at the Château de Lauzanac. The Broughs bought their hilltop pile of luminous white 16th-century stones in 1988 and restored it

lovingly, adding a lofty tower. Beyond the gravely entrance courtyard, a path leads to the garden's ancient cedars and linden trees and a swimming pool. The stones of Lauzanac sing of Mediterranean cypresses and olive trees, a super feat considering that they used only local masons and carpenters with whom they had no language in common. Christopher, with his green thumb, bulldozed the surroundings into a lush English park with lots of flowers and a kitchen garden. You should try his tomatoes. And his *haricots verts!* The sheep graze in the field below.

As for their tourist crop, the Broughs renovated the farm buildings into several two-story one-family units, cheeringly done up by Sally Anne with chintzes and bright colors, comfortable chairs and pretty, practical kitchens. After a swim, the tourists can sip their drinks near the pool and enjoy an orange sun sinking behind the hills beyond, and perhaps catch a glimpse of Henriette, the Broughs's 15-year old daughter, galloping about on Gauguin, her horse.

The prize-winning winegrower -- a woman

Patricia Atkinson is a golden-haired, golden-voiced grandmother from London with a figure like Brigitte Bardot. A former banker, she and her husband decided to move to *la douce* France and bought a vineyard near Eymet, in 1990. Atkinson was going to work it himself, but came down with a debilitating disease just afterwards, keeping him in London.

Patricia was stuck with 5 hectares (about 12 acres) of vineyards. She knew nothing about vineyards. The vines were old. It would take two years before they produced. She engaged an oenologist for the final mixing, but learned to do everything else herself, cutting back in January, spraying in May, picking in the fall. It either rained too much or not enough. She was stung by wasps called vinegar flies. She was kept up all night stirring the 3-meter high vats because the alcohol level was too high, perched on top of a 12-foot high ladder. She fell off the ladder and broke her leg in three places. French neighbors, when they heard about it, came over and said, "We'll do your cutting and spraying this year."

In 1994, her sweet white wine, Clos d'Yvigne Saussignac from the semillon grapes, won her a *"coup de coeur,"* the highest award of the prestigious *Hachette Guide des Vins*. Her Clos d'Yvigne Saussignac won it again in 1995 and 1996.

Patricia calls this wine her "liquid gold." To produce it is a long watch of good nerves to choose the right moment to pick, extreme care in the picking, and vigilance from the pressing to the vats, the control of their temperature, to the final resting place in oak barrels. After two years, it's ready to be drunk, at best with foie gras, and two kinds of cheese, Roquefort and Brie de Meaux.

` She has been so successful in selling it (for FF 200 a bottle) that last year she bought 15 more hectares of vineyards.

I went to see her during the *vendanges* on a hot sunny October day in 1999. I found her deep in the vines with a team of pickers, her friends. Wisps of blond hair kept falling in her face as she clipped bunches of wizzened grapes that were coated with a hairy fuzz, like something left too long in your refrigerator.

"They have to look like that," she said. "It shows that the concentrate of sugar is just right, with a perfect balance of sugar, protein and acidity. We call it noble rot. We have to pick carefully, not take the green ones, or the puffed-up ones, leaving them for later, when they have the noble rot too."

She cut off a bunch and a puff of hairy dust went up. Patricia looked radiant. "Luscious dust!" she said. "A cloud like that and you know you've got great grapes."

Savoir-Flair Tip No. 210:
Rural French people give similar dinner parties to Parisians

If you're invited to dinner by your local Monsieur Bottin, the French mistress of the village château, or resident English, the food will be similar, and not different from Paris dinners. The tableware will vary, but there will be the same number of courses (entrée, perhaps a second entrée, meat dish, salad, cheese, dessert).

Savoir-Flair Tip No. 211:
After 2 pm, don't expect lunch at a country restaurant
More Country Living Savoir-Flair Tips

Normal store hours

Stores in the countryside generally open at 9:00 am and close at 6:30.

Stores in villages, even supermarkets, close for lunch in rural France.The exact hour of lunch closing, like the hour of opening in the morning and closing in the evening, varies and has to be learned in each place.

Lunchtime

Only the huge hypermarkets are open at lunchtime. Other stores will lock up tight at 12:30, perhaps until 4:00.

Restaurants

Renie O'Callaghan, expecting to be served lunch at 2:15pm: "One day we drove to Carennac because we had read the book by Anne Barry, *At Home in France,* and heard from others that it was a beautiful village. We arrived about 2:00 hot and hungry. The restaurants were no longer serving lunch and the small markets were not yet open. We had to make do with a soft drink and a candy bar." In the evening, they start serving about 7:30.

Days

Banks are probably open on Saturday and closed on Monday. Almost everything closes in Eymet on Monday except Madame Lopez and the supermarket, which will be closed all day Sunday (not Madame Lopez). Other stores are usually open on Sunday morning.

The News

3 Chemin de la Monzie, 24000 Périgueux
tel 33 5 53 54 56 36, fax: 33 5 53 08 17 73
e-mail: adverts@french-news.com

Rental suggestions in the Eymet area

• Christopher and Sally Anne Brough
Château de Lauzanac
24500 Eymet
tel 33 5 53 22 98 22, fax 33 5 53 27 97 83
e-mail: château-on-the-hill@wanadoo.fr
• Mark and Ségolène Dauger
Château de Lamothe
47330 Feranac
tel/fax 33 5 53 36 98 02
e-mail: lamothe@worldonline.fr
• James Pattinson, real estate agent
Agence Immobiliere du Perigord,
1 rue Calmette, 24105 Bergerac
tel 00 33 5 53 57 11 03
mobile number 06 89 30 55 80, fax 33 5 53 57 98 92
• Eymet Immobilier, John Coshall, director
7 rue du Temple
24500 Eymet
tel 33 5 53 23 98 89, fax 33 5 53 27 10 76
e-mail: eymetimmo@easynet.fr

- Richard and Bee Crow
La Paynaud
Ste. Eulalie d'Eymet
24500 Eymet.
tel 33 5 53 58 35 38, fax: 33 5 53 57 62 51
For rentals all over France, check out
- The Internet: http://www.holidayrentals.co.uk/pages/doc00994.htm
- The English magazine The Lady,
39-40 Bedford st., London WC2E 9ER
tel 44 20 77379 4717, fax 44 20 7836 3601

Supermarket shopping

It can turn into a treasure hunt. Take your time, this should be part of the fun of a new place.

- To detach a shopping cart, you'll need a 10-franc coin.
- You'll have to weigh your vegetables and fruit yourself. You put it in one of the plastic sacks in rolls near the fresh-produce counters, place it on the scales, push the picture-button of the produce you're weighing, tear off the price and stick it on the plastic sack.
- The milk in cartons and not refrigerated (*lait longue-durée*) is sterilized and stays good for weeks. Fresh milk is often in some completely different area that demands a search. Ask someone for "*lait frais*" and check the date on it. Fresh milk with a red screw-cap is with cream (*lait entier*), with a blue screw-cap is skimmed (*demi-écrémé*) and with a green screw-cap (extremely rare) is totally fat-free (*écrémé.*).
- The different varieties of cream in the U.S. don't exist in France. The French use *crème fraîche*, which is slightly sour, in and on everything. You can buy sterilized cream in a little carton (*crème liquide*) and whip it, or you can buy already-whipped and sweetened cream (*crème Chantilly*) in an aerosol container.
- Butter (*beurre*) marked *demi-sel* is is very salted.
- You have to bag the groceries yourself.

The O'Callahans on supermarket shopping

"Since food shopping is pretty much visual, I didn't consider this would pose a problem," said Renie. "I spent a good 15 minutes just trying to make out which box in the dairy section was butter. Then there was the decision to make--demi-sel or not? And what does demi-sel mean, anyway, half salt?

"Luckily, some kind soul helped us with purchasing fruit and vegetables, showing us how to weigh them on those scales with pictures. We were also impressed by the way they handle the shopping carts. Put a coin in, unchain the cart and after finishing with it bringing it back to a certain spot and get your money back. No shopping carts scattered around the parking lot in France!"

Conclusion

The French, living more slowly, have learned the advantage of living more deeply. In science, in art, in technical and industrial training, they know the need of taking time and the wastefulness of superficiality.

Edith Wharton, *French Ways and Their Meaning*, 1918

Il faut donner du temps au temps.
(You have to give time to time.)

François Mitterrand, and most Frenchmen

Give time to time? Anglophones coming to France have deep trouble with this. If you're in a speed profession like Rob Chaddock, a software engineer, then the trouble is *really* deep.

"Paris is a pipe dream," he said. "It's romantic, the world's most romantic city. And then you get here... and it's not convenient, it's difficult You can't call home for sympathy. Sympathy? For what? For living in Paris? Are you kidding? You can't say it's hard -- no one will believe you. Friends come by and say they could live here better than you.

"The timetable is different and frustrating. A day in the U.S... you make a list of what you need to do, and then you do it. In France, you get through half. Ideally, the shortest distance between two points is a straight line. There's not an even remotely straight line in France.

"And then... after a while, you realize you have to jump off the train. Stop rushing. Live each moment. Then life becomes different."

Now back in Washington, Rob misses giving time to time. He misses his local tradespeople. He misses cafés. "I miss the casual meetings of people and the discussions that develop. I miss the long dinners, the arguments, the talk of politics, world problems. "

Gail Chaddock wrote this about Paris in the *Monitor* after their return:

As an American, I'd grown up thinking that a queue is an obstacle between me and something I want, such as seeing the first four minutes of a movie. We have express lines in the United States. We have automated tellers, drive-thru windows, bank-by-phone. All this is to avoid lines, because our time is too valuable to waste standing around.

Not so in Paris. Here, lines are just an excuse for a good conversation. Take McDonald's. The lines at any McDonald's in Paris are long, and not just because the employees haven't mastered the knack of tossing three things into a bag at the same time. There are conversations going on at the head of that line.

"What goes with a Big Mac?" asked one prospective diner. It didn't seem that such a question could possibly prompt a long response. "Fries or more fries" would about do it, especially since the fries were French. As it turned out, there was quite a lot to be said about Big Macs.

Much of *Savoir-Flair* is a how-to book about the French sense of time... time for politeness, for getting to know people; time for the unexpected, the unusual and unplanned; time for the pleasure of talking, or eating, time for strolling down a street or going to the market, time for going to the theatre -- or time for whomever was most in need of it.

No doubt things have speeded up in the last few years in France. Parisians are talking on their cellular phones in the streets, on trains, in restaurants. Government institutions and most companies have Web sites. The French invented the Minitel and the microchip for credit card security. But the human connections are still what matter, both among friends and strangers. French *savoir-vivre* is about giving time to time. The way this plays out for you, a foreigner, can be stirring, and sometimes life saving. I'd like to end this book with examples of what Shellie Karabell in her walk around the Marais in Chapter 9, called French tenderness.

You can see it everywhere in France. For instance, standing in a queue for a Métro ticket. When it was her turn after a long wait in line, New Yorker Jean Matthews asked the ticket agent a question and was totally bewildered by the answer in a cascade of French. An elderly Frenchman noticed her confusion, and left his place in line to ask her, in English, if he could help her out.

You could have been walking along the rue du Bac at just the moment the optician, Madame Dupont-Valmaure, rushed out of her shop at no. 36 to call to a young woman passing by, Elizabeth Turché: *"Madame, j'ai le lapin de la petite!"* (I have the little one's rabbit!) Two months before, in need of dark glasses, Elizabeth, an American married to a Frenchman, had been there with her little baby, Julia, in a stroller. While Elizabeth tried on various pairs of dark glasses, Julia's soft little toy rabbit had fallen on the floor. It wasn't the cuddly teddy bear she took to bed, so that night she didn't make a fuss about it. The next day, Elizabeth noticed that the rabbit was missing. She decided against a probably hopeless search for it in the various stores they'd visited that day.

Now, months later, here was the little rabbit. She stared at Madame Dupont-Valmaure. "You mean -- you remembered whose it was -- and kept it all this time?"

"I knew you lived in the neighborhood, so I was sure that sooner or later I'd see you," she said simply.

A little farther down the rue du Bac, at the rue de Grenelle, is a well-known *poissonnerie* (fishmonger). This is where the no. 69 bus turns right from the rue du Bac onto the rue de Grenelle, but is almost always blocked by a car parked at the corner, despite a thicket of municipal parking obstacles and "No Parking" signs. It's always several minutes of honking before the car drives off. The no. 69 bus drivers have made use of this interlude over the years to get to know the neighborhood tradespeople. If you're having some coffee at the café opposite the *poissonnerie* during one of these incidents, you will probably notice that the driver of the no. 69 bus isn't disturbed; he left an order with the fishmonger the last time round. Then you see the fishmonger running out with it to the bus, a nice big fish carefully wrapped so as not to disturb the delicate noses of the passengers.

Another day, in November when it was quite cold, you might have seen Sally Murray walking around the Latin Quarter in too-thin clothes. Expecting warm weather when she left Alabama in September, all she'd brought with her was jeans, sandals, shirts and a jeans jacket. She soon had an attack of bronchitis. One day on the way to the Métro, she had a violent coughing fit. An elderly woman selling souvenirs opposite the Métro, whom Sally had smiled at and nodded to every day as she walked by -- but who had never nodded or smiled back -- crossed the street, excused herself and said she hoped Sally wasn't offended, but could she buy her a coat? Sally was horrified and embarrassed, and finally explained that she was a tourist enjoying Paris, and had had the choice of buying a coat or spending the money on staying a bit longer, and had decided to stay longer. The woman nodded and from then on, she smiled and waved each time she saw Sally.

Kim Chevalier, a graphic designer from Boston, is married to an Englishman whose work with a British software company enables them to live in the Pyrenees, in Ariège. She took her baby, Pascale, with her in the car to pick up Claire, her older daughter, from kindergarten. She left the baby sleeping in the car seat while she went into the building to get Claire.

As she helped Claire into her jacket, a peasant woman came into the kindergarten carrying Pascale. "I was shocked," said Kim, "and asked her what was wrong. 'Oh, the sun came out and was in her eyes. She didn't like it, so I brought her in to you,' she said. "

And if you suddenly get sick in France?

Traveling to Paris from Rome, Tricia Perron, the research scientist at the University of Kansas we met before, had an attack of acute pain in her abdomen which turned out later to be appendicitis. She wanted to get home to her doctor fast. At the airport in Paris, she tried to change her round trip ticket from Kansas City to Frankfurt to a ticket to Kansas City via New York. The agent explained that a one-way ticket from Paris would cost more than her round trip ticket, and that, anyway, the next flight was overbooked because of a canceled flight to Boston. Tricia described the pains and how desperate she was to get home. "The agent shuffled some papers and was writing something," Tricia said later, "then she handed me an Ambassador class ticket for New York and said, 'Take this and don't tell anyone.'"

In a TGV, on his way to Nice with his wife and four children, Newell Wright was incapacitated with pain from a kidney stone attack. A French gentleman on the train called an ambulance with his cellular phone. "When we arrived," Newell said, "he asked us if we trusted him to take my four children and all of our luggage to our hotel, while Julie and I went to the hospital. We let him do it, and after the stone passed in the hospital, he came to see how I was doing. He then took us back to the hotel, where we found our four kids and all our luggage. His name was Patrick. That's all I know about him other than that he lives in Nice."

Jo Schaffer, from upstate New York, was in the dining car of a Paris-Madrid SNCF-TGV express to Madrid when the husband of an English couple at the same table started showing signs of a stroke. He couldn't get his fork as far as his mouth. He said inappropriate things like, "Tell the chauffeur to come back later." Then he collapsed. The conductor phoned ahead to a hospital in Bordeaux. The train made an unscheduled stop in Bordeaux, where an ambulance was waiting for the sick man. The conductor helped his wife to unload all the luggage into the ambulance.

Julianne Guthrie, the Indiana consultant-analyst at Notre Dame who likes to tour France with her mother, sometimes in a bus, hurt her ankle falling down on the steps of the tour bus near Nice. The doctor at the Nice hospital put her on crutches and she went on with the tour. In Reims, after visiting the cathedral, Julianne and her mother made another visit, this one to the underground public *toilettes* across from the cathedral.

"Getting down the steps wasn't a problem," said Julianne. "After I finished, I figured I would get a headstart going up the stairs so that my mother wouldn't have to worry about me. But I simply couldn't get the hang of the crutches going upstairs. A Frenchman saw me struggling and hurried down the stairs to me. He picked me up and carried me up the stairs. Then he took my crutches, went down to the foot of the stairs and demonstrated the use of crutches on steps."

Sometimes travelers' so-called misadventures in France seem as if the tour guides must have planned them.

Sarah Brown, a teacher from Brownwood, Texas, went to France for the first time a few years ago with two lady colleagues. They were all about 30. None of them spoke French, though Sarah had a few words. They were all passionately eager to see the Monet museum at Giverny near Vernon, about an hour to the west of Paris, and boarded the train in Paris in high spirits. They had a lot to talk about, and not having seen the account of the "Sixth SNCF Tale" in *Savoir-Flair*, they didn't pay attention to the stops and sailed by Vernon. This is what Sarah e-mailed me about their adventure, not exactly a misadventure:

A Frenchman, a businessman on his way home after a week in Paris, overheard us and asked if we had missed our stop. I confessed that we had, and asked him in my broken French for advice. He said we could get off at the next stop and wait for the return train. But, he said, since that would take a couple of hours off our trip, and that was his station, he'd be glad to drive us to Vernon, which, I believe, was about a 30-minute drive.

We discussed this for a couple of minutes, a little uncertain. After all, a strange man.

He then interjected that he would have to go to his house first, and tell his wife. That decided me that he was okay. My friends, who hadn't understood him, told me that it took less time for me to decide to get in a car with a strange man than it did for me to order my meal in a restaurant. (That actually is true.) Anyway, we went with the gentleman, who informed us -- as soon as we got in the car -- that he was faithful to his wife. We echoed the same sentiments about our spouses and all was well. We went to his house, a cute little bungalow on the bank of the Seine, where his wife invited us in for coffee and a chat with their parrot. We then all piled into his car -- not the parrot, of course -- and were off to Giverny.

It was the most beautiful drive I have ever been on, through the very countryside which had been the subject of so many paintings that we loved.

Our hosts told us, as we were driving, that they had lived there all their lives, but they had never been to Giverny. They were looking forward to going as much as we. When we arrived, they bought us drinks at the café, and then spent the afternoon walking through the gardens and posing for photos with us. After several hours, they drove us to the train station and stayed until they knew we were on the correct train.

I have never received such gracious hospitality. They took a complete afternoon on a long-awaited weekend, and carted a group of American women around. They were funny and kind, and very concerned that we make it back to Paris safely.

All right, you say, *but*... It's been raining every day. People bump into you on the sidewalk. "I get so sick of it," said a librarian from Boston, "that I just stand there and say, 'Okay, come on, knock me over!'" The French are Latin and "get in your face" when they talk. "Don't they know where to stand? It makes me very uncomfortable," said an executive from Toronto. And the cars -- "The drivers here are absolutely mad," said London antique dealer Shirley Kennedy. "In London, they slow down if they see you coming from 200 feet. Here, they speed up." As for the smiles --"So they think we're hypocritical to smile? Then why do they say *enchanté* all the time? My doctor said it to my mother -- my husband -- everyone!" said an artist from Melbourne. Places you want to see are hard to get to. At the new Francois Mitterrand Library, you have to climb a million steps up. It's slippery in the rain. You can't find the right entrance. When you do, you have to walk another million miles to get anywhere... and so forth.

Yes, but where else can you walk without a map following the red and white hatch marks on a path called the GR 9 from the Belgian border down to the Mediterranean? Path GR 1 goes around Paris for about 350 miles through little villages close to Paris but in the countryside.

Where else can you jog mid-city on an old elevated railway line (to Vincennes), much of it planted with bushes and trees and little pools, and end up in a thriving open market (Saint Mandé)? In what other major world capital, coming out of a movie on Saint-Germain-des-Prés about 5 pm, might you be held up crossing the street by hundreds of happy roller bladers... with a police escort?

What other city cares so much about beauty that -- like a beautiful woman hiding a recent facelift -- it paints an enormous screen to hide the scaffolding of one of its major monuments, the Church of the Madeleine? And the screen is so much like the building itself that from far away, you don't notice the difference.

This Paris cares so much about its trees that it is the first city to design an effective electronic monitoring system to fight car and dog pollution and keep them healthy. In 1998, each of its 90,000 individually-planted trees lining 4,800 streets was embedded with a computer chip. This is the Paris which is repairing the street lamps on the Pont Royal, in fact, the lighting of all the bridges.

Have you noticed the elegant brown cross-bar railings around street corners to prevent you from crossing except at the zebra stripes? The green and silver fences around the construction spots? There are no unsightly fire hydrants, but grates in the sidewalk that the firemen lift up to connect their hoses to the pipes underneath.

And what about the designer clothes of the firemen, even when you see them jogging in the Luxembourg garden? Dressed for a fire, they look like Roman gladiators in their fine casques.

As for music... people playing musical instruments all over Paris. Winnie Hawkes, whom we first met in a wheel chair in Chapter 2, was stopped by a policeman for speeding. She broke into an aria from "Tosca." The policeman asked her to finish the song -- and didn't give her a ticket.

Ian Heard, the artist from Cornwall who designed and illustrated the cover of *Savoir-Flair*, also sings and plays the guitar. Visiting Paris with his wife, Eve, he stopped in at a café near the Père Lachaise cemetery for a cup of coffee at about 8pm, standing at the counter. Suddenly a woman in her 60's at the other end of the counter, not particularly well-dressed, began singing an aria from "Carmen." Just like that. After she got through, Ian, a tenor, and not a shy one, couldn't resist answering with another aria from "Carmen." Then he switched to a folksong dear to the hearts of Frenchmen, "Belle Virginie." The woman at the other end of the bar joined him. Everyone clapped.

Robert Lovenheim said at the end of the Introduction, "Maybe everything in France doesn't work. But *life* works."

It does. I hope you agree.

A Parisian writes about his city

...cette harmonie majestueuse entre la langue, le style, l'architecture, le théâtre, la mode, la musique, l'art politique, militaire et qui fait que tous les "arts" semblent alors dirigés par un même chef d'orchestre invisible. Moments prédestinés sous Périclès, Auguste, Louis XIV, où la création rencontre comme par miracle une sorte de perfection diffuse.

...this magnificent harmony between language, style, architecture, theatre, fashion, music, the art of politics and the battlefield, which seem to be directed by the same invisible orchestra conductor. Moments fore-ordained by divine decree under Pericles, Augustus and Louix XIV, where creation miraculously converges with a kind of radiating perfection.

Claude Imbert, director of *Le Point*, in *Le Figaro, 2000*

About the Author

Polly Platt, a native Philadelphian, will tell you that her journalistic career peaked as an editor of the Wellesley College News and that then it was downhill as feature writer for the Philadelphia Evening Bulletin and later as reporter for the New York Post. She moved to Paris in 1967. Her curiosity about France began before that, when she was christened. Officially her name is Mary Cordes Platt, after a great grandmother descended from a Huguenot, Antoine Cordes, who escaped to Charleston from Cordes-sur-Ciel, a small medieval village in southern France, after the Revocation of the Edict of Nantes in 1685. She has seven French grandsons.

In 1986 she incorporated Culture Crossings, a training company for executives and their spouses transferred abroad. Her French and American multinational clients include J.P. Morgan, Air Liquide, General Motors, Lafarge, 3M, Dassault, Microsoft and the American Embassy in Paris. Her international bestseller, *French or Foe?*, took off from Anglophone observations in her seminars. It has been published in French (Bayard Press, Paris) and in Japanese (TBS-Britannica, Tokyo).

With over 100,000 copies in print, *French or Foe?* has become the reference for French and American multinationals, international real estate agents, travel agents and the language programs of high schools and universities. A multimedia version is being produced by Robert Fisher, chairman of the language department of Southwest Texas University.

She still gives cross-cultural seminars, and since the publication of *French or Foe?*, she has been invited to be the keynote speaker at numerous corporate and Franco-American events. When asked whether she prefers speaking or writing, she hesitates and says, "I love to make people laugh, and when you give a speech, you can see them and hear them laughing, which is awfully nice. Getting letters is awfully nice, too, when people tell you that you've helped them in their lives, and writing can be exciting as well as agonizing, but you're all alone."

She loves getting mail at polly@pollyplatt.com... which might give her an idea for a third book. Her Web site is www.pollyplatt.com.